T0082957

The Author *of the* Worlds
(Revised)

The Author *of the* Worlds

(Revised)

Matthew Theisen

THE AUTHOR OF THE WORLDS (REVISED)

iUniverse books may be ordered through booksellers or by contacting:

iUniverse
1663 Liberty Drive
Bloomington, IN 47403
www.iuniverse.com
844-349-9409

ISBN: 978-1-6632-3556-5 (sc)
ISBN: 978-1-6632-3557-2 (e)

Print information available on the last page.

iUniverse rev. date: 02/04/2022

Contents

1

Lucifer's Latrine

Sing, Ganesh, of the turbulent decade,
and lighten my consciousness from a shade
to the second millennium's last years,
and write of Charles Standing Horse and his peers.
Rapid City, in South Dakota's state,
is where the tale starts, unraveling fate.
On a Sabbath morning, Reuben awoke
to the noise a brother made from a choke
of bile from the night's before alcohol,
and brothers gathered to talk in the hall
to plot getting their sibling from the house,
and escape listening to their parents' grouse.
They brought him on their shoulders while he shook,
a towel round his waist, with a begone look.
The balding brother cleaned the bathroom mess,
and they set the boy on his bed to dress
him in his Sunday church service attire,
like he was an angel leading the choir.
Stan let his fellow brothers do the chore,
and stepped to Reuben, pretending to snore.
Stan: "Awake, sweet prince, from dreams of the moon;
put on your suit and tie, we shall leave soon."
Reuben: "He is still in the age of boys.
Why have him drink when he should play with toys?

Chemical use will keep him from growing,
look at the bald one. Where are we going?"
Stanley: "To Hell if we are not careful,
and you once enjoyed a beer bellyful.
It is best he learn from us how to drink,
practice the art to not barf in the sink.
When he begins to party in earnest,
will soar above pals and not turd his nest."
Reuben: "That is a valuable thing,
and I am certain like you he will sing."
Stan leaned close and blew smoke in Reuben's face.
The balding one was first down the staircase
to distract kin while others brought the youth,
who had his first try at gin and vermouth.
Reuben paused when outside, by the car door,
inhaling the thaw of manure's odor.
The month of April brought unfolding life,
despite a looming drought that promised strife.
The others got into the pickup truck,
and the balding one and Reuben were stuck
as comrades to drive to an acreage
that the eldest son lost on a mortgage.
He had taken loans for vacation flights
to Las Vegas and their casino lights.
New farm machines were bought with what was left,
then the bank foreclosed, leaving him bereft.
His girlfriend took their child and fled the lair,
Reuben would laugh if he bothered to care.
A law firm bought the land, and subsidies
from the realm kept the soil barren of seeds.
The house stayed in the Jacobs' family,
where the sons hid a missal homily,
stolen each month from their church to be read
aloud over bongs in case those who bred
them asked for the *Gospel* guide of the day
when they arrived home from new Eden's play.

The boy was carried in on their shoulders,
like a triumph march for wounded soldiers.
Stan approached Reuben with a cigarette,
and said to his brother without a threat:
"For some reason we are always at odds.
Take a puff. As Christ said, we are like gods,
and what we put in our mouths is not bad,
it is what comes out that drives people mad."
Reuben turned and walked to the empty field,
disengaged from his brothers like a shield.
Stan shrugged and went into the house, at war
to offer peace or to crush Reuben's core.
As Reuben walked he remembered a time
when he laid in the field, watching corn climb
to the Heavens, and Stan wandered the maze,
searching for Reuben hidden in the maize.
When found, they wrestled, breaking corn aisle stalks,
then laid there, watching the jet-fighter Hawks
pass over from the military base
necessary for the armament race.
At the end of the field his sight was seized
by viewing a dark god's hunger appeased:
stumps jutted forth, not work done by beavers,
but for the cause of progress believers.
The few trees left looked out of place, forlorn,
as if pondering they would soon be torn.
Some trees stood, like stakes, bereft of branches:
Hermes' border pillars to mark ranches,
like the wood used by Vlad the Impaler,
now the symbol of a farmer's failure.
The irrigation rig was also sold
in an auction that broke the Jacobs' mold
as outstanding ranchers and smart farm-hands,
who sunk to the level of peon-bands.
Reuben stood on the bank, gazed at the stream,
his hand on a tree, which fell like a beam.

He shred the bark, observing the fungus,
and believed that there were those among us
who did not care how quickly the scenes changed,
and were lost as nature's script rearranged.
Reuben: "On television there are scenes
that shill this chemical as a safe means
to rid the world of bugs and choking weeds,
a new, evolved defoliant of seeds,
like used in Vietnam, to spread cancer
through the Heartland. I am taught the answer
is to love those who spread such reckless hate,
desiring control of each mental state."
A passing crow laughed at him with a caw,
and he felt bile humor rise in his maw:
"Scarecrow Muslims would only bring about
the unveiling they sing for with a shout."
Reuben clambered down the bank and stripped nude,
like when a boy, playing with his parents' brood.
The water was cold and his skin tingled:
good memories and bad mixed and mingled.
He began to see spots before his eyes,
red swirling round with cosmic enterprise.
On the far bank, in the sun's silhouette,
appeared a creature the first gods beget.
It shimmered in shapes, and seemed a vast range
of beasts and humans with a seamless change
as a stalking panther, then humans who danced.
Reuben watched it closely, his mind entranced.
It altered to a deer, a dog, then horse,
and seeing he was near the power source,
Reuben tried to keep it in his vision,
but it vanished with a blasting fission.
At the far shore was a tree on the bank
branching the top edge where its roots still sank.
In a quest to see mystical matter,
Reuben quickly climbed the makeshift ladder.

His torso scraped raw from a contusion,
he found a frog, adding to confusion.
He took off his glasses and wiped at tears:
victim of cosmic pranks or schizoid fears.
Near the bank snaked an asphalt trail for bikes,
or so folks could walk out of town on hikes.
He stepped through some trees, which were not damaged,
pursuing the being who had imaged
itself as energy in consciousness,
pellucid and anti-matter darkness.
The budding trees, bent in conversation,
seemed to laugh at his bared situation.
Reuben approached and felt among strangers:
playgrounds being built and homeless mangers,
which would also function as a cook-site
for picnickers to avoid a rain's blight.
He returned to the bank, went down the tree,
and lay on the sand, wishing his soul free.
At dusk he dressed and walked back to the house,
sure at least one brother would be a souse.
They were gone, and Reuben knew the next day
they would get him for school along their way.
Reuben had not eaten, nor did he find
any food to quiet his racing mind.
The refrigerator was stocked with beer,
towards which he felt a repulsive fear.
Stan's pipe was on the living room table,
an ornate ape to make life a fable
wherein Stan plotted to be with rangers,
sent to foreign lands to battle dangers.
Next to the pipe was Stan's non-fiction book
about Vlad Dracul and how he forsook
conventions of war to induce terror
in Muslims fighting for their emperor.
Dracul was better known as a vampire
than a Christian for The Holy Empire.

Reuben did calisthenics, dreamed of Gog,
and at dawn, watched a damp billowing fog.
He went out the backdoor, gazed round, then sat,
and was approached by a one-eyed tomcat,
who dropped a mangled crow at Reuben's feet,
then groomed himself, purring pride at his feat.
Reuben: "The gods want me to break my fast,
but I do not want this bird for breakfast."
Stan arrived with the boy and some school clothes;
if Sunday's best were soiled it would bring oaths
of vehemence from their mother and dad,
nor were such suits part of the teenage fad.
Stan drove with speed into Rapid City
so gravel roads spurred clouds that were gritty.
In English class Reuben became aware
that Bernard Levi could not help but stare
at Reuben as if he were the full moon,
out of place at day, but praised by a loon.
Studies that morning began Shakespeare's play
Romeo and Juliet. The Friday
before, they had finished *Antigone*,
a tale which wracked Reuben with agony.
Following class, Bernard asked him to meet
in the school's cafeteria, and eat
with Charles Standing Horse after study-hall.
Reuben replied with an affected drawl:
"Why is there sudden interest in me?
All I know of you is that you agree
our teacher is a bumbling loudmouth goof.
I may sound cruel but I am aloof."
Bernard: "Your character has a strange glow,
as if the lead actor in a stage show,
but I respect your wish to be alone,
though this place makes me want to cry and moan.
I need all of the comrades I can get,
even some partners-in-crime to abet."

Reuben laughed and said he would meet Bernard
to question if he understood the Bard.
Bernie chose a seat near Camille Ann Woods,
who smiled at him, thrilling his outcast moods.
Study-hall done, he nervously asked her
to dine with him, hoping passions would stir.
Camille: "I know it sounds rude and pouty,
but you guys are unruly and rowdy.
While I dislike the school's cliques, I have friends,
so do not take it hard or need amends."
He wondered if she was a lesbian,
and went to have lunch with Charles and Reuben.
Charles came with a gold hoop pierced through his nose,
saying he was like a bull led to woes
of a meat-packing plant to be processed,
and thus Charles' evolution had regressed.
He ate an orange without peeling it,
and talked with Reuben of their brother's wit.
Maddox, Charles's brother, was friends with Stan,
who were so close they seemed to form a clan.
They rose in sports, winning with distinction,
and hunted the freshmen to extinction.
Reuben: "I remember my first swirlie:
they said my long hair made me look girly."
Bernard: "I am not up on this jargon.
I just got here, waking to lingo's dawn."
Charles: "They stick our heads in toilets and flush,
giving themselves a bully's junkie rush."
Bernard: "Why does the school allow such things?
I have enough problems without those stings."
Reuben: "They count on the pecking order
to enforce the strict upper-class border.
The faculty cannot smack around brats,
so juniors and seniors crush us like gnats.
Where are you from to not have had a part
on being a crushed victim from the start?"

Bernard: "I was home-schooled until last week,
when my mom caught me in a porno peek."
Charles: "It does not sound like a vacation,
rather a graphic sex education."
Reuben laughed; Bernard, in shame, hung his head.
Stacy Kurtz approached their table and said:
"Next week our class will be seeing a flick
on the play that is my favorite pick."
Bernard felt his mouth begin to water,
she sent him on sex-crusades of slaughter.
Charles: "Good, a movie. Then I can find sleep.
Films lack the symbols of dreams that go deep."
Stacy: "But I just told you it is great.
'Tis about two gangs and their love of hate."
Charles: "Neat, another updated version
to which I have an active aversion.
Instead of reading *Moby Dick* why not
a flick of sharks being blown-up and shot?"
Bernard: "Please ignore him, he is uncouth.
Films are metaphors of our nation's truth."
Stacy: "Do you know who wrote *Moby Dick*?
Try to think of the answer real quick."
Charles: "You think your presence here is a gift,
and I am sure it was Jonathan Swift."
Stacy smiled happily and sang out: "Wrong!
Stick to comic books that are not too long."
Stacy walked away, swiveling her hips,
and Bernard refrained from licking his lips.
Charles: "So you have been pushed out of the nest
to read tales of suicide and incest.
My hormone-raging adolescent fears
have a monkey-wrench thrown in to grind gears.
First, Oedipus, who loved his mom so,
then doomed Juliette and her Romeo.
I do not bring my Tarzan books to school,
because snots sneer and say I am a fool."

Reuben: "The saved ones seem to heap scorn on
those whose trail wanders with every new dawn.
I was taught only Christ brings happiness,
and it is bought at a scapegoat expense.
So we are charged with making others pay
for their sins until they see the right way.
Religions act as gods' machine lever,
and for perfected souls the wars sever
human qualities that are kind and good,
leaving us roaming the polluted wood
of former Edens, so we are compelled
to heil fuehers to gain where we once dwelled."
Bernard: "Perhaps extinct wild predators
force open the reincarnation doors
to be reborn as humans in cities,
preying on weak to murderous ditties.
I read a Hindu book, *The Song of God*,
and we deserve what we get, though we laude
higher powers with gifts and sacrifice,
wrapped in illusion's contrary device."
Charles: "Killing the human raptors brings peace,
but innocence would die too, giving lease
to a backlash whipping us, unperceived,
for what we have created and believed."
Reuben: "I find my parents elated
school trains me to be domesticated.
With no enforced peace I would go feral,
crazy as monkeys trapped in a barrel.
As the saying goes, sex civilizes,
and search for a mate trivializes
to looks, smell, udders, or tinted hair-plaits
for narcissistic love or polar traits.
My life centers about breeding programs:
hybrid corn, cattle, and the perfect hams.
When the rut ends, lead the bull to slaughter
to prevent him mating with a daughter.

We usually hire a chief stud,
because he humps 'til he falls in the mud,
and is too dangerous to keep near cows,
though some weary old boars we pen with sows."
Bernard: "I like myths of hunting wild hogs,
'tis part of our evolution from trogs.
They painted the past and hoped their future
huntsmen craft was blessed by Mother Nature."
Charles: "I thought Jews put an exclusive cork
on bottom-feeding animals like pork."
Bernard: "I refuse to be orthodox
and eat kosher foods: matzo, bagels, lox.
When Christ exorcised Legion into swine,
he had to pay their owner a claim's fine
because a Jew lawyer took on the case,
and used the laws to keep Christ in his place
by finding his work an undivine flaw,
as possession is nine-tenths of the law."
After soccer practice that afternoon
Charles drove Bernard through the lot like a loon,
using the spare keys to Maddox's car,
pretending to be a stock driver star.
When baseball practice was finished, Maddox
punched Bernard twice, who ate dirt from the shocks.
A rally gathered as the brothers fought,
a young girl yelled, joyously overwrought:
"Punch him in the face and make blood drops flow!
Stop dancing around and give us a show!"
They circled, feeling adrenalin rile,
quite aware of each other's combat style.
A clout from Maddox landed on Charles' head,
making him see pure lights; then Maddox said:
"Just apologize now and we will leave,
or learn the fear of god so you believe."
Charles: "All you have on me is age and weight,
this goes beyond brotherly love and hate."

Another punch made Charles reel and near fall,
then he charged with a majestic war call.
Charles slammed Maddox's head on the car trunk,
and a dent was made with every clunk.
Stan considered stopping the fierce assault,
but the fight grinded to a sudden halt.
Maddox threw his brother off and kicked him
in the stomach, and while his mind was dim,
skillfully tore the gold hoop from Charles' nose,
causing him to deflate from fighting pose.
Maddox randomly flipped the hoop to Stan,
who kept it as if by destiny's plan.
Bernard picked himself up, spitting out grass,
while murmurs of approval swept the mass.
Offering Charles his hand, Maddox bent down
to grant largesse from his champion crown.
Charles shouted obscenities, but his throat
had thick layers of a bloody bile coat.
Camille stepped in and helped Charles to his feet,
with Bernard aiding they walked from defeat.
Stan: "So your brother has a new girlfriend
to salve his wounds and put him on the mend.
If she is with him she must be a whore,
because all fools know your tribe is the door
to a low Hell of damnation stink pits,
where home-codes are lost like a crazed bat flits."
Maddox: "Your girlfriend drinks with the park bums,
which is why, when with her, I use condoms."
A tense moment of glares between the two
was broken by Stan offering a brew.
Maddox: "I have to get home before Charles
to tell what happened and dodge my mom's snarls.
Fortunately, my father is shacked-up
in a hotel, drunk and weak as a pup."
Stan: "You should stay with me and not go home.
I have seen your dad's rabid froth and foam

when he flashes to Vietnam action;
if she phones him you might be in traction."
Maddox: "He pays for sins as a white man
civilizing us from our tribal clan.
He tried to force my mom to change her name,
and we called the cops to further his shame
when she was pregnant with Betty and said
she would marry Dave Standing Horse instead."
Stan: "You are vexed by the fight, I can tell,
because you rarely speak of your life's Hell.
Come along, we will run around the track
until your guarded frame of mind is back."
As the two began to circle in pace,
Charles was led to the bus by Camille's grace.
She took stacks of tissue out of her purse,
and applied them to his nose like a nurse.
Charles weakly struggled with her hands at first,
then with cries of agony, wept and cursed,
his pride shattered by curious classmates,
whom Bernard held back, as if guiding fates.
They hurried Charles onto the bus before
officials asked details of the fight's lore.
Bernard held Charles between them on the seat,
and she cleaned the wound 'til they reached her street.
She took Charles with her, saying he lived close,
as some females recoiled, thinking it gross.
Clara Standing Horse was by the window,
and ran to her second son to bestow
a healing touch, then saw his damaged face
needed stitches to keep the skin in place.
Camille told the story of what she saw,
her high voice quavering with nervous awe.
Clara: "Did I raise him to be hostile?
Perhaps. We must get to the hospital.
I do not have enough for taxi fare,
my car broke down. Can your mom drive us there?"

Camille: "I shall check and see if she will,
or I could give you a ten dollar bill."
She went home and had her safe-box unlocked,
then her mother approached the door and knocked,
saying: "Why do I not rate a 'Hello'?
You usually come in and bellow."
Camille: "I need cash to help the neighbors;
I know you think of them as drunken boors,
but they must go to the hospital quick,
and do not need your lecture's wordy trick."
Dana: "Young lady, do not use that voice
while you are under a roof by my choice.
There is blood on your clothes. Are you all right?
Should I call your father at his worksite?
Just calm down and tell me everything.
Have you suffered some unfortunate sting?"
Camille rushed through the story of the brawl,
and asked her mother to not force a stall.
Dana: "You believe I am a base snob,
but I am not part of the racist mob
that would turn away people in dire need,
unless they are drunk on liquor or mead.
It just seems best they stay with their own kind,
made in God's image but different mind.
I will take them to the hospital now,
while you do homework, using your brain's plow,
but first get out of those clothes and shower,
and try not to think of me as so sour."
Dana Woods said a soft prayer to Jesus
to be led by his will as he pleases,
and that her car seats be free of bloodstain,
as cleaning them would bring vehement pain.
Bernard went home, his mind in disorder.
Too often he broke decorum's border,
forcing his mother to make decisions
in moments akin nuclear fissions,

bothering her until she exploded.
So he saw himself clearly, and noted
he was no longer an infant at breast,
and must use his wits when pushed from the nest.
He took a tome from his mother's bookshelf
that she read while gestating his mixed-self.
Rachel Levi had explored various
religions when young, and took serious
thought that one can change the environment
by altering psyches with the intent
to improve the world with good energy,
'til she earned her psychiatric degree.
Bernard carried the volume to his nook,
closed the door and opened the obscure book:
Ganesh was given the duty to guard
a cave's door. The elephant-headed bard
fulfilled his father's task against demon
hordes and gods' troops who sought Shiva's semen.
Believing they needed his spawn in wars,
they tried to get by the master of doors.
Ganesh made their bodies fall in a heap,
but knew the din would disturb Shiva's sleep.
Ganesh also had a selfish reason
to prevent breeding, though not of treason:
as Shiva's child he was the favorite,
and would not share holy opus merit.
His father gave him a direct order
to keep noise from entering the border.
To fulfill the pledge, Ganesh stopped the fight,
and the gods and demons were quick to smite.
Seizing Ganesha, they cut off his trunk,
in tearful shame he ran to Shiva's bunk,
who wrapped the proboscis round his waist,
and thanked his son for helping him stay chaste.
Then they watched the nose merge with Shiva's loin,
'til Shiva unraveled it from his groin.

Ganesh brought it to a new paradise,
where it would tempt humans with good and vice.
Gods and demons realized their error:
humans would outgrow great powers' terror,
and not accept enforced obedience,
rather join Shiva in his cosmic dance.
Bernard closed the book and felt he was trapped
in an ancient oracle scribes had mapped.
He thought: Humans are resilient creatures,
yet fragile in evolving new features.
Changing clothes, we think we are diverse
for the audiences who hear our verse.
Such a frenetic pace leaves us hollow,
as greed's reinvention makes us shallow.
I pick up on characteristic styles,
thinking a walk in their shoes a few miles
will adopt their attributes as my own,
reaping benefits from seeds they have sown.
Earth is now the fallen angels' latrines,
over-fertilized and raped by machines.
Poisoned water forms awful birth defects,
inherited land is what form reflects.
So the day draws to an end with a spark
of revelation giving souls a mark.

2

The Games

For months Stan and Maddox were clean and dry,
including Stan's cigarettes on the sly.
They exercised together in routines,
planning to join America's Marines.
Three days prior leaving home to be trained,
a party was held, and as kegs drained,
they set up a stage for one last rock show
where revelers camped and nothing would grow.
Amplifiers and lights had strands of wires
hooked to the house to play the modern lyres.
"Mad Dog" Maddox on drums, Stan screamed a crow,
and when he saw Dee he picked up to throw
a condom filled with rotten eggs to wreck
her finely coiffed hair spilling past her neck.
Stan and Maddox laughed as she fled in tears,
and Stan said since she no longer had school peers'
pressure she could date Maddox, a half-breed,
which was why she broke Stan's sexual need.
Maddox: "Do you require a drawn-out map?
She chose me because you treat her like crap."
They banged tunes and people drifted away,
then Stan saw Reuben and said they would pay
one-eighth of the profits for him to play.
Reuben: "Only if you adopt a style

that does not make people's guts puke a bile."
Stan agreed and Reuben took lead guitar,
and that Friday night he was Heaven's star.
Camille watched him as he hit the right chords
that seemed to awaken the lightning lords.
The low sky was dashed by electric volts,
like a stallion, unbroken by man, bolts
from saddles and seems a force of nature,
so the clouds clashed as a living creature.
Yet no rain fell from the summer heat-storm,
and Reuben was inspired by a sweet form,
Camille, who had arrived with some classmates.
They avoided parents' questions of fates
with lies the girls were at each other's place,
leaving behind them no evident trace.
Reuben played a last song and walked off stage,
and Stan quickly followed, twisted with rage:
"Wait a second, champ. Where are you going?
They love us now, and the crowd is growing."
Reuben: "Keep your money. I do not care.
You have the rhythm of a drunken bear."
Stan threw him against the amplifier,
which shrieked like a Valkyrie's brimstone fire.
Reuben straightened and unslung the guitar
from his shoulder and swung as if to scar
Stan, but only grazed with the fearless blow,
as the crowd pushed in to see the new show.
Stan: "You near broke my head like an eggshell.
Now learn the pain of a fallen angel."
Reuben held the guitar as a war-club,
like a lion king protecting his cub
from a male who wishes to chomp fresh meat,
and bring the lioness to quicker heat
to mate with the new master of the pride,
for blood-love of her cubs and milk has dried.
At the silence, Stan looked at the storm-clouds

which had parted, leaving no wispy shrouds.
Then he shrugged and opened arms to embrace
his brother, saying in drunk cheerful grace:
"You are blessed by Christ in this storm's wild stir,
and I pay heed to his barometer."
He put forth his hand to secure the deal,
which Reuben quickly shook to find Camille.
The audience let him through with praises
for his guitar playing in smooth phases.
They patted his back and offered him grass,
proud he stood against Stan. He found the lass
in the backyard at a picnic table,
looking sweet and fresh, and he felt able.
Reuben: "I have seen you before, though where
I cannot say. What brought you to this lair
of Pan's drunken iniquity and vice
where they search for a virgin sacrifice?"
Nina: "Then only I am qualified,
because she had the sex gods mollified."
Camille: "Ignore the junk-mail she sent,
at times she is Rumor's embodiment.
We were in the same English class last spring
that Bortz conducted, where you would not sing,
so she only called on those with raised arms
to kiss her rear, lulled by her noisy charms."
Reuben: "That sounds eerily familiar.
We were like trained chimps, perhaps sillier.
If we massed the group consciousness at hand,
in a few millenniums we could band
together and compose a masterpiece
akin those from England, Egypt, or Greece.
I am Reuben, part of the Jacobs' line.
Who are you with eyes that so brightly shine?"
Camille: "I know your name, it is famous.
Here are Denise and Nina, sit with us.
I am Camille Woods, and I am impressed

at how the sky and your guitar addressed
the audience in rolling waves of sound,
like an ocean breaker that gains high-ground."
Reuben realized she was not ready
to leave her friends, so made himself steady
in his resolve to be at ease and talk
with pleasure and not be aloof or balk.
After several moments of school chat,
and how teachers often seemed like a brat,
Camille said they were to sleep in the field
in a nylon tent as a weather shield.
Reuben: "The house is empty, come with me.
It is not a hotel, so stay for free."
The young women nodded at each other,
and Reuben planned to outwit his brother
by closing windows and locking the doors,
though Reuben would rise early to do chores.
In the house, Camille's two friends acted scared,
and returned to the fields to tent they shared,
but Camille said she was going to stay,
and Nina laughed knowingly with a bray.
He and Camille went upstairs to a room,
and standing up they kissed in the dark gloom.
Reuben latched the door then returned to her.
O, sweet first love that makes our passions stir!
When their clothing had been gently removed,
he thought of the future, and it behooved
him to say: "I think Stan has condoms here,
and I will not hurt you, my precious dear."
Camille: "Your strong body and spirit haunt,
and we can do other things if you want,
but I am not prepared for full sex bliss,
though we can ravish our forms with a kiss."
So Camille and Reuben were at love-play
'til drained, then slept to the new morning's day.
Reuben left to do his chores, but his heart

was with Camille as if they did not part.
Stanley was sleeping in his car, curled up,
his hand still holding a plastic beer cup.
Reuben tapped on the window and Stan woke,
then jabbed Reuben's chest with a finger poke,
saying: "What do you mean to lock me out?
Oh, I feel ill, going through a beer-drought,
then hitting the sauce again much too hard,
so my thinking is like a splintered shard.
You better leave or there will be a fight.
I wonder if you bagged a broad last night."
Reuben: "I will care for the cows today,
but need you to be silent of my play
with the girl, because our parents prejudge
the pursuit of females due to the sludge
our stupid brother brought on, with regret
of worthless seeds for a child to beget."
Stan: "Go ahead and take my pick-up truck.
If you get caught with no license, tough luck."
He milked the cows, and led them to pasture,
while Camille lay in bed, feeling rapture
sweep through her with fond waves of love and joy.
Then she argued that he was just a boy,
who knew no difference between hormones
and true passions she felt with sighing moans.
She showered, then to have something to do,
washed the bedding and her self-image grew:
"I no longer play house with a toy doll.
Strange, but I crave a taste for alcohol.
Just a little, to enhance elation,
the common drug for our fast-paced nation."
Bernard Levi woke a few hours later
from dreams of being with a Jew-baiter
who called Bernard an evil Christ-killer,
part of the twelve tribes' lineage pillar
of Chosen People, who fell by the side

due to Ishmael's spawn of rising tide.
Bernard thought perhaps the cause of the dreams
was maturity breaking former seams
that held him in one dress code, as it were,
which bound him at birth by karmic capture.
He showered and shaved, his hair thick and rough,
and made scowls at the mirror to look tough.
He chose a thick book from his mother's shelf
of the Hindu way of knowing true self.
Rachel Levi came out in her bathrobe
and asked her son of his religious probe:
"Why this interest in things so far-flung?
It is balderdash and you are too young.
All it did was confuse my path in life,
and not finding god, all I had was strife."
Bernard: "I think the best tales are Hindu,
and what is it you would like me to do?
Play video games until my eyes bleed?
Perhaps if you had not over-used weed
you would have gained a consciousness of light
instead of a haunting haphazard blight."
Rachel: "My past is none of your affair,
and when you speak to me you best take care,
or I will send you right back to your dad,
knowing full well it will not make you glad."
Bernard did not rise to the occasion,
and left as she pled the cause of Zion.
At a quick pace he cycled out of town
to avoid thoughts of ways to put her down.
He reached gravel roads and was getting tired,
when he saw a stream of cars, and was fired
by wonder to follow them to the lot
of the Jacobs' clan to see what was wrought.
Bernard saw Charles, walking without a shirt,
then he was lost in clouds of gravel dirt.
A car of young women pulled up to Charles,

and one said to him through the dusty marls:
"You are kind of cute. Would you like a ride?
Party with us 'til synapses are fried."
Laughing, Charles hand-signed, feeling demented,
aware that another girl commented:
"Are you crazy? He is one of those Sioux,
and has been drinking since the age of two."
The girl responded: "What makes you so great
that you can afford racism and hate?"
Bernard caught up with Charles at the driveway,
where a youth stood collecting the kegs' pay.
Bernard: "I have not seen you since school closed.
Are you avoiding me as I supposed?"
Charles smiled: "I like you, but you are needy,
and in my in-most self I am greedy."
As he spoke a circle of laughing crows
descended around him, then they arose.
While Bernard massaged his legs from their cramps,
Charles handed the guardian four Food Stamps.
The collector turned to Maddox nearby,
and informed him of Charles with a loud cry:
"Your idiot brother wants to get in
with Food Stamps, a stereotype Injun."
Maddox approached and took the paper-bills,
staring at Charles in a contest of wills.
Maddox: "The next time you steal Food Stamps, Chuck,
you will wish that you were an unborn muck.
Our family needs those to eat, you slug.
What are you doing with that gallon jug?"
Charles: "Mom took Betty to her soccer match,
and your self-righteousness is a bad batch,
since mom gave me these so I can have meals,
and I am not the one who blithely steals.
The empty milk jug is for beer, of course,
and it looks like I have found a main source."
Maddox: "I do not want to see you here,

so go out in the fields to drink your beer."
Bernard followed Charles to a flowing keg,
that he happily saw did not renege.
They found a site far from the stage and crowd,
and they shared the jug though Bernard was cowed,
thinking so much beer would leave him helpless,
but he was spurred on by Charles' fearlessness.
They drank and laughed, telling tales of childhood,
as if sudden light had brightened their mood.
Charles did his animal imitations,
and Bernard poured forth Soma libations,
saying: "The gods are drunk, as they should be
when playing with the worlds. Accept this fee,
and if you battle over it to doom
that is because 'tis our nasty heirloom.
Look at how the spirits serve their own ends.
Is there a god left who at least pretends
to not need a votive from believers,
detached from the joyous and the grievers?
A god who does not enforce stupid laws
like a vile judge, but is the Causeless Cause?"
Charles: "You think the spirit is a theory,
which proves you are smart, but I am leery
that giving cerebral approach a chance
might have me miss life's mysterious dance.
This barren field will be fertile again,
whether by God's design or a human.
You take it upon yourself to critique
unfolding tales, when 'tis love you should seek.
Choose a god with your discriminate mind,
it may open doors or kick your behind.
Perhaps you need a girl's trophy hickey.
Yet I understand why you are picky:
humans tend to run with a herd instinct,
blotting consciousness to become extinct."
Bernard: "I need someone here to take notes

on how the majority rules with votes,
for we are brilliant in our current shapes,
worshipping Bacchus of fermented grapes.
Seems everything now is manufactured,
water, soil, and air are spoiled and fractured.
We past the survival of the fittest
to be judged by our credit interest:
too greatly invested to disengage
as we watch the wars for oil burn our stage."
Charles: "I think artificial selections,
though used for hybrids and rigged elections,
is a mere phase of our development
to fulfill the Great Mystery's intent."
Bernard: "Jews believe in Abe and Sarah,
Hindus in illusion of Samsara.
Drifting life's deathly sea, I need a wharf.
Excuse me a moment, I have to barf."
Meanwhile, Reuben and Camille found passion
with each other in an artful fashion,
then embraced in exhaustion with soft words,
as if smiled on by satiated lords.
Camille: "I am good at debate and such,
and I was scared that you would want too much,
so I would have to fight off your desire,
yet we were able to dampen lust's fire."
Reuben: "Among the barnyard stock foreplay
does not exist, but we have found the way
to appease one another and quench thirst,
and in my heart you will always be first."
Camille: "Do not say those things for my sake,
because I do not want us to be fake.
Young love and lust are easily entwined,
when souls do not have a discerning mind,
'til it is too late and lives are shattered,
and we lose what we thought greatly mattered."
Reuben: "I am not along for the ride,

dearest one. Come on, we will go outside."
Stan and Maddox were preparing four bouts:
a wrestling match, then running the field routes,
cars used in a demolition contest,
and Frisbee throwing to decide the best.
As they formed the combat engagement rules,
Bernard and Charles stumbled towards them like fools.
Reuben and Camille emerged to applause,
holding hands, shamed by cheers from the crowd's maws;
then he grinned at the folks in the backyard.
Slightly aware, venom poured from Bernard:
"Oh, so I am not good enough for you.
With him 'tis nothing to have sex and brew."
Reuben laughed, thinking them some funny jokes,
but when it went on with derisive pokes,
Reuben grabbed Bernard and rattled his head
'til Charles stepped in and touching Reuben, said:
"He is possessed by beer and not to blame.
Let him go to deal with when you are tame.
Think back and remember your first cheap buzz.
His mind is full of cobwebs and lint fuzz."
Reuben pushed Bernard to the ground and stood
over him in a moment of dark mood,
saying: "If I see you again today
I will make you regret the price you pay.
It is no honor to defeat a drunk,
but I stand for no insults from a punk."
Embarrassed, Camille walked to her friends' tent,
but they had left that morning, tired and spent.
She returned to ask Reuben for a ride,
and saw Charles leading Bernard as he cried:
"The awful ravages of demon rum
has me tell lies, though called a truth serum.
How can I ever show my face again?
Perhaps it is an oracle's omen.
Beer did not make me like the Romantics,

following Lord Byron with my antics,
or like an opiated Coleridge,
have my psyche open to Heaven's bridge.
Instead, wreck parties like the Mariner
lost in life's deathly ocean: a sinner."
Charles laughed, handing Bernard the gallon jug,
after which, gave him a tobacco plug.
Charles: "I want to see you vomit some more
while I dance around your purged vacuum core."
Soon Charles joined his friend laying on the ground,
and Bernard reached for him, with arms wrapped round.
In his mind, Charles could see the Elders laugh:
regressed from a bull to a shaky calf.
His free will was gone, sucked out of his soul,
and he roamed mazes, searching for a role.
The streets were twisted, the buildings askew,
then he met legions of a ghostly crew.
Aware that they were homeless and in need,
he broke away to his parents with speed,
but Clara was draped in a swirling mist,
as if to guard against desired incest.
So he turned his thoughts to a higher realm,
and found Bernard with his hand on the helm
of a craft like a cosmic entity
divided to an expanding city,
with forests razed for population's greed,
then Charles realized they were all his seed.
Bernard smiled, relinquishing his helm's post
for Charles to assume control of the Host.
The worlds seemed to shudder under his rage
as he flipped open *The Book of Life's* page.
Rising as a storm, the planet dust seethed,
and through its consciousness Charles lived and breathed.
Bernard moved quickly to steal it from him,
and Charles passed on as the lights became dim.
Bernard: "You are the beginner of life,

Prajapati, the source of love and strife."
Leaving the voice behind, Charles went upwards
until he found the room of written words
that shape all of the galaxies' actions,
whether peaceful life or karmic sanctions.
An elephant-headed man-child waited,
and when he saw Charles he was elated.
A woman appeared from the open book,
and when they approached each other a look
of love passed through the three, and they embraced,
shining with brilliance, which a third eye graced.
As their minds drifted through Samsara's loam,
Camille Woods asked Reuben to take her home,
but he was selected the referee
by contestants, accepting his decree.
Camille: "When will all of this be finished?
If I am not home I shall be punished,
and could not go out with you on a date,
crushing my spirit, for last night was great."
Reuben: "I do not have a car license,
so I share your problem in common sense.
I will find you a ride when this is done,
but I wish to see whose pride is the sun.
'Tis a good match, and one of them shall lose
to hang his head while rumor spreads the news.
Stan has recovered and does not look sick,
so just wait here and the games will go quick."
The crowd made a ring around the contest
of wrestling to decide who was the best.
At his weight-class, Stan won championships,
but Maddox was known for his python grips,
which he used to strain the muscles of foes
like a taut string that releases arrows
to pierce the hide of a rampaging bear,
though such means of hunting has become rare.
So Maddox made his opponents feel aches,

wearing them down until they got the shakes.
As they circled, moves within moves and feints,
to Reuben they shone as if wrestling saints,
like the match Jacob had by the river
that shattered his hip, making him quiver,
but he would not let the angel-man go,
'til it blessed Jacob with a new name's glow.
So they seemed, as he held the winner's purse.
Stan grabbed Mad Dog, but he got a reverse
and pulled Stan down with a half-nelson yank.
Maddox held him until Stanley could crank
his legs round Maddox' ankles and escape.
Then moving so fast Maddox saw no shape,
Stan picked him up and threw him on the ground,
no longer at play, like boys full of sound,
rejoicing with their close friends for the fun
of seeing who is king under the sun.
The wind was pushed from Mad Dog's diaphragm,
then felt his nose receive a head-butt ram.
He grunted with pain, Stan rose to applause,
but Reuben announced Stan broke wrestling laws
with a clout when Maddox was in defeat,
which was poor sportsmanship, for he was beat.
Stan helped Maddox up, who gasped for his wind,
and when he got it, said Stan had not sinned.
Maddox: "We did not have a sanctioned bout,
so let us move on to the runners' route.
I am ready for people to be set
at the field's end so we do not forget
how far the distance, and pace ourselves thus,
and neither can cheat, creating a fuss."
Sharon Dieson and Phil Nert volunteered,
and rode his motorcycle, straightly steered,
to the end of the field to be judges,
fostering against neither one grudges
that would lend favor to Maddox or Stan,

showing a Hermes' like skill as they ran.
During the first quarter of the long race,
Maddox jogged along at Stan's striding pace,
but when they reached where there were no camped tents,
Maddox opened all his energy vents.
As a gentle breeze suddenly turns storm,
the Heavens darken and one sees no form,
except for what is brightened by a jolt
of the sky's lightning, so did Maddox bolt.
He turned round at the far end of the field,
well in front of Stanley, who would not yield.
He finished behind by many meters,
gasping for air like a foal that teeters
on its new legs, and cannot get bearing,
'til the mind and muscles merge for sharing.
As they drank water to replenish sweat,
Stan had a rash urge for a cigarette.
For over two months he had been smoke-free,
and argued with the temptation to spree,
thinking: I no longer want that habit,
because in the Marines I must be fit.
So he exercised his free will and won,
and when they had recovered from the run,
they got two Frisbees from Maddox's car
to decide the disc-toss champion star.
Knowing the skill did not depend on strength,
Stanley spun the Frisbee an awesome length.
Maddox also had a talented throw,
but it went too high and the current's blow
made it veer to the left and fall yards short,
like a listing ship cannot find a port.
For the final match of the contest shows
they got hammers and broke out cars' windows,
and cleared the barnyard for what was to be
the space for a demolition derby.
They prepared for whatever the fates dealt,

both eschewing his respective seatbelt.
Reuben yelled go and they stomped gas pedals,
rammed into each other, folding metals
as if it were melted to liquid ore
that bursts from a volcano's molten core.
Not heeding the whiplash they crunched into,
Stan saw the radiator-grille punched through
the engine of his truck, and knew its doom.
Maddox backed-up for maneuvering room.
Stan tried to chase him while the truck still lived,
peering through steam as reality sieved
from known to unknown, skewing perspective,
making Stan hesitant and selective.
He could not see Maddox, then a fierce clip
on the right side made Stan bite through his lip.
He bailed from his truck, spat out streams of blood,
consciousness dimming in waves of a flood.
The sounds in his head were a percussion,
and vaguely knew he had a concussion.
He was led to the doorsteps by Cal Hawn,
and came to as if facing a new dawn.
Reuben was caught between being concerned
or happy his brother got what he earned.
Maddox: "So we are even with match points,
and we feel the aches in muscles and joints.
Shall we divvy up the party proceeds?
We proved to be equal in strength and deeds."
Stanley held his head for a long moment
to find the precise words of his intent:
"I cannot accept this series as tied,
damaged though I am, it prickles my pride.
So I say we have one last match of skill,
though a blood-debt is incurred by a kill."
Maddox laughed, shrugging shoulders with a sigh,
deciding it was a good day to die.
Maddox: "I am too weary for races,

but perhaps lawn darts at twenty paces
to see who can aim them closest to win,
and whoever is stained with the most sin
places faith that he does not risk the wrath
of wind gods aiming darts on a death-path."
After a thought, Stan shook his wounded head,
and a moment later Calvin Hawn said:
"My dad has two spears hanging on a wall
from Africa where he went to install
peace among tribes who slaughtered each others'
neighborhood clans: children, men, and mothers.
In Rwanda it was a bloody mess
that the outside nations did not address
until thousands died under machetes,
with rapes, murders, and gross atrocities.
It still goes on, my father had to leave,
each tribe wanting to rule as they believe
they are meant to do, as their heritage
is the best gene-culture on the world's stage.
Before my dad fled, in order to live,
they granted gifts, 'twas all they had to give,
as their society is truly sick,
where we are headed with modern music.
They are fine spears, with heads made of iron.
I can take them from the nails they hang on."
Maddox: "We could throw them at a target
and whoever hits the mark wins our bet."
Stan: "That seems the way of a girl or child,
but I have a heart gone savage and wild
because of pride and no gain of glory,
so let us go on and finish the story,
and if one of us is struck by the spears,
the other is champion of the peers."
Maddox: "What sort of game are you playing?
It would be premeditated slaying.
I have no mind to throw a spear at you,

I would end up imprisoned, my life through.
Come, let us agree. You know I am right
that you would go free because you are white."
Stanley sneered: "You only play the race card
to defer a task you think is too hard.
Have we not had scrapes before with the law?
Did they treat being Native as a flaw?
This weakness does not become you, Mad Dog,
squirming from duels like an impaled lab frog."
Maddox: "That is easy for you to say
because you are still loved as the sun's ray
after three months of storm-clouds' slashing rain
that floods the streams, bringing heartache and pain.
Crops are washed away, the animals starved
before the butchers can have the herds carved.
The last time we were caught drunk and driving
it was only through your father's striving
on my behalf that my record was cleared.
He would not feel the same if you were speared.
I doubt he would have lawyers defend me
while being judged by an all-white jury."
Reuben approached them, followed by Camille,
who sensed new passions could no longer feel
the giddy heights of first touch's magic,
instead, had foresight of scenes turned tragic.
He brusquely ignored her pleas for a ride,
so she sprinted into the house and cried.
Stan: "Perhaps you are right. The worst of sins
is white people being killed by redskins
than the opposite, which is a pity.
From your view it is a racist city,
so I will take a solemn oath and swear
that if you kill me, and lay my soul bare,
you shall not be caught in a legal-feud
with courts or among my family-brood.
Reuben, bear witness and make it be true,

that none of our systems has Maddox rue
his actions by their hatred taking vent
with what may occur in today's event.
Calvin, go get the spears while we arrange
the contest before our hearts have a change."
Maddox: "I will swear by my own beliefs
that if I lose and suffer death's dark griefs
my kin will not hound you for a blood-price,
as I have already beaten you twice.
My brother is drunk somewhere with a Jew,
but Reuben can tell Charles when he comes to.
Christ is your ultimate reality,
so make a sacred oath of fealty
if you are slain I am not liable,
and I want your right hand on the *Bible*."
Stan: "We will go and draw up a contract
so neither is to blame for how we act."
They went into the house and Reuben found
Camille wiping her eyes, tears without sound.
He took her hand and led her to a room,
giving her time to haphazardly groom:
crushing away tears and combing her hair,
then she fixed on him a blank aplomb stare.
Reuben: "You know I am preoccupied,
and do not have time to find you a ride.
I wish there were something more I can do.
Perhaps your friends can cover your curfew.
Last night was bliss, which I do not regret,
but it pains me now to see you upset."
He leaned close for a kiss to make the peace,
but Camille would lend no more love to lease.
She backed away and stood up from the bed,
and walking out the door she turned and said:
"Last night is done, our appetites sated.
Insincere apologies, so stated,
insult us both and break like weak alloys

under your belief that boys will be boys.
I do not know you well enough to nag,
so if you want to tell the guys and brag
of our encounter, feel free to do it.
I am done crying and throwing a fit."
Reuben sat pondering and Stan appeared,
gazing at his brother, then smiled and jeered:
"A little trouble in Paradise, eh?
Listen closely to what I have to say.
You should have offered her fresh apple-pie,
because young females are the kind who cry,
and, when down, want offered food and nurture.
Do not ask me why it is their nature."
He searched a drawer and found Charles' loop ring,
and pierced his left ear, ignoring the sting.
Stan: "My truck is yours if I lose this bout,
but I must be confident, free of doubt."
Reuben: "The wits are battered in your skull,
for you already wrecked your vehicle.
Perhaps we should wait, if Maddox concurs,
a few days 'til your mind no longer whirs."
Stan: "I have had worse hangovers by far,
and feel I follow my destiny's star.
You worry too much and lose today's gifts.
Popularity always wanes and shifts,
because people trail any fad or trend.
I live in the now with Christ as my end.
I want to rise above chaos and reach
the eye of the apocalypse to teach
there is but one path to true salvation,
which we depend on in our loved nation."
Reuben: "Whatever is right, I suppose.
Though how a Christian fits a soldier's pose
I do not comprehend, nor do I care
if you can have a justified warfare."
Stan: "Use reason, which is why I admire

the Sioux, though they lost and are in a mire.
Without war, we would be ruled by Hitler,
with life as a recurring nightmare blur.
My German background cringes from such fates,
and a nuclear holocaust means states
must steer the hostile countries from the course
of dropping atom bombs, though we use force.
We need great men in the military,
not scum like Oliver North, with nary
a trace of good conduct, who sold weapons
to Iran, raising them from roles as pawns.
It pained me when Reagan told insane lies.
We must be careful choosing who will rise."
Stan hung a rosary about his neck,
then looked in the mirror to image-check.
They went out the backdoor into the yard,
and for the first throw Maddox drew high card.
They went apart twenty paces and prayed
to their Maker Beings who were unmade.
The throw from Maddox was straight but too high,
going over Stan's head, who gave a sigh.
He nodded in relief as the crowd gasped,
and did not taunt Maddox, instead Stan grasped
his spear and cast it in a perfect line,
crunching Maddox's chest, who fell supine.
So life ended for Maddox Standing Horse,
and his spirit went soaring on its course.

3

Plotting a Course

For three days Charles fasted on his house roof,
while prosecutors said they had no proof
that Stan Jacob had committed murder,
so Judge Tanner issued a court order
letting Stanley join the military.
The Natives' voices were not contrary,
for Maddox needed no stand-in lawyer
in the life and death of a warrior.
Charles sought a vision of his own, not shared
with people and tribes who might be too scared
to realize life is open-ended,
and only true needs must be defended:
clean air, good food, along with pure water
should be preserved from industry's slaughter.
Charles saw an ancient oracle was mapped,
designed by aliens to keep men trapped.
Only women bring forth the needed tale
to prevent humans from being for sale
to the high-bidder of the war machine,
in all the dressings of religious sheen.
He felt himself engaged in sweet pleasure
that was greatest of all Earthly treasure,
yet her joy was higher for the balance
of labor's product: love and pain enhance

the creation of children with senses,
who come into world with no defenses,
except the antibodies from the source
of all life-giving perpetual force.
So Charles sat and prayed for continuance.
Should he seek revenge or try the ghost-dance?
He could not kill Stanley in a fair fight,
nor did Charles wish to lose Mother Earth's sight.
It comforted him, and he felt he owed
it to her blessing to have his seeds sowed.
Yet when he felt sure of his decision,
and ready to embark on the mission,
came a troubling query of who would pay
for the child to be raised on Earth's stage-play.
Charles blinked at the question and realized
that systematic welfare subsidized
baby-raising until the eighteenth year,
when no longer children and forced to steer
their repayments owed to the government
as soldiers for corporations that meant
to expand the global economy,
and people lost free will's autonomy.
Or the choice to be sponsored by the state,
with a convict's record and prison's fate.
Charles: "Can I have a career and children
or will I run away from the burden?
'Tis irresponsible to not support
a family, yet blame the white man's court
for social injustice, then use their fare
to bring forth my spawn, saying it is fair.
One must adapt to changing perspective,
using discernment to be selective.
Am I so important I think my genes
can overcome the infernal machines?
Or will I be serving devious ones,
feeding the monsters my daughters and sons?"

He sought inspiration for an answer,
and his soul became a spinning dancer,
no longer concerned with money matters
that bind a commonwealth 'til it shatters.
Charles showered and dressed for the funeral,
and was approached by his father, not full
of liquor, though his eyes were streaked blood dots,
and his red nose was swollen with veins' clots.
Harold Peen: "It is good to see you, son.
I check into treatment when this is done.
That damn liquor has got the best of me.
If I were sober, Stan would not be free.
Perhaps we can file a civil law case,
though that would fail to take your brother's place."
Charles: "And what would you buy with the blood-price?
Get drunk and flashback to slogging through rice
paddies, and maybe burn down a village.
I know you will not send me to college.
You are on chemical dependence wards
so often they leave open the fence-boards
to let you in and out, learning to soothe
our family with your lies, slick and smooth."
Harold's first instinct was to grab the boy
and shake him until Harold felt the joy
of releasing his pent-up frustration
for feeling discarded by his nation.
Then he saw himself looking in Charles' eyes
and felt a lightning bolt to his surprise.
He wavered a moment, seeing his life:
the woman he loved another man's wife,
a son who hated him, the other dead.
Hoping he showed no weakness, Harold fled.
When summer's heat turned to autumn's cool breeze,
and a multi-colored robe donned the trees,
one Friday, Dave Standing Horse left his job
to visit Pine Ridge, feeling a jug's throb.

He sped down the reservation's highway
to buy more beer at the town of White Clay,
America's most deadly two-mile stretch
the Lakota maneuver to fetch
beer because the tribe had banned alcohol,
yet it lures them on like the Siren's call.
Dave Standing Horse did not see a carload
of revelers weaving about the road.
He was killed instantly, his stunned spirit
flew from his form, torn and shunned by the hit.
The next day Clara received the bad news.
She fell apart, and could not pay rent dues,
with no life insurance or job pension,
so she drank wine to ease heartache's tension.
Charles could not bring her from the Void's abyss,
and they received an eviction notice.
Charles left young Betty to pack their items,
fleeing his mother's agonized systems
of love and hate and the final release,
searching for immortality and peace
with wine that brought her to the brink of death
to face the horror and draw her last breath.
He stayed with the Levis until Clara
sobered from her vile drift through Samsara.
He chose Bernard because Charles' other friends
were Lakota who drank to blackout ends.
Two months after her husband's collision,
she sought for Charles from the homeless mission.
She embraced him, but he was reticent,
and sniffed her features for alcohol's scent.
Rachel and Bernard left the living room.
While Charles played with the animated doom
of video games, Clara spoke her mind,
trying to grasp why her son was unkind.
Clara: "I am ready for your return,
and am sorry it took so long to learn

that I must exist in the here and now
and not ponder dark griefs of why and how.
We have a private room at the shelter,
and my brain is not hazed helter-skelter.
You and Beatrice are all I have left,
and without you both my soul is bereft.
They have been kind to take you in their home,
but I promise you that we will not roam."
Charles sniffed and put down the remote control,
not wishing to shed an assumed proud role,
but when he saw his mother softly weep,
he felt love in his heart begin to creep.
Charles: "Bernard and Rachel treat me with care,
and we can wrestle in our underwear,
as Maddox and I did when we were boys,
before he met Stan, the killer of joys.
Bernard opened the doors of religion
that seem to curse our people and region.
God spurned Adam and Eve the Tree of Life,
only by progeny through man and wife
can immortality be gained on Earth.
So, to be contrary, a virgin birth
made Christ the eternal life elixirs,
hung on a branch by crucifixers."
Clara: "My mind does not think of such things.
What you speak is a mournful dirge that sings
the righteousness of the world being torn
by good and evil, and that I am born
to destroy the trees to create my cross
for a polluted haze of words that gloss
actions by preaching Earthly life is sin,
so we must make it Hell to put fiends in.
For my worst self it might be the right place,
but I try to love you with a sweet grace.
Part of me wants to protect you from harms,
yet with free will comes superstitious charms,

which you alone must choose to face life with,
be it pipes, feathers, or a *Bible* myth."
Charles: "I am grateful you came here for me.
Perhaps being homeless can set one free
from constant consumption of what is next
to sate appetite in a spew of text
that advertisers bounce off satellites,
filling the airwaves with their noisy blights."
Clara: "I filed the forms with child welfare
so we can get out of the homeless lair.
You can stay here if you want until then,
for my spirit feels healthy and open
since you accept me with my faults and all,
and I am so happy that I could bawl."
Charles: "I will stay with you and make the best
of the situation at your behest."
So for three weeks Charles stayed at the refuge,
and noticed how some people played the stooge
from disinfectant cocktails or huffed dope,
yet kept his fortitude, not losing hope.
Stanley joined the Army's Special Forces,
the best at running obstacle courses,
stoic in life without food or water,
becoming a soldier sent to slaughter.
There came a chance to show his bravery
when Saddam Hussein enforced slavery
upon Kuwait, a neighboring nation
of Iraq, where he held the chief station.
Questions about a quick loan to Hussein
from global banks gave the war a bad stain.
Did satellites miss Iraq's troops gather
at Kuwait's border for raids, but rather
allow Hussein to use the armament
he bought with money America lent
for his ongoing war against Iran,
with the Pentagon arming Hussein's clan

in conspiracy to get at the oil
in deep reserves beneath the region's soil?
Despite doubt of the politicians' shows,
one thing could be certain: gas prices rose.
President Bush called for world unity
to restore Kuwait's throned sovereignty,
declaring it an attack on freedom
and democracy, pounding a war-drum.
Nor did the George Bush faithful understand
that Kuwait was ruled by a monarch's hand.
So the United Nations collected
and General Norman was selected
to run the operation, Desert Storm.
Stan Jacob felt ready and in great form,
deployed to kidnap or kill the tyrant,
once a friend with his anti-Iran rant.
When the Coalition made their attack,
an official's first-cousin in Iraq
told the unified troops he would help them
if they installed him in their new system
of Iraq's government, as they arranged
to replace Saddam's rule, which was deranged.
They accepted Al-Shailah's proposal,
which he swore upon with his very soul.
Saddam had look-alikes through the nation,
trained as him to foil assassination,
but Al-Shailah's cousin was kept posted
on the true Hussein, as oil-fields roasted
due to Iraq's retreating spiteful spleen,
and folks cheered the Coalition on-screen.
What the audience could not watch was Stan's
squad being briefed on capture or kill plans.
Iraq's army had folded, yet no truce
had been reached to avoid the tightened noose.
Perhaps lives would be spared if they could thwart
Hussein to be sentenced by a world court

to be a cell-mate with Panama's chief,
a Bush-friend jailed as a drug-dealing thief.
Al-Shailah's house was found by satellite
and Stan's squad took a helicopter flight,
and as it hovered they slid down rope-strips
in the stillness of night, but with sure grips.
Al-Shailah, his graying beard near torn out
by anxiety of a bloody bout,
led the squadron to where Saddam would meet
his officials the next morning to eat
breakfast while discussing ways to use tact
for ending the war with a peace contract.
Stan felt ill at ease, his instincts ensnared,
and spoke to his chief to have concern bared:
"This goes against military training
to not post scouts, and the night is waning.
Why not put men at each window and blast
him when he comes? I feel a net is cast."
Specialist Candon did not try to hide
his contempt for Stanley when he replied:
"I was told you were the best of your class,
but I see your fear like an empty glass.
As a favor I have brought you along,
because my chief praised you with a war-song.
Yet I see you are not fit for combat,
as nervous and loud as a feisty cat.
Al-Shailah has done his part with no leaks,
betraying Saddam while kissing both cheeks,
and we have done this sort of thing before,
so shut-up now, I will argue no more."
They waited and soon heard Baghdad awake.
Stan knew his reputation was at stake,
and he must comport himself with control,
or soldiering would be a short-lived role.
Loud running footsteps approached from the hall,
and in a foreign tongue there was a call.

Candon fired through the door at unseen foes,
and Stanley jumped through some first-floor windows.
He landed on the heads of Saddam's guards,
who fired at Stan's squad, ignoring glass shards.
A shell through his arm, Stan dropped his rifle,
but adrenalin caused pain to stifle.
Each act seemed clear, with courage to bolster,
as Stan pulled his pistol from the holster.
On his back in the garden posies Stan
squeezed the trigger, killing the nearest man,
who fell on Stanley, cushioning the blow
from a grenade's shock and explosive glow.
Stan waited for the debris to settle,
body parts, charred wood, and twisted metal.
Then he pushed the corpse off his wounded form,
and ran from the aftermath of the storm.
He would avoid the safe house he was told
to meet at, for his squadron had been sold
and betrayed, so he had only the thought
of survival or death if he were caught.
He climbed the wall surrounding the estate,
and shot a guard, who died cursing his fate.
Sprinting through Baghdad's wealthy neighborhood,
Stan had no time to think of bad or good,
but as he neared a Tigris River bridge
came thoughts of retribution's cold porridge,
and he vaguely knew he would serve it well,
so they suffered like the spirits in Hell.
He jumped in the river and swam downstream,
his arm numb and heavy like the log's beam
that he lifted in training with his squad,
so he began calling to Christ as God,
unfocused, though he felt like a knighted
crusader while his prayers were recited.
Several miles downstream he climbed ashore,
feeling the disease of Babylon's whore.

Stan cleaned his pistol the best that he knew,
and dressed his wound so no infection grew.
He trudged through sand to a nearby village
that his troops suborned but did not pillage.
Before Stanley's air-lift by the medic,
he told his leading officer the quick
details of how the mission had gone wrong,
his squad slain by Hussein's murderous throng.
Commander Foley wiped sweat from his eyes,
shrugged his shoulders and said to Stan's surprise:
"Saddam accepted our offer last night,
and retains his power, so ends the fight.
A White House stooge aborted the mission,
against my word and without permission.
You need not know more than that, young soldier.
Now go and have doctors fix your shoulder."
Jacob was stunned and wondered if he too
would be killed to silence the betrayed crew.
Stan: "So they worried that we would succeed
and end Hussein's nightmare realm of bad seed,
making a pact to save him so he rules,
sending us to death like heroic fools.
Why were we not communicated with?
We could have escaped, avoiding death's scythe.
What is to become of me? A morphine
overdose to feed the starved war machine?"
Foley: "You think we cull flocks like shepherds.
Shut-up now and I will forget your words.
This goes beyond our duty or one life,
for a truce will save our troopers from strife.
You have two choices: you can pursue this
and your action will be called cowardice,
jumping through the window, leaving your squad.
Or you can have people respect and laude
your efforts for freeing Kuwait and oil,
with medals and parades on our own soil."

At Berlin Stan laid in a hospital,
mulling Foley's candor, and felt hostile.
Did Stan have the means to kill everyone,
or could he accept war as games and fun
for the leaders of the military
whose talk of conviction went contrary
to their foul deeds of intrigue, gaining wealth,
preying on their loyal soldiers with stealth?
As the nurse put in a pain-killer tube,
Stan decided he had played a dumb rube.
From ever on he would control the stage,
and none would have him at disadvantage.
He thought Christ had not abandoned the world,
but evil flourished, its banner unfurled.
Kirk Sanders, wounded in the leg, approached
in a wheelchair with a topic he broached:
"I am glad I got out of that Hell-hole,
and am so crazed for sex, would sell my soul.
I feel leashed and controlled by these dog tags,
and we could not even have girly mags.
Muslims say we are too caught up in sex,
while they go through seventeen wives and vex
any attempt by women at free will,
and if they try it, might end up like road-kill.
We free their countries so they can enslave
females as in a Neanderthal cave,
knock them out and drag them along the ground,
meek and subservient without a sound.
It is strange to travel from one nation
that bans alcohol at my post-station,
because it is forbidden by Islam,
then be in Germany where we can slam
drinks as much as we like in a beer-hall,
and get good and drunk until the last call."
Stan: "We like to free countries for a price,
gambling with soldiers like a game of dice.

Hitler or Hussein, what does it matter?
We are the world's cops as chiefs get fatter."
Kirk: "I am uncertain if I agree,
but it does us no good to be angry.
What you need is a blonde Aryan chick
to drain stress rather than a needle's prick.
I will be released in another week,
then aim for a thrill-pleasure's highest peak.
Should we not win any willing females,
we can find a cathouse, it never fails."
Stan: "During my father's Vietnam tour,
he caught a social disease from a whore,
so he made me promise that I would not
do the same on a foul back-alley cot.
But I will go along to see Berlin,
for that is the heritage of my kin.
Besides, I am so wrathful I might beat
a whore to feel victory in defeat."
Kirk: "You need to find a way to annul
your rage and not take it so personal.
Or were you part of the troops that were massed,
and by our own damn weapons were nerve-gassed?"
Stan: "No, I was lucky to miss that show,
and I hope our government will bestow
more care on them than Vietnam victims
doused with Agent Orange on leaders' whims."
Kirk: "They bought it from a corporation,
with taxpayers' money in our nation.
Now we support veterans with cancer,
but no one I know has the right answer.
The cycles turn with every person's fate,
we are destined to become what we hate."
That evening Stan had a prophetic dream,
which ran through his psyche without a seam.
The world's nations were at wicked levels,
the righteous meek whipped by laughing devils.

The Heavens roiled in a filthy smog haze
that was unpierced by celestial rays.
As scorching lava flows from a hilltop,
so bubbling blood spilled from the human crop,
reaped by the hate hidden in hearts of men,
changed to monsters to fulfill an omen.
Yet Stan was paralyzed by emotions,
loathing the weak retarded his motions,
and if he took a stand against the shades,
could be crushed or, like them, a form that fades.
He hid in the dark of his painkillers,
then his groin burst lights from seeding pillars,
and he was returned to the gruesome scene,
watching his children be torn by obscene
brutes who laughed and leered at Stan's impotence,
who fancied himself a man of good sense.
He prayed for relief from his self-bondage,
and to bring an end to the wicked age.
A light appeared in the sky to release
Stan from his chains and fulfill promised peace.
As he rose he noticed others as well
fighting off the dungeon restraints of Hell.
Together they battled demons and freed
souls lifted to the sky as Christ's blessed seed.
As the war went on Stan's mind became blank,
so caught in fighting-rapture his soul stank.
He cleaved the head of a monster who shrieked
at the terrible mayhem Jacob wreaked.
He grabbed a shade's pike and shattered the form
of a beast who howled like a monsoon storm
as it rages through the sea to reach shore,
and folks have hope when they near the eye's core,
believing it has passed, and go outside
to face the churning typhoon's seething tide.
At the beast's howl the other demons ran
to focus their attack on war-wild Stan.

Four released souls joined him, and back-to-back
they circled and destroyed the demon pack.
As the bodies piled high, the men lost ground,
and as their hopes ebbed came a lovely sound,
fragile and distant, as if from the sky,
barely audible over Stan's war cry.
Then Heaven ripped apart with a great glow,
as if with spotlights to guide the staged show.
Smiling, the author of the worlds appeared,
and replied to the shades who mocked and jeered:
"The world is granted to become your stew,
but these are not meant to perish by you.
Without innocence to prey on, you might
turn your regard from the harrowing plight
to structure a world that you understand,
not letting your vengeance get out of hand.
For you felt wronged by those who had good lives,
and butchered and robbed your children and wives.
Now this land is yours and we wish you well.
Your story-tellers will aid where you dwell."
As the demons nodded in agreement,
Stan felt rebellious at the arrangement.
Stan: "We can conquer this territory,
and spread the good news of your son's story.
Just send more soldiers to help us create
a place of blessing as your favored state.
The worlds must be as one under your rule,
left to their own device they play the fool.
Give us authority in your son's name,
and we will not disappoint or cause shame."
The author of the worlds extended light,
and sundry souls restored the land from blight.
The corpses vanished under grass and trees,
flowers blossomed and they felt a cool breeze
that took away compulsions to battle,
and wild beasts appeared as did meek cattle.

The demons exhaled noxious fumes and changed
into creatures of love who rearranged
their circle round Stan and his fellow souls,
becoming aware of new nature's roles.
His four warrior friends held out their hands,
but Stan Jacob heeded his own commands.
They looked at him in pain and flew away,
as his desire continued for the fray.
He faced enemies, but they passed through him,
then his mind ached and senses became dim.
For this he blamed God and forsook his faith,
realizing he was a homeless wraith.
His goal became to have his mischief spread,
bedeviling foes 'til they crowned his head.
He saw a serpent and entered its shape,
and blotted its consciousness with a drape.
Slithering along, he found a female,
lovely in form, whom he wished to assail.
Stan woke in a cold sweat and wiped his brow,
glad to be present in the here and now.
He did not have long to ponder the dream,
as Foley walked in to recruit a team
of Special Forces to prevent intrigue
against the international oil league.
Most troops would withdraw, but work would remain
to keep oil flowing and keep down Hussein.
Businessmen would be protected from fights,
and weapon inspectors guarded at sites
that were secret, and Stan could relay
information to prevent devil's play.
Guards were also needed for diplomats,
and Coalition oil-war bureaucrats.
Jacob listened closely to the sale's pitch,
and found himself longing for home's safe niche.
Stan: "So it is time to fill the coffer.
Such is war, but I reject your offer.

I do not think myself too grand or high,
but I did not join to become a spy
for a corporation to gain profit,
and my sore shoulder wound makes me unfit.
So I would like to be discharged at once,
as I am not a complete foolish dunce
fighting giants who are in fact windmills,
producing energy like oil that kills
crazed crusaders, whether by wars or smog.
The pollution is bad enough to fog
the senses and minds and make goofy loons
like Don Quixote. I will not join goons
who sold me and laid my faith in ruins."
Thus ended, for a time, Jacob's career,
his mind clouded with resentment and fear.

4

In the Shadow of the Cross

In the summer's furnace-blast heat Charles called
Camille Ann Woods to ask if she had crawled
out of the introvert shell of her mind
to partake of some joys that she might find
with fellows who regretted their abuse,
desiring to make peace more than a truce.
She was hesitant when Charles informed her
Reuben and Bernard sat on a sharp burr
in their mistreatment the previous year,
one was sex-stupid, the latter on beer.
When she asked what they would do, Charles replied
go swim, and Bernard would give her a ride.
She still felt betrayed, but Charles was such joy
that her anger left like a weak alloy,
which melts away from the precious metal
with bright sparks in a shape-shifting kettle.
She agreed and twenty minutes later
Bernard arrived, hairy as a satyr,
wearing sandals, swimming trunks, and no shirt,
and he did not try to be coy or flirt.
Dana Woods greeted him and closely asked
questions to find if intentions were masked.
He wanted to please, but felt in the lurch
when Dana queried if he went to church.

Bernard: "That is something I wish to do,
but am Jewish and probably Hindu.
Though I work hard to keep an open mind,
I doubt god had books personally signed."
Dana: "'Tis a shame you do not believe,
but I see Camille is anxious to leave.
This talk of religion bores her to tears,
but I am glad to meet her high school peers."
Bernard: "'Tis strange that she loves to debate,
yet avoids religions tied to our fate.
Perhaps she knows something she will not share
for fear we will twist it to our own fare.
Humans are brave or egoists to spread
enlightenment banquets like wine and bread."
Dana: "Have fun and remember the doors
to church are open with incense odors."
Camille: "Maybe that explains why you smoke,
to commune with ghostly souls, though you choke."
They drove to the Jacobs' farmhouse with talks
of the drought that was destroying corn stalks.
Then she asked if Charles would put on a show,
and grant weird knowledge like a soul's window.
Bernard: "Now he walks, runs, or rides a bike,
says 'tis unhealthy to even hitchhike.
Apparently he took a solemn vow,
which has not made him holier than thou,
to never drive again due to the blood
of fossil fuel releasing a flood.
He believes there are many oracles,
and those we choose have their own miracles,
depending on the energy put in,
with results doled as a blessing or sin."
Camille: "Now that we are turning sixteen,
it is curious and almost obscene
that he does not want a driver's license
to make him lazy and pollute good sense.

We all have to do our part to keep pace
with global warming to destroy our race."
They laughed about impending extinction,
whether it was true or science fiction.
Reuben was waiting with his b.b. gun,
shooting rodents a cat chased on the run.
When his lord lost interest, the tom-cat
sat down to groom, then dined on the fresh rat.
Reuben sat beside her in the front-seat,
and she felt old thrills, despite their defeat
by her prior wrath and calculation,
which placed her above his farm-boy station.
She put her arms round each and gave them hugs,
and was glad to see smiles rather than shrugs.
Driving through the field to the shrinking stream,
Bernard talked fervently of Brahma's dream:
"We are all part of a god who must wake,
and when we know reality, forsake
the moving atoms, which do not sit still.
Yet we must pay our karmic levers' till,
so we are reincarnated for moves
in perpetual motions' stage-play grooves."
Reuben: "To me, Brahma is just a cow,
who does not ponder much on why and how.
If she dreams it is not a profound one,
munching alfalfa under the sun
is her paradise, along with her crew.
Om turned backwards is a meaningless moo.
As for motions, tell that to my brother,
for he is lost in many worlds other
than this one of third-dimensional force,
thinking he is Death who rides the pale horse.
Pipe dreams from smoking vast amounts of dope,
leave him strung-out stoned with abandoned hope.
Mostly he reads Dracula comic books,
and when we urge life, gives us nasty looks.

Sometimes he gets angry and blows his lid
with tirades like a gangster on acid."
Camille: "'Tis sad he suffers such a pox,
but my heart still mourns and sings for Maddox.
Your Jacob clan was the town's royalty,
but Charles and I share a deep loyalty.
When we were young, we sometimes played a game
of hide-and-go-seek, before there was shame
in having a Native as a close friend,
then school started and play came to an end."
Bernard: "Perhaps before Stan slits his wrists
you could get him to see psychiatrists.
'Tis safer to be on a legal drug,
and he may cease to be a strung-out thug.
It seems the children who are not obese
are on steroids to enhance muscles' crease,
and both styles take prescribed medication.
We are junkies in a lotus nation
like Odysseus fled from in his schemes.
Brahma, on a lotus, unravels dreams."
Reuben: "I do not know your metaphor,
my interest is in Egyptian lore.
The Jews broke away from the incest knot,
which wrecked the pharaohs' line with stupid rot."
Bernard: "Abram and Sarah pretended
they were siblings when they were befriended
by the Egyptian pharaoh, who took her
as a wife, so Yaweh's wrath was a spur.
In-breeding leads to harsh blights on the land,
turning life-giving Earth to dusty sand.
Perhaps we need the Hispanics' bloodline,
sturdy stock we accept as a good sign.
If the Spanish Armada had not sank,
and the English smacked them a nasty spank,
we would read Cervantes, who died the year
his English counterpart did, Will Shakespeare."

Camille: "I do not know what books you read,
but I judge no words, rather by your deed.
Intellect is fine, but only prepares
the mind for worlds beyond our daily cares.
We are insular units, not the stars,
and when we reach for them our life has mars
that are tenfold when we mislead others,
though each of us is Christ and Earth Mothers."
Bernard laughed: "Yes, if there are infinite
incarnated worlds, then the definite
chances are we each enact every role,
depending on the status of our soul."
They parked and slid down the bank to the stream,
and she was glad god quit being the theme.
Camille was at peace, not feeling jaded,
and the water was warm as they waded.
Reuben splashed around like a sea otter,
then poured on Bernard a bit of water.
Reuben: "You have now been fully baptized,
and true paganism is realized,
so worship that tree before it falls down,
and grace your head with a poison oak crown."
They heard laughter and looked to find the source,
and Reuben once more thought he saw the horse
which he had witnessed the previous spring
that promised glory, though it left a sting.
He put on his glasses to see the ledge
and view that which surpasses all knowledge.
Charles stood on the ridge like at a door-sill,
then stripped naked and jumped off for a thrill,
falling from the sky as a lightning streak,
with barely a small ripple in the creek.
Reuben thought: The water is too shallow.
He will die as a field that is fallow
and barren because seeds are denied Earth.
So his neck will break shortly after birth.

He and Bernard rushed through the stream to find
Charles, who had evidently lost his mind.
In the mad search, Camille stayed near the shore,
her eyes closed, whispering forgotten lore,
but her prayer was disrupted by a pull
that carried her under for a mouthful
of water, and she feared some kind of shark
or leviathan had left its tooth-mark.
She struggled and felt hands pull her to air,
then saw Charles laughing at his wicked dare.
He hugged Camille and kissed her on the lips,
which Reuben viewed as the apocalypse.
Charles: "I knew there would be a wild battle,
like bulls fight to be the king of cattle,
so I distracted you to circumvent
before the lust in we males found a vent."
He held her in his arms and Bernard laughed,
but Reuben felt the pain of envy's shaft.
She took Charles by the hand to shore and wrapped
a towel round his waist while Bernard clapped,
saying, "Brilliant show, one I did not miss.
Only you survive falls through the abyss.
If there is ever a true rebellion,
I will help you unseat Heaven's lion."
She and Charles held hands, absorbing the sun,
while the other two played football for fun.
Then they sat on the sand and discussed tales
of their private hunts for elusive whales.
Camille: "I fancied myself eloquent,
with a memory like an elephant,
but when I got to the finals at state
I found myself frozen in the debate.
The theme was the electoral system,
and like a tomato left on its stem
overnight in autumn's first blasting frost,
my head went numb and our debate team lost.

I may prefer a personal contest,
where my own view matters and is the best."
Bernard: "Trophies are always nice to have,
during bad times they can act as wounds' salve.
Yet 'tis difficult to keep perspective
in a world that seems wholly subjective.
My mother has a psychotic client
who communes with ghosts and is ebullient.
She prescribes pills, which he says he will take,
but more often than not he tries to fake
normalcy when he goes to appointments;
says the Son of Man blessed him with ointments.
Perhaps the world needs such goofy, kind folks
to remind us of the illusions' yokes
that we bind ourselves to with various
distractive tools which seem nefarious."
Reuben: "Farms and ranches have gone high-tech.
We want convenience or we feel neglect.
Some politicians invest in food-land
as corporate subsidy crops expand.
Now Food Stamps are a common currency
for small farmers in our democracy.
We try to escape, but the chance narrows
as we near the age of ruling pharaohs.
The land is theirs through eminent domain
to strip-mine or field a new hybrid grain,
and grow petrol for their gasoline shops,
which wrecks the soil by not rotating crops."
Bernard: "So we all have our own stories,
embattled with foes, searching for glories.
What about you, Charles? Do you have a gripe
of how the whites tried to destroy your pipe?"
Charles laughed and rolled over on his stomach,
but his voice had an emotional lack:
"Every act has a polar contrary,
and for me karmic force does not tarry,

I get what I deserve, like it or not.
But life will change for Natives sunk in rot
when the Great Mystery decides 'tis time
to return stories of reason and rhyme.
Unlike most races we do not allow
one leader for us to blindly follow.
Many voices speak the truth among us,
going our own ways if there is a fuss
of one person choosing from many paths,
for we select our ways, weaving our swaths."
Camille: "You are communal and mystic
individuals, not a statistic."
Bernard: "This could soon be the Sahara,
with resources plundered for Samsara.
We create vast illusions for profits,
one of them being we are god's prophets,
ensnaring people to achieve our goals
by preaching we will benefit their souls."
They talked through the evening, as the moon rose,
and darkness blended with the shadows.
What little remained of the trees seemed dense,
betraying the foursome's optical sense
to believe they were in a large forest,
yet made to feel welcome as a houseguest.
Charles: "Perhaps they have accepted their fate,
and enjoy company on their estate,
wanting nothing from us but some quiet,
having been force-fed a toxic diet."
Camille: "The authorities give us cross
messages that pollution's waste and dross
is worth it to have jobs and long careers,
yet instill in us global warming fears."
She hugged Charles and he swam to the far shore;
Bernard thought him a pagan god like Thor,
controlling the elements of nature,
yet doomed to fall from his noble stature

when the war for powerful status things
destroys with the greed that Ragnorok brings.
Bernard: "We near the twilight of the gods,
relying on companies for seedpods.
You are right, Reuben: the agrarian
culture is dying, and sectarian
groups are rivaling for herd believers,
with iron rods as conscienceless reivers.
Yet Camille is right that as work-foes' till,
we require debates to express free will.
There seem to be more satellite forums
to speak against politicians' war drums,
but there is a lack of well-informed views
because the tirades become the big news."
Reuben: "Come on, we will go see if Stan
has burned his mind on dope like a fry pan."
They clambered up the creek-shelf to the car,
each convinced in their shows they were the star.
Charles saw a crow and his perspective changed
to that of the bird who so freely ranged.
A frog hopped in front of Charles with due haste,
and within its mouth Charles could seem to taste
bugs it had consumed to propagate genes,
without mom's milk because no tadpole weans.
Charles: "So the fish eat what the frogs have sown.
In a few years I will be on my own.
I have to learn the predator instinct,
or run the risk of becoming extinct.
The Iron Curtain is being unveiled,
and Eastern Germans are no longer jailed.
Yet there is cause for repetitive strife,
as the aged will not die, but cling to life.
The old generation is but a drain
on health resources, yet they feel no pain
because they are given medical care,
but begrudge poor workers socialist fare,

saying it is too near Communism,
which they pray is destroyed atheism.
The old vote for whoever will promise
health care as they lay in a diaper's piss;
tottering like babies, still they can drive,
as troops die for oil and pharmacies thrive.
New progenies think the old ways are done;
the aged fear death yet pray Armageddon
arrives with its choir and Heavenly glow,
then they can smugly sneer, 'We told you so.'"
As Charles walked he pondered his future task,
and it seemed he wore a medicine mask:
a buffalo head that could gather strength
for those whose faith would go to any length
to be free of maladies' afflictions,
and go beyond the senses' addictions.
Meanwhile the trio went to the farmhouse,
where Stan had become a drunken stoned souse.
Stacks of comic books and pornography
indicated his mind's geography
in self-seeking search for vapid pleasure,
which he described as his worthy treasure.
Reuben: "Mom asked me to check on your health,
and if you had regained your former stealth.
You once were strong, which is hard to believe
seeing you in this shape, so we will leave."
Stan: "Tell mom some kind of fabled story
of a hurt soldier and faded glory.
Please forgive the mess and my distraction.
I am a paralyzed force of action.
'Tis sad that my favorite companion
are the channels of my television.
Our nation is run by a candy-ass,
who I will not fight for, instead smoke grass.
To win a war one must induce terror,
and bring constancy as a light-bearer.

Profit alone should not be the motive,
but an enduring faith beyond votive
candles in a church for divine guidance
on how to lead our foes through death's grim dance.
If rivals are sadistic and cruel,
match the calamity with fearsome rule:
chop off heads, destroy a few minarets,
'til they know you will make them have regrets
for rebellion, as Genghis Khan once did,
but we are up for sale to the high bid."
Camille: "We are not a blood-crazed empire,
with offerings made to gods on a pyre.
The voice of the people guides our nation,
not the *Bible* gleaned for destination.
Charles thinks there are outer space aliens,
who are here to collect on unpaid liens.
I, though, accept only authority
from my heart and the laws of our city."
Stan: "Ah, the voice from a safe place above,
who thinks it can reason foes into love.
In truth, only a standardized order
can change foes' hate and desire for murder,
and that form must be born of violence,
when dissenters are dead or in silence.
If America will not do such things,
despite the concurring evil it brings,
then other nations will, and wreck our land.
While we talk of democracy as planned
for all people, other states hatch a plot
that forces enslavement for the world's lot."
The youngest Jacob appeared from playing
in the barn, holding items and saying:
"I found this tree branch that looks like the cross
Christ was hung on to save us from great loss,
and here is a blessed marijuana plant,
that proves our god's love is benevolent."

Stan: "You idiot, that bud is not ripe,
and I want no partners to yell out hype
that I cultivate an illegal crop,
which I am certain the police would stop.
Now return that scarecrow to its right place,
but the plant you can keep by my kind grace."
The child dropped to his knees with lifted arms,
entreating in a voice shrill with alarms:
"Stan, you have so much and I so little.
We can cut the profits down the middle.
My friends would be happy to buy some bud,
even if it lacks power and is crud."
Stan: "Great. Wasted youth want me to sell dope.
Such a pact sends me to Hell without hope.
'Tis a nation of fanciful escapes,
whether it is dope or fermented grapes,
or gadgets that we can manipulate
to make us feel in control and inflate
egos so we become satellite lords,
and like our president blurt foolish words.
Then feel disoriented when we find
we cannot control the communal mind.
While the third-dimension crumbles apart,
we seek therapy with gloom in our heart.
Two in three Yanks need a mind-overhaul,
the rest of us are headed for a fall."
He stood and took the scarecrow from the boy,
and stabbed it through the guts of Stan's loathed joy.
The television exploded in shards,
killing images of insipid bards.
He turned and walked to the down-stair's bathroom,
and without a word he began to groom:
shaved his beard and cut his shoulder-length hair,
when done he started cleaning the foul lair.

5

Solemn Oaths

The following spring a heavy snow fell,
and after the ring of the last school bell
Charles made his way home, pretending to be
an Eskimo shaman whose soul, set free,
ranged in search of a vision for his clans
by fasting, no chemicals to lay plans.
As he walked, a car-full of young female
Natives steered toward the curb of his trail.
Tina Forpana rolled down her window,
with a charming smile and eyes like a doe.
Tina: "Charles, you look like you need a ride,
and Tammy is in back, your future bride."
The young women laughed and Charles stopped his pace,
while Tammy White Owl hid her pretty face.
Tina: "She has light skin, which you prefer,
and she tinted her hair to crimson fur.
Your Christian beatific virgin lore
in pursuing Camille starts a race war.
The whites only give their women to blacks,
as pay for slavery and lynch attacks.
Too often our men end up in prison
due to dope, booze, and a bad decision.
Once there, they become the wives of cellmates,
devolving to blob bisexual fates.

You do not seem the type for that lifestyle,
though you are gay with your wit and bright smile."
Charles: "Why try to shame me into actions?
I take no side in divisive factions,
and do not like being told I need sex
to prevent a bloody prison rape hex.
For even those men can go on breeding
once released with the urge to plant seedling."
Tina: "Oh, come on, I was just joshing.
We need to do Tammy's laundry washing,
and her mom left whiskey at their hotel.
You can use a few stiff drinks, I can tell."
Charles looked at the snow mounds blocking his way,
and chose to release his vows for the day.
He thought: Odd how it seems to be arranged.
There are forces at work that want me changed.
Perhaps I cannot will myself to light
without experiencing others' plight
by letting them give me a helping hand,
if it is as my destiny has planned.
They drove several blocks, sliding in snow,
Charles feeling attraction for Tammy grow.
Arriving at the hotel, Charles got out,
as did Tammy, but Tina said the route
home would be awful if she stayed too long,
or had any cocktails, which could turn wrong.
Tina: "Charles, it is time you got a clue,
go perform everything I wish to do."
She snorted a laugh, steered into traffic,
and Charles felt tingling that was terrific.
They went in the room and Tammy mixed drinks,
then they gave a hearty toast with glass clinks.
Charles: "Is your family coming back soon?
I prefer not being viewed as a goon
making sly advances on a daughter,
drunk on way too much whiskey and water."

Tammy: "My mom fled to her cousin's lair
to hide from a man who will not search there.
He beat her while they were on a bad drunk,
so she is taking the cure, like a monk,
at the Rosebud Res, with perpetual
faith in the medicine man ritual.
She wants me to get an education
to bestow grace on our Native nation,
so she left me here to attend classes,
and drink whiskey that tastes like molasses.
She took my siblings, thinking I can fend
for myself, her broken heart on the mend.
Plus she had paid two weeks' rent in advance,
and the hotel took a 'no return' stance."
Charles: "You seem beyond teen adolescence,
and if I bother you with my presence,
inform me and I will let you alone,
for I feel my senses sway as if blown
by the blizzard, which moves me as it will,
yet I find the adventure a great thrill."
Tammy: "Come and sit on the bed and watch
the politicians kick it up a notch.
If we were stranded in the Donner Nest,
and they were with us, not being honest,
telling lies how they could rescue our fleet,
they would be the first people we should eat.
Instead, they are just images on-screen,
and we love dirty fighters who are mean,
so long as they have a mild ambience,
and to truth a studied ambivalence."
Tammy stretched her legs and rested her head
on Charles' shoulder, who took a drink then said:
"They promise deals to snare souls to a cord,
like Bill Clinton, a kind of pre-Jew lord,
Baal, the original come-back kid,
chopped-up every autumn as the god bid,

to make the soil ripe, then resurrected
in spring. Phallic monuments erected
in a land's capitol is nothing new,
but people resent his wife as a shrew.
If the Babylon lord wins, an attack
is destined for the land now called Iraq,
smiting those who betrayed belief in him
by evolving to faiths of the Muslim.
Americans respect dirty fighting,
if they win profits from viral blighting.
The Jews' freedom from Egypt were fictions,
created in tales based on convictions
of those who were distinct in Babylon.
To make themselves unique, they formed Zion,
without hanging gardens or ziggurats,
which gods descended to visit their brats.
Pyramids are artificial mountains,
Sinai's peak arranged the Jews' social pens."
They held each other watching images
of corporate men acting as sages.
Soon Charles was kissing Tammy on the lips,
paying no heed to political quips.
Clothes began being removed with wonder,
and Charles hoped he would commit no blunder.
Tammy: "Please give me a moment to think,
I need to wash up and put down this drink.
The television folks are watching us,
and will alert my mom, causing a fuss."
Charles laughed at her visionary mind-set,
and while she cleaned herself he was beset
by a storm of emotions on what acts
he should choose to tell his mom of the facts.
Charles dialed his house, deciding to lie,
but when Clara answered he felt too sly,
and simply told her the truth, leaving out
alcohol and his first sexual bout.

Clara asked of his vow for no oil use,
and was he playing some game, fast and loose.
Charles proclaimed his current activities
were not debauched springtime festivities.
Clara: "Since you are riding in cars now,
I will drive there, with no guff of a vow.
I shall be there shortly so be ready,
for I can drive fine, my hand is steady."
Moments later, she called to say a foot
of snow had her bound, he had to stay-put.
Tammy: "It seems the forces are at work
to keep us happy, so we must not shirk
in our duty to the powers of love,
who bless us on Earth and Heaven above."
So began a long night of young passion,
which seemed too brief with its fleshly ration,
feeding lustful fires many times over,
'til their spirits disengage and hover
their bodies, spent and drained yet still entwined,
seeking little deaths in the two-backed grind.
Finally they slept in deep dreamless states,
unaware Charles passed his genetic traits
to Tammy's body for new life to groom,
though her mind could not fathom that Fate's loom.
At dawn there was pounding upon the door,
and the young lovers awoke, stiff and sore.
At the entrance, she looked through the peephole,
and saw Arnold Staggen, built like a troll.
Her mother's ex-boyfriend, released from jail,
demanded his clothing in a loud rail.
She said they had been thrown in the garbage,
which drove Arnold through the door in a rage.
Tammy fell and he grabbed her by the hair,
causing Charles to leap in a devil's dare
on Arnold's back. Charles dug at eye-sockets,
and bit Staggen's ear, who freed her lockets.

He threw Charles off and rubbed his scratched eyes.
Charles kicked at Arnold's shin, and at the cries
of agony, Charles grabbed a full bottle,
and yelling a war-cry at high throttle,
smashed the glass beaker over Arnold's head,
who collapsed on the carpet as if dead.
Tammy quickly shut the door and urged Charles
to get dressed and leave before caught in marls
with patrolling police, sure to arrive
at the hotel suite like bees to a hive,
heeding the commands from a dispatcher,
for neighbors heard the fight's immense stature.
They dressed swiftly and parted with a kiss,
feeling an elan leap through the abyss.
Charles began walking but did not get far.
A block from the hotel a police car
pulled to the curb with a blasting siren,
and Charles thought it was the boatman, Chiron,
to ferry Charles into a Hades' scene
of the legal system, corrupt and mean.
At the shouted words telling him to halt,
Charles decided he would take the whole fault
for the hard beating his foe had suffered
to keep Tammy unexposed and buffered.
Yet Charles kept walking despite the order,
his mind changing to that of a hoarder,
remembering all the good things life held.
Like at Christmas when he and Betty shelled
shrimp in the kitchen sink for a banquet,
and how his mother gave him a blanket
she had quilted from his favorite clothes,
and taught him to accept that which he loathes.
Only by knowing the situation
as it is, without capitulation,
can he work to improve his story-line,
not holding grudges with a baby's whine.

As Charles thought of these things he felt detached,
his senses soaring as mind's door unlatched.
Distantly he heard the command to stop,
and turned to see a gun aimed by the cop.
Charles walked further, then heard the warning shot,
and knew he would join Maddox in a plot
at the graveyard, being embalmed worm stew,
if on that path Charles chose to continue.
Death could be an intriguing cruise, he thought:
one where enlightenment cannot be bought,
and stories are told of every nation,
with animals speaking in elation,
using voices raised with pure harmony,
not sold or killed for pleasure and money.
The Book of the Dead would open its runes,
and he would clearly understand their tunes.
Yet he also knew such an afterlife
could not last long due to spiritual strife.
He would be sucked back into toiling greed,
perhaps a panhandler for daily mead.
It was best to stay in the life he knew,
with a mother guarding him while he grew.
Charles fell and laid like the ancient Earth mounds,
as police gave contradictory sounds:
"Do not move. Stand up. Keep your hands in place.
Stay still. Turn around. Let us see your face."
Feeling led to the slaughter like mild sheep,
Charles' arms were wrenched and the handcuffs bit deep.
He gave only his name, having no card
as written by a bureaucratic bard.
Nor a Social Security number,
because Charles fathomed it would encumber
his freedom in the computer era,
with satellites prayed to, circling terra.
Tammy was led out, crying and handcuffed,
and dragged to a car to be shoved and stuffed.

Officer Tratz: "A man is dead in there,
and you act like you truly do not care.
Think of your mom and the pain of her strife.
This will steal at least ten years of her life."
Charles: "I gave you the number of her phone.
Just read me my rights and leave me alone."
His age was determined by a phone call,
and Charles was taken to Juvenile Hall:
photographed, finger-printed, and strip-searched,
his reputation forever besmirched.
Clara and Beatrice visited him,
and he told his version, stoic and grim,
editing the sex banquet, and after
he was done, Betty had nervous laughter.
While Clara wept the three held hands and sighed,
feeling their emotions rise like the tide
ebbs and eddies of the orbiting moon,
which folklore says makes a man a crazed loon.
His family's energy helped remind
Charles that life should not be stuck on rewind.
The past was done, he must live in the now,
and not be concerned with why, when, and how.
Clara: "Perhaps you could get a hair-cut
so you do not look like a half-breed mutt.
You can pass as *wasicu* with your skin,
and get a lighter sentence for your sin."
Charles: "It seems pointless now to continue
a vision quest in a courtroom's venue.
I broke my solemn oaths, and I must face
white men's judgment to put me in my place.
I will get a hair-cut, and call Bernard
to donate his fine clothes. Though it is hard
to play their legal system's game of Hells,
there is a power at work that compels.
My act was no sin, yet I shall be meek.
I thought false humility for the weak.

Now I see it is how the system whirls,
with global leaders whose intrigue unfurls."
At Charles' bond hearing the judge refused bail,
and ruled Charles be tried as an adult male,
for Tammy White Owl had changed her story
to make her seem remorseful and sorry.
Often she turned it over in her mind
to look her best, and truth was hard to find.
Charles loathed her, but his mind a warrior's,
realized she did as told by lawyers,
whose job was to win the case at all cost,
despite her being traumatized and lost.
At least she did not accuse Charles of rape
to avoid a slut stigma and escape
her mother's wrath for promiscuity,
which they had practiced with acuity.
Tammy was released to her mother's care,
and went in hiding at their Rosebud lair,
refusing to return to testify.
Her clan found it easy to justify
the slaying of Arnold for his abuse.
Charles was released from the death sentence noose,
yet he still faced charges of man-slaughter,
for the court used Arnold as a martyr.
But when his past was unveiled as shady,
dope-making and assault on his lady,
it was hard to find media support
for Arnold as a victim by the court
The Levis had a lawyer acquaintance,
much respected for his communal stance
in free *pro bono* work among the poor,
and he took Charles' case, opening the door
to self-defense for his cause in action,
and Charles was freed with five years' probation.
Fall equinox was passed celebrating
with friends and family, and Jew-baiting.

Bernard: "Now you see why we have law books
in the *Bible* to stone or free our crooks.
Perhaps you owe Arnold's kin a goat-herd,
though in this era it would be absurd.
Did they try to turn you into a snitch?
Some people do that in hopes to get rich.
There are so many covert agencies
who act like they make royal regencies,
battling with each other to gain support
to run the system and the Supreme Court."
Charles: "I was not approached by any spies
that I was aware of, to my surprise.
Though one inmate continued asking me
about my case, and perhaps charged a fee
for relaying the data to the guards,
when we were done playing a game of cards.
The others would not sit with him and chat,
probably knowing he was a cop-rat."
Bernard: "Paid informants are now the norm,
with immunity for a crime-spree storm.
The career criminals likewise get wealth
from taxpayers by an gencies' stealth.
Covert leagues expect honor among thieves,
paying for what only a fool believes.
The reason I ask is I have some weed,
a crop from Reuben with a potent seed.
I know you have to pass the urine test,
and will not bother you or be a pest.
I just want you aware that we get high,
so when we do it you can say goodbye."
Charles: "Five months I sat in a cell to rot,
nor will I return to that life for pot.
It was a difficult lesson to learn
amidst the party cults that roil and churn.
I suppose I shall have to find new friends,
as once revelry starts it never ends."

Bernard: "I can keep it under control,
and with grass can play a different role,
expanding consciousness with it as guide
above my fellow humans' bleating tide."
Charles: "That is the lie of hazy pipe dreams,
and soon you will be caught within its schemes.
You now believe life is an illusion,
made by the Hindu gods in collusion.
Then comes a day when it will not matter
what you do, feeling your psyche shatter.
But enough of this. I shall not lecture
how you should arrange your own mind's structure."
Bernard: "Perhaps you are right to critique
the desire for escapism I seek.
I abuse my mom's use of Jewish tools
that take me hostage at our Sabbath shuls.
'Tis strange how we chain ourselves to a link
that we hope will free us, instead we sink."
Late hours they spent talking in Charles' bedroom,
and how he was lucky to avoid doom.
Or, as Bernard mentioned, Charles might be meant
to have roles that fulfill the gods' intent.
As the night waned they moved to the front-porch,
watching the sun rise as the Heaven's torch.
Enjoying freedom, Charles heard the crickets
singing with him, hidden in the thickets.
His non-fossil fuel vow seemed childish,
yet taught him about an Ideal wish,
and not expect life to follow his plans
as if he were a star to loving fans.
The ensuing years would be quite intense,
with a twenty-year suspended sentence
hanging over him as a guillotine,
and the rat-maze seemingly Byzantine.
Charles: "I will have to perform monkey tricks,
now that I am stuck in the system's mix.

Yet I can enjoy the beauty of dawn
and the smell of dew exhaled on the lawn.
The space aliens continue their work
on oracles making us go berserk."
Bernard: "So will begin another age,
and they want your genetic lineage.
Perhaps our chakras are tiny space ships
that guide us through our diverse cosmic trips.
Unlike me, you will be culled from the stock
and taken to a newly-made Earth's dock.
I prefer to think of it as a brew
concocted by gods who have plans for you.
The very devil is in the details.
With that, it is time for me to set sails."
They shook hands and Bernard went home to sleep,
while Charles thought of ways to mend Earth's up-keep.
Though he would no longer take solemn vows
easy to forsake by a stirring rouse,
he believed his duty was to restore
Earth's simple pleasures that humans abhor.
He had judged the older generation
as major consumers of the nation,
yet sometimes frugal from the impression
of the 1930's Great Depression.
He went in the small house and cleaned dishes,
the first time in months he had no wishes
to be above humans in their despair,
glad he could partake in the party's fare.
There was a trapped mouse with a broken neck
under the sink. Charles tossed it in the dreck,
saying: "Sorry, but your choice was not right
in being betrayed by your appetite.
Perhaps I can get a cat from Reuben
to keep varmints from invading our den.
Taxpayer funds support labs to clone mice,
who breed quick as lightning and carry lice."

The telephone rang and Charles answered it,
not knowing his life would soon be re-writ.
Tammy White Owl said she had heard the news
Charles had been released, and hoped her ruse
of hiding at the Rosebud Settlement
had helped him, for such had been her intent.
Charles: "Telling the truth would have worked better,
and freed me sooner from bounded fetter."
Tammy: "I was too ashamed of our acts,
and did not properly recall the facts.
I did not want a bad reputation
by an out-of-control situation.
You are free now and that is what matters,
and want you to know before the chatters
reach you with their rumors, which are flagrant,
that with your child I am five months' pregnant."
There was a pause, then Charles heavily sighed,
yet, for some reason, he was not surprised.
He was still paying for a night of fun,
and wondered should he have a gene test done.
Charles: "I assume this phone call is a sign
annunciating the child will be mine.
Just what is it you expect me to do?
When I needed help you took wing and flew.
Obviously I cannot trust your word,
and pretending I love you is absurd.
I will do what I can for the child's sake.
No living soul should think 'tis a mistake.
What I ask is you stay off alcohol,
as booze makes an embryo's growth forestall.
I will not take care of a water-head
and would leave it in the woods to be dead."
Tammy: "I have something that is my own.
You were a donor when the seed was sown.
I will allow no one to interfere,
so keep your suggestions and stupid fear.

I did not phone you so we could bicker,
and you are the one to avoid liquor,
because you were like a rampaging beast,
striking Arnold until his breathing ceased."
Charles: "'Tis strange how your memory grows dim,
as I did it to protect you from him.
But if you want to play as a mother,
I will not refuse your urge. Why bother?
It is not the same as playing with dolls,
when a babe cries in a diaper it fouls.
I predict that within a short time-span
your mom will be guardian of your clan,
and you made pregnant by another man.
You will add to lineage confusion
with your pell-mell sexual profusion."
Tammy: "To Hell with you and your forecast.
I merely wanted our bygones be past,
but you let the bile humor in you rise.
You will end up a cook, burning French-fries,
not even good enough to keep that job,
amounting to nothing, a useless blob."
Yet as her tirade went on, Charles felt glee
that she had changed to anger from her plea
to be understood for her betrayal,
which had raised his ire, causing him to rail.
When he began to laugh at her insult
of how he had joined a White Goddess' cult,
her voice became more wrathful and she sobbed,
feeling alive as mating instincts throbbed.
She started laughing too, and they relaxed,
letting emotions wane as they had waxed.
Charles: "Now that we have that vitriol out,
let us be reasonable and not pout.
When we combine it is a collision,
so you have to make your own decision.
We form one another in images

of our desires, as if writ on pages,
demanding flesh to put it on stages.
But now there is an innocent involved,
who is not a mere problem to be solved.
It takes more time and nurture than I have,
so let us be polite for wounds to salve.
I will try to be less of a prophet,
and if I find work, shall share the profit."
Aware that she could not ask any more,
the talk ended with civil demeanor.

6

The Dance

The school's homecoming dance was the next week,
and Camille let the information leak,
in hopes the rumor mill would reach Reuben,
that her passion for him was not hidden.
But he wanted a woman whose intent
was to express through sex more fulfillment.
He was also unsure of how to feel
when it came to emotions for Camille.
Were they friends or lovers, and did he care
to analyze it and lay his soul bare?
So he asked Gloria Bask to the dance,
and she awaited the night of romance.
Bernard and Camille also made a date,
and Charles went with a girl who had no mate,
but wanted to go to be with comrades,
so Charles played her game of dressing-up fads.
He had told no one of his child to be,
for Bernard would talk of Samsara's bree,
and Clara lecture her disappointment,
which could be expected from a parent.
Charles stayed humorous, though stricken with guilt.
As when a river becomes blocked by silt,
and pollution flows into backwaters
to poison our future sons and daughters.

So damming his spirit caused Charles to change,
and he spent long hours wandering the grange,
mood ebullient, then darkness descending
to make him laugh with choked tears, while sending
a mixture of prayers and foul curses
to the four directions of life's verses.
He desired total control of their songs,
and mete karmic justice for all the wrongs.
He regretted the spilling of bad-blood,
yet prayed for a Noah's Ark fiery flood.
He might spare his white friends, if they would join,
so long as they promised not to purloin
seeds of humankind stemming from his loin.
He tried not to revert to his old ways,
but soon he was praying with the sun's rays,
alone in the hills of Rapid City,
fasting in hopes of a revealed ditty
spanning generations, gender, and race,
bestowing on Charles a Heavenly grace.
While classmates reveled with no sacrifice,
parades, football games, dressed in artifice,
Charles felt his young shell held an ancient soul
that knew darkness and light, yet had no role
in the modern era of distractions,
which people fought for in diverse factions.
Baal Clinton was doing his utmost
to win the country's presidential post
with promises of a new covenant
between voters, god, and the government.
Those who were wise enough not to trust him
chose a candidate whose chances were slim
because he formed an independent bloc,
and talked like an alien high on grok.
Bush simmered, not believing he could lose
after such support for his Iraq ruse.
Surely people preferred a well-staged war

than a leader who had no moral core.
Better to deal with the devil one knows,
than an unknown factor running the shows.
Though Charles detached from policies of state
Bernard wrote scenes for Charles to illustrate
a comic book about a Jew hero
who was first born in the time of Nero,
and lived for centuries, watching cycles
revolve in preparation for Michael's
war with evil, all merged in a dragon,
whose front-man was the Beast, Ronald Reagan.
Charles did the drawings of Captain Zion,
whose sidekick was a Heavenly lion.
They wrecked foes with an espionage coil,
while making side-deals with Muslims for oil.
Charles expressed doubt on the term "towel-head",
and Bernard nodded, agreeing, but said:
"You can always tell the villain in flicks,
if white they say "nigger" in tired old shticks.
Blacks have logo hats, like a business name,
of a civil right's leader who reached fame
by spear-heading the Black Islamic State,
killed by their prophet to manipulate
power and control over the women,
with tirades against whites as an omen
of the future, unless Negroes unite
with Islam's banner and put up a fight.
The hats help clear bad blood, and like a trend
will quickly dissolve and come to its end."
Charles: "The Black Muslims are too controlling
for normal folks who are just fad-trolling,
and the Black Islam prophet, Farrakhan,
is a goon with weapons like Genghis Khan.
I would go to Africa, were I black,
where I could rape women and not catch flak
for being a rampaging animal,

with no deep ponderings on which to mull."
Bernard: "Why go there when you can make cash
talking to white crowds of your cocaine stash?
So you cannot sing or play instruments,
just get onstage and shout your hatred vents.
Music machines will provide background noise,
and anyone can do it who employs
a riff and rap about slapping bitches
so hard they require hospital stitches.
There is a lot of money to be made,
talent-less thugs are a capital trade,
receiving awards as geniuses free
to do as they like, taught as poetry.
The black gangsters prey on their own people,
like cannibals at a lord Christ steeple,
then brag about their lore, with souls for sale,
and warn their paying crowd not to tell-tale
because the legal system is the yoke
of oppression driven by all white folk."
Charles: "'Tis hard to respect an audience
who offer their women to violence,
but if we create such a comic book,
we should give it a sarcastic outlook.
Otherwise we would sink to their level
of filth where I do not want to revel."
Bernard: "To be fair, I had Zion sing
of the beating police gave Rodney King.
He was crazed on dope and fled a crime scene,
and the thumping cops gave was on each screen.
It may be true we get what we deserve,
but that savage attack hit a raw nerve.
The police will be forgiven their crime,
for I doubt they shall do any jail-time.
I imagine King can win a lawsuit,
and perhaps the beating was worth the loot.
Our nation has a strange duality

of throwing money at brutality
because bestial instincts are still mental,
though we believe ourselves kind and gentle.
Destiny can be reached by a quick car,
and unbalanced budgets show what we are.
Decent jobs are too few or underpaid,
buying from foreign lands stuff we once made."
Charles: "So this comic has an agenda,
like the Nazis used for propaganda.
I have no interest in politics,
because once manure flies it always sticks
to the one who flings it and the target,
and as you say, we deserve what we get.
Deregulation is the new mantra,
with the federal bosses as Santa
in gifts to bail out the Savings and Loan,
who cheated investors of what they own
by lobbying Congressional members,
but in twenty-years no one remembers,
and chances are that by then one might win
the presidency washed clean of his sin."
Bernard: "You see? You know more than you think.
I prefer to believe we will not sink
to electing one of the Keating Five
to direct our nation in a nosedive.
I am not sure if our memory fails
to allow rearrangement of the tales.
What we need is Ganesha, who recalls
with his elephant-head, the god of walls,
everything we do as we roam the maze
for the rewards that attract and amaze."
Charles: "Rats succeed in a labyrinth feat,
as history unfolds, a dull repeat."
Bernard: "Ganesh mounts a rodent war god
whom Hindu tales blend to come from one pod.
Now that global society is near,

people can see foreigners as their peer.
Yet as Berlin's wall comes down we react
by finding new enemies in Iraq."
Charles: "The deniability factor
means the hiring of a half-baked actor.
Edicts issued are difficult to trace
back to the source of the puppeteer's face.
Rooting out the rot has no true merit,
though the media acts as a ferret,
digging through dirt for us to have a glimpse
of the diseased political whores' pimps.
You do not have to give me any proof
the president's rat-race is for a goof.
Whether good or evil, why be judges?
But once in power they settle grudges."
Bernard: "Of course they resent the public
for long campaigns with dirty boots to lick.
When we see sideshow freaks we tend to laugh,
whether at a state fair's two-headed calf,
or a sick pathological liar
with stickers to promote a dream empire.
They must get weary of eating corn-dogs,
and talking to farmers viewed as drunk trogs.
The winner gets revenge with war tactics,
for making him do monkey-trick antics,
sending sons and daughters to fight for oil.
So we shape each other in ceaseless toil.
Do we act as gods judging a cockroach?
My mom takes a more cerebral approach:
evil is just chemicals in our brain
misfiring neurons, making us insane."
Charles: "Yes, truth is becoming subjective,
depending on a person's perspective.
Candidates need cockroaches' endurance,
but I must prepare for the high school dance."
Bernard: "Tonight will be innocent fun,

and let me know when your drawings are done
so I can put them on my computer,
with safety against a virus looter.
You can keep the suit you wore at trial
if you do not puke on the bathroom's tile,
praying to the porcelain god we know
does not forgive or have grace to bestow."
Charles: "If I am the only Native there
I will leave early to avoid the stare
of people who think I am invading
celebrations for folks of white shading.
I would like at least one dance with Camille,
but thought I should check to see how you feel."
Bernard: "I forced my ego to deflate,
as for her 'tis only a pity date,
though she refused to admit or confess
she wants to see Gloria in her dress.
Camille's pride is pricked, and envy follows
that Reuben has new worshipping hallows
to a female who enjoys sex and lust,
like a pagan goddess with a big bust.
I might be jealous of Reuben as well,
but I do not wish to explore that Hell.
If you dance with Camille, the cowboys' rage
might be provoked to a high-racist stage.
I am not used to cultural tension.
It is silly to have apprehension
every time one sees people of color,
and it makes my wits seem weak and duller.
I suppose 'tis a Jewish heritage
to learn and adapt to control the stage,
writing the *Odyssey* as Jacob's age.
Stealing tales from the Greeks' tribe of Danaan
to supply the history of Canaan,
shaping from our own craft a shrewd sinner.
We will drive to your place after dinner."

At the dance, when Camille saw Gloria
in Reuben's arms, swept in euphoria,
Camille thought she would drown her hate with wine,
and asked Bernard to get some by design.
He told her there was beer in the car's trunk,
but was having too much fun to get drunk.
They briefly argued, he gave her the keys
to be rid of her and the angry pleas.
Bernard's favorite song was being played,
and he saw the night's plans getting waylaid.
He said to Charles: "Great. Now I have to deal
with her vomiting an expensive meal.
Do you have any homophobia?
The urge to dance is in my tibia."
Charles: "Me? Not really. Come on, let us spin
to this Hellish music raising a din."
They danced in-step like mercury fluid
shifting in fusion, then parting amid
crowd comments that they were flaming faggots,
who should die and be eaten by maggots.
Stacy Kurtz was intrigued and grabbed Bernard
to gavotte with her, while Charles was shoved hard
by Tracey Arngton, a brutish fellow,
stunned that Charles pushed back with a fierce bellow:
"What is your malfunction, you idiots?
I will take you down to a size that fits."
Reuben stepped between them as the fight brewed,
and used diplomatic wits that were shrewd:
"Tracey, he is on probation, and jail
awaits you both as the end of this tale."
He pulled free of Reuben and swung a fist
that hit Charles so his eyes saw a dull mist.
He dropped to a knee, and shook his head clear,
then rose against his pecking-order peer.
His instincts thrived and reason was annulled:
he ran at Tracey's legs, grabbed them and pulled

him to the floor. Charles kicked wildly and punched,
knowing blest joy when Tracey's nose crunched
with the impact of Charles' fisted knuckles,
not caring if he would soon wear shackles.
However, Tracey's bulk was too massive,
and they struggled, the audience passive,
watching as the competitors battled.
Tracey forced Charles to the floor and straddled
his legs as he tried to knee Tracey's groin,
Charles tasting blood, with flavor like a coin.
Tracey pinned him, reared back and cocked his arm,
throwing a fierce punch that did Charles no harm,
for he saw it coming and moved his head,
Tracey broke his hand on the floor instead.
Tracey grabbed his knuckles and at his moans,
the circle parted for the chaperones.
Charles laughed as Tracey was taken away,
but the typing teacher grabbed Charles to say:
"You have two choices: you can leave right now,
or we phone the police to end this row."
Charles argued that Tracey started the brawl,
but could see he was destined for a fall,
so he joined Camille in the parking lot,
trying to make her consciousness unknot.
He told her of the fight while she drank beer,
and when she cried he wiped away the tear.
Charles: "You are a melancholic drinker,
in cobwebs of a passionate thinker.
While it is a way to clear out one's mind,
you may release any monsters you find."
Camille: "If I do that it will be puke
when my stomach and brain suffer a nuke.
I admire how you are so defiant,
and do not play an industrious ant.
We need people who are not worker drones,
after our lineage is shaped as clones.

Can you make sense or am I slurring words?
Soon I will be singing in flight with birds."
Charles: "I shall try not to take advantage,
though driven mad by a spermy blind rage.
I will sit in front to not be tempted,
because no human has lust exempted."
Camille: "Oh, Charley, you are not like that.
Will Bernard forgive me being a brat?
Like he would say, I have found a new shtick,
getting drunk as a hopeless romantic."
Charles: "A person can enjoy suffering
with all the misery one's mind can bring,
especially if one feels that the wrongs
should prevent others from dancing to songs.
Some can package existential angst tales,
and sell it to consumers for retails.
Free will to deliberately immerse
oneself in misery is a commerce.
Perhaps you can reshape your diary
to show the Hell you go through, with fiery
condemnations of the pain in high school,
using woe as a literary tool."
Camille: "How you know things is infernal,
though I like to think it is a journal.
I am pegged as an introvert bookworm,
who quietly judges others as form
without content or knowledge, which I have
to use on perceived slights as a balm salve."
Charles: "At least you wound no one but yourself.
I admire those who read from a bookshelf.
Stories are part of our evolution,
helping to instigate revolution.
I suppose if I want to stir up such
among Lakota I should get in touch
with the mother language and traditions
beyond entertainments' false renditions."

Camille: "Cultures are strange double-edged swords.
How to package them yet stay true to words
is a woe I do not have to deal with
because my people have their own set myth
to be repackaged, of course for profit;
and, like Mormons, follow any prophet.
Have they tried to win you with Heaven's bribe?
'Tis their work, thinking the lost Jewish tribe
migrated to America and saw
Jesus Christ emerge from Earth's Hellish maw."
Charles: "Every once in a while they arrived
at our door with the beliefs they contrived.
When my mom was drunk she would let them in,
and argue about Original Sin.
She had a belly-full of poisoned fruits
force-fed to her by the boarding-school brutes.
She sees now Christians battle over us,
so she tells them to leave without a fuss."
The two talked and Camille stopped at five beers
to not make drinking one of her careers.
She also had to make an allowance,
finding that she had a low tolerance.
Feeling giddy with the alcohol bliss,
she leaned over the seat, gave Charles a kiss.
He returned it and as their passions rose,
Bernard and Stacy left the dancing shows.
They caught the two in a lovers' grapple,
as if lips were a forbidden apple.
Charles and Camille were jolted with surprise,
but Bernard laughed while Stacy hid her eyes.
Bernard: "So now you two are locked at lips.
Charles, get in back for more convenient grips.
I hope we do not require a beer-run.
Did you drink it like Attila the Hun?"
Camille: "I had a few, so rest easy.
Spread no rumors, we are not that sleazy.

Does she think we are good enough for her,
or whip us hard like an egg-sucking cur?"
Bernard: "If you turn into a mean drunk,
I shall have to lock you in the car trunk.
I feel like a cock with too many hens.
She joins us for a party at Reuben's."
Stacy: "I am at the third-level tiers
in the ranking amongst our high school peers,
so I went to the dance with just my friends,
and will put on a veneer that pretends
we get along fine, Camille, for the sake
of the night's fare, which I wish to partake."
Camille's mind was silent soliloquies,
then she offered Stacy apologies.
At Jacob's farmhouse the beer quickly flowed,
and soon cars were lined-up along the road.
Reuben's plan to get Gloria alone
was dismantled since the party had grown
out-of-control, and he was somewhat pleased
he was the source to have Bacchus appeased.
Bernard and Stacy went up to a room,
locking the door so their love-play could bloom.
Camille began drinking wine, fast and hard.
After vomiting she searched for Bernard
to take her home, but she could not find him,
so passed out in his car, her senses dim.
Stanley, who had purchased the alcohol,
dropped to his hands and knees so he could crawl
among the young women, sniffing crotches.
Seeing him, Charles' face went wane with blotches,
and stood in a corner, releasing screams
as memories of Maddox, like in dreams,
raced through Charles' fierce mind, demanding vengeance
to even the score of karmic engines.
Stanley stood up and Charles saw the gold hoop
hanging from Stan's ear, and the entire group

parted like the tide on a breaker's shore
when the storm-gods shake Earth with a downpour.
Charles felt paralyzed and could only shout,
as if from his mouth demons were cast out.
Stanley approached him with a smirking grin,
and unlatched the gold earring's holding pin.
Stanley straightened Charles' tie and suit collar,
and when his voice faded from a holler,
Stan said: "I think you should have this token.
'Tis all you get for oaths we have broken."
Charles' desire for revenge told him to fight,
yet he also had the urge to take flight.
He prayed for the proper course of action,
and responded in a second's fraction.
He took Stan's palm that held the gold earring,
and closed his foe's fingers around the thing.
Charles: "Though you wish to shatter my psyche,
'til we end this matter, keep the trophy.
It is more than that which I am after,
as it will not return joy and laughter
to my kinfolk, stolen in the contest,
nor relieve the aching in my mom's breast.
There will come the right time when we throw down
a gauntlet in which one of us shall drown,
losing the senses and feeling adrift,
looking through our past life, trying to sift
good from evil, still attached to objects,
and if Fate has it so, made Hell's subjects."
Stanley: "Those are fine words and I agree,
but I believe Christ pays my worldly fee
if I am penitent, as he so taught,
paying for my sins with triumph he brought.
There is always reaction to movement.
Displaced particles met with bereavement
can send one into a whirling tailspin.
I learned pain and hate only make me grin.

Though it may not be proper etiquette,
it helps me live without lasting regret.
You best leave before I am laid to waste
on whiskey, which when I have its taste
become nasty and crazy paranoid,
hounding for a fight you cannot avoid."
Charles gazed at the looks of the revelers'
and saw the confrontation had allures
for them in hopes of watching blood be spilled,
and have atavistic longings fulfilled.
Cornered and frantic for his next movements,
Charles breathed deeply for several moments,
then he brushed by Stanley and walked away,
hearing behind him raucous laughter bray.
He went past Bernard's car and saw Camille
dry-heaving the remnants of her last meal.
He thought: My curse upon all whom are white.
If lucky, she will not be raped tonight.
He walked through the wastelands and heard the call
of a cougar coughing, which made him stall.
The creature approached him as if by plan;
Charles tried to enter its thoughts as human,
but the cat growled, and Charles saw in his mind
the ability to change shapes and find
the primordial source of all creatures,
and went in the beast with altered features.
Through the darkness the two walked side-by-side,
and when they reached the creek's bank, the cat cried,
leaving Charles to sit on the ledge to think.
He slid down the bank and watched a wolf drink
from the stream, and Charles also quenched his thirst,
believing he was the last and the first
hunter of the expanding universe,
teaching the animals their language verse.
Its lolling tongue hanging, the wolf panted,
then they lifted their voices and canted

a song in howls to the force of nature,
which seemed to them a hymnal of rapture.
Charles crossed the stream, looked and the wolf was gone,
and desired to have a new form to don.
He climbed the far bank and laughed at the mud
smeared on his clothes. An adrenalin flood
had him dance in circles, spinning with joy
and abandon as when he was a boy,
learning the steps from Elders at Pow-wows,
who gave gifts The Great Mystery endows.
When exhausted, Charles laid down and rested,
asking stars if he was being tested.
Senses alive, he heard soft padded feet,
but did not worry if it was a feat
for him to accomplish in hopes to shed
the corporate distractions in his head.
He felt a tongue licking the sweaty sheen
off him and knew he could beat the machine.
He saw a curious coyote smile
a mischievous grin that had Charles rile
from supine pose and scratch the canine's ear,
who ran pursuing the tail on his rear.
He thought: So the vast cycles continue,
and we search for light or change of venue,
chasing in hunt for what we feel we lack,
with a smog-light from a nuclear stack.
Energy fogs our senses with misuse,
believing our own lies and intrigues' ruse.
I must learn to function with discernment,
and use experience in each movement,
with many past lives for me to draw from,
a killer, homeless, and dancer to drum,
I am of value to society:
an animal with no false piety.

7

The Bard of the Bardos

Charles knew that he was a unified soul,
and despite varieties of the role
he was playing with the characters' cast
he knew future plots would become the past.
So he began dividing up his life
as if armed with a spiritual knife.
When with friends he laughed and stayed humorous,
while at sweat-lodges he tried to impress
Elders with insight to the spirits' realm,
as if his hand was steady on the helm.
Amused by his attempts to be profound,
they let him babble his vacuous sound,
for at least he worked to expand language
beyond the typical young adult's age.
Charles felt as if his soul lifted a cowl,
and tried to be kind to Tammy White Owl.
He saw too many women had been left
to taxpayers' money, or live bereft
with children, and the endless argument
of support by ranks of the government.
Charles wanted to will himself to success,
yet as he partook he saw much excess.
It seemed perpetual adolescence
defined the era's outlook and essence.

Older generations often complained
that the young had no self-control, nor reined
in their desire for ever increasing
appetites the old believed was leasing
the future with debts they could not afford,
yet they too played with gadgets, as minds poured
through gears as if to a satellite lord.
Charles focused on scientific study,
and cognitive thoughts became unmuddy.
The dark energy of modern physics
could be the evil in metaphysics:
between electrons, protons, and neutrons
is where the shadow falls in sunlight dawns
of new epochs that revolve like the past,
despite molecules reflecting light's cast.
He came to believe the world could shape-shift,
and love of technology caused a rift
between humans and their life-giving source,
as aliens conspired for Earth's course.
It seemed too many sins went unpunished,
and wealthy people's work was near finished,
as the Earth staggered from their labors' stains,
they could escape in space ships from death pains.
Yet to such scum many had surrendered
their free will for the convenience tendered.
Charles refused to be so dominated
in a filthy cage that was gold-plated.
Perhaps he was meant to shift karmic gears,
and become the greed-mongers' nightmare fears.
First, though, he would have to pay the blood-score,
and send Stanley's spirit to Chiron's shore.
Charles realized revenge would be bitter
if such schemes did not make the world better.
To serve a higher good was his purpose,
so did not let his rage build to surplus.
He went about his business and school work,

watching Native friends go slowly berserk.
They would not pursue an education;
liquor's promise was an obfuscation.
Charles broached the subject with his friends the night
of school term tests to perceive their insight.
Charles had finished the comic book drawing,
and though Bernard was weary and yawning,
he said: "Our bodies are mere fleshly dots,
most of our essence is in certain spots.
Hindus call them chakras. They are divine
if we keep them pure and heed the gods' sign.
Yet by our means the world is polluted,
scenery rebels for what we looted.
Some think angels do it at god's commands,
and thus wash blood, like Pilate, from their hands.
Maybe our aligned chakras are space ships
for an exodus and apocalypse.
The cosmos has no end to conniptions,
ask Reuben. He studies the Egyptians."
Charles turned to where the other was nodding,
who asked for patience if words were plodding.
Reuben: "I have studied that ancient sites
were chosen for stars in religious rites.
The sphinx was a vagina to give births,
pyramids were breasts to nurse to high-berths.
Female structures caught male energy rods
in various forms referred to as gods,
who were all related, and so incest
between the pharaohs and sisters seemed best.
The Egyptians had stomach deities,
hearts and livers, too, like the fealties
by modern humans to pharmacy pills
for digestive tracts and sexual thrills.
So we all pay for our inner-working
we dare not fathom, where shades are lurking.
We appease the depths with medications,

or twirl shadows with Soma vacations.
People like us gather for a huddle
to brag of fishing in a mud-puddle,
and the ones that escaped from our harpoons,
which may evolve to spoil the promised boons."
Charles: "We believe in demand and supplies,
and our prayers are answered with replies
from those in power who concoct new faiths,
and former gods are homeless spoiler wraiths.
People wanted a god to maim and kill,
he even took that pain, paying sin's bill."
Reuben: "Organized religions and states
are often entwined for their single fates.
For now, Americans have their own choice
in selecting a god to hear their voice.
Akhnaton decreed there was but one god,
and made the Egyptians worship and laude,
naming it Aton, who became the Jews'
Adonai, as all languages infuse.
When the Pharaoh died, some loyalists stuck
to their beliefs, and were chained to the muck
of slavery, though some fled to Canaan,
stealing the *Odyssey* from the Danaan.
Judaic, Christian, and Islamic faiths
are bastard children of pagan god wraiths.
The tales of begotten are full of noise,
Solomon, Christ, and Ishmael were boys
spawned by questionable reputation,
who went to Egypt, the pharaoh's nation."
Bernard: "With some luck Baal and his mate
will not be able to consolidate
more power in the presidential post,
reforming country as king and queen host.
The states have already given away
much control to corporate puppet's sway.
In the era of eminent domain

The Homestead Act is nulled by those who reign.
Strange, only a few hundred years ago
Natives could move as they please, on the go."
Charles: "Now humans escape in fantasies
from the third-dimension to be at ease,
while the world around us becomes poisoned,
the gods receive mixed messages we send.
We think we earn deities' lenience
in their gifts of gadgets' convenience,
programming ourselves to be consumers,
we spin out destiny like Fate-loomers.
What choice will you make now that school is done?
It is expected we take some action."
Bernard: "We go diverse ways, as we should.
I to a college for work that pays good.
Perhaps earn a degree in business math
as an honest book-keeper so the wrath
of god does not make me a perversion,
a Hell's accountant Saint Peter version.
I will likewise take computer courses
for a brain run by satellite forces."
Reuben: "My dad has the house deed on hold,
though barren fields around it have been sold.
Stan now says he is going to marry,
and is rejoining the military,
so the house is mine to live in until
my father retires from farming the till.
He wants to be certain I know the trade
when I inherit the business he made.
My half-wit brothers do not deserve trust,
they would gamble our future and go bust.
One bought a house mortgage with credit cards,
now his debt chases him through trailer-yards.
Another is a hand for landscaping,
his only solace is booze-escaping.
They all thought they would be autonomous,

but fell from the heights to that of a mouse
running the corporate maze for rewards
to end up on loony or cancer wards
for constantly inhaling noxious fumes
of bug-spraying and fertilizer dooms."
Charles: "Does that mean you will go organic
and add hysteria to the panic
of people who worry of what they eat
in hybrid cloned food and hormoned stock meat?"
Reuben: "No, to compete with larger farms
I must inject the cows and pray no harms
come to the consumers via the dope,
though prayer seems useless despite my hope.
What of you, Charles? We talked of our futures.
How will you deal with your dual natures?"
Charles: "Yes, having a career seems quite fraught
with piling-up money that goes to naught,
for our work has a direct opposite,
or so it appears by what Fates have writ.
We say we work to bear a family,
repeating it as if a homily,
yet think nothing of spending into debt,
convincing ourselves, as told, to accept
gadget luxuries into vapid lives,
so we become worker drones in bee-hives.
We are eked enough opium honey
to buy Soma and cars with our money.
This, people conceive makes them free to roam,
since the world is unsafe to walk from home."
So the conversation turned on topics,
including the science of light optics.
Charles slept on Bernard's couch and the next day
phoned his cousin, Manny, to find a way
to Rosebud to see Charles' newborn daughter,
but Manny's truck was sent to the slaughter.
He had received some money for the junk,

and was ready to go on a binge-drunk.
The two hitch-hiked to the reservation,
which is a legal sovereign nation,
which was pressured to give up that status
for state police to confront any fuss.
Natives had many a tribal member
in jails and prisons, which could dismember
tribal unity so whites could move in
and claim the land by court's jurisdiction.
The loss of civil rights through felonies
made the settlements easier to seize,
for the cavalry would ride in to save
the Natives from a terrible crime-wave.
Government officials would take the bribes,
called lobbying gifts, to destroy the tribes.
So funds were withheld from tribal police
in hopes violence would greatly increase,
and Natives give in to the government,
who would send Earth resource looters intent
on destroying what was once held sacred
turned to wastelands of a synthetic grid.
Charles was aware of these things but unsure
if he could face the wrath he would incur
were he to battle against backroom scenes
of America's business cog-machines.
A truck stopped, like at docks for a sailor,
and he and Manny jumped in the trailer.
There were six young men going to Rosebud,
passing round a pipe of green potent bud.
The driver, Darren, drove to Tammy's place,
and said to consider it their home-base
for a return trip to Rapid City
in two days, because they stirred his pity.
Manny and Charles approached the house and knocked,
a moment later the door was unlocked
and Tammy leapt into Charles' arms, then gazed

at his outer features, and seemed amazed.
Tammy: "I did not think it possible.
Do you fast like prophets in the *Bible*?
You are even thinner now than before.
What are you trying to get at the core?
And that mustache has really got to go,
it looks so shabby, not fitting your show."
Charles said: "You have not seen me for a year,
and this is your greeting when I come near.
Meet Manny, who rode along, my cousin.
Now I want to see the fruits of my sin.
As Christians teach, good can come from evil,
so let us be at peace and stay civil,
not passing remarks about each other
that makes her choose between dad and mother."
They entered the house and went to the crib
where Sally slept, dried milk on her pink bib,
which Tammy removed and the infant stirred,
so they were rushed away without a word.
Tammy led them down to the living room,
and presented her mother's beadwork loom,
saying dream-catchers were her next projects,
as Sally learned to focus on objects.
Tammy: "Let her sleep now. She is too tired
to be poked and hugged by whom she was sired."
Charles sat on the sofa and looked around,
commenting the house was clean and he found
that to be a most notable surprise,
and Tammy's mother must be on the rise.
Manny opened his backpack and produced
a bottle of booze for them to get juiced.
Two hours later Sara White Owl returned,
greeting Charles with a smile 'til she discerned
the three were half-drunk, and told them to leave,
for her house was dry, hoping to achieve
a Lakota language college degree,

and they must go elsewhere for their drunk spree.
Tammy apologized but her mother
said she was not angry, so why bother
with phony amends that were an insult,
just leave quickly and she would find no fault.
They tottered to an aunt's house down the street,
who welcomed them in with a happy bleat:
"At last relief. Your brothers and sisters
are acting as mini-monsoon twisters.
I feel like doing some serious harm,
breaking their legs or removing an arm."
When she was done speaking in a whine's grouse,
Tammy walked her siblings to Sara's house.
Manny sat down but Charles was ill at ease,
thinking the wooden house a waste of trees.
Kara Wilburtson, sensing Charles' distaste,
said to ignore the foul wallpaper paste.
Kara: "Every family needs a place
to remove masks and show an ugly face.
I let this house be whatever folks want,
setting free the spirits which always haunt."
Charles took a chair and sat on the front porch,
feeling the whiskey leave a trailing scorch.
The house, to him, was too much of a wreck,
and for two days they drank on Manny's check.
In what became perpetual motions,
people came and went in search of potions.
When the money and alcohol was gone,
Charles lay quivering on the weedy lawn.
Darren arrived and he said Sara told
him where to find them, and asked if they sold
their souls for a glass of watery beer,
or worse, their rumps, and turned out to be queer.
Manny laughed but Charles felt so sick at heart
that all he wished was to quickly depart.
Darren drove to a house of a relatives,

who welcomed Charles and Manny, where Natives
sat watching a film while others played cards.
Darren offered wine, saying it retards
the pain within of an abysmal life,
and when they said no, he pulled out a knife.
Six men leaped upon the unwitting pair,
and Darren told them with a smiling glare:
"You have two choices: either join our gang
and there will only be a brief scar pang.
You can deny us and still have the marks
so you cannot swim with other gang's sharks.
Not only that, but we shall likewise stomp
you so bad you will have no teeth to chomp."
Charles struggled and said their souls would be cursed.
Darren nodded and said Manny was first,
so Charles could see his cousin broke and tame,
and would think twice as knife was held to stove's flame.
Their shirts were torn off, the knife was heated,
and Charles accepted he was defeated.
Dragged to the floor, one sat on Manny's head.
The blade caused his skin to blister, then bled.
Charles called out to the female audience,
who did not like charred meat, so burned incense.
He said: "We Native people should not act
in such a brutal way to have a pact."
Karen: "How do you know what is proper?
You merely play as a Native-shopper,
taking what you want from our heritage,
as a museum Indian onstage,
not knowing life on the reservation,
just coming here for a drunk vacation.
You think you bless us with your appearance,
slumming with the bums at a Pow-Wow dance."
Charles: "Do I know you? Have we met before,
and I scorned you, so you even the score?"
Karen: "I have seen you with the white kind,

and you are a legend in your own mind.
Were you as holy as you like to think,
you would not come here with whiskey to drink.
You are getting what you rightly deserve,
and we are the karmic levers which serve
to mete justice and power to our clan,
for you are not a true medicine man."
Charles shuddered at the venom of her words,
and knew he thought himself above the herds
of animal packs and humanity,
and 'twas time to pay for his vanity.
Ah, he thought: belief in our Native pride
takes many forms, both outer and inside.
After Manny was scarred with the gang's sign,
one youth held him down, nor did Manny whine.
A group approached Charles with a heated blade,
who fought their strong grips and uselessly flayed.
Like matadors torturing a young bull,
Charles was fiercely thrown, landing on his skull.
He saw bright bolts from dancing Thunderbirds,
and passed into realms that go beyond words.
A world of sweet harmonious music,
with no discord, healing the lame and sick.
Yet as Charles watched Thunderbirds soar in flight,
he desired to expand power and sight,
and see what else was in the universe,
then white angels dropped on him with a verse.
The sky grew dark with a brewing battle,
and wild buffalo became meek cattle.
Grabbing hold of Charles, a Thunderbird cried
Charles was meant to be the sacrifice ride
to another level of cosmic planes
awaiting them to live on the Great Plains.
Other voices told Charles not to listen,
but rather continue, and to hasten
Heaven's warfare, eager for a climax,

and those who used free will received an axe.
Uncertain on what to do with the storm,
a moment later Charles returned to form.
Manny grabbed the neck of his foe and squeezed,
crushing his throat 'til he collapsed and wheezed.
Manny stood, drawing a concealed knife,
and the women screeched like a warning fife.
Manny threw himself on his opponents,
swinging the thick blade with deadly intents.
He ran at Baylor and slashed at his throat,
and the blood-flow covered him like a coat.
Then turning fast, Manny kicked Darren's chin,
breaking his jaw, sending him in a spin.
David pulled Manny's legs to bring him down,
but he was stabbed at the top of his crown,
so he released Manny and fell aside
like the others, who parted as a tide
that reaches a stony jut near the shore,
which sea breakers part at as waters pour.
Charles pulled free of the man holding his arm,
and wishing to do him bodily harm,
Charles used Darren's dropped knife to stab his chest,
feeling a surge of adrenalin crest.
The blade went in below his shoulder bone,
and he went unconscious with a low moan,
but Karen grabbed a knife and blocked their way,
screaming at both there would be Hell to pay.
Manny: "You are a crazy, stupid slut.
Stand down or you will get one in the gut.
I did not pound on these broken fellows
to be beaten by a bitch who bellows
doom and destruction. Why, just look around,
and see there are no men to stand their ground."
She made a firm swing, but Charles grabbed her wrist,
and broke her nose with a shattering fist.
She fell to the floor with a bleating sob,

and she was the last defense of the mob.
Three other women watched from where they sat,
with verbal abuse that Charles ate dog scat.
Manny and Charles opened the door and ran,
quickly in pursued by the vengeance-hot clan.
The pair ran through backyards, nude to the waist,
hearts pounding wildly, and victory's taste
within reach as pursuers fell behind.
Like famine weakens wolves chasing a hind,
too long without food in the winter's blast,
the wolves know they must break their weary fast.
They spot floundering in ice a young doe,
and the hunt starts over thick fallen snow,
but one wolf has lost too much strength and fails,
and his status falls among the pack males.
So Manny and Charles were quick to elude
the gang who swore upon them a blood feud.
The pair made it to Sara White Owl's place,
and relayed the tale of the deadly chase.
Sara said they could not stay at her home
as a kind of driftwood washed up on loam,
for she wanted to live in that region
without the vendettas of a legion.
Charles was wounded by her ambivalence,
but Manny raged with a florid incense:
"Lady, hard of heart and slow in the head,
is it your wish to see both of us dead?
We barely fought free with our fists and knives,
and now you seek to sacrifice our lives.
At least give us a ride from the slaughter,
for Charles is father to your granddaughter."
Sara: "If you had not gotten so drunk,
they would not have treated you like a punk.
I can smell the alcohol on your breath,
as you pursue it even onto death.
Wait here and I will settle the matter.

I know their matron, so stop this chatter."
Sara left and Charles went to his infant,
stroking her head with a soft humming cant.
Tammy came from her aunt's house and found them.
Charles gently wiped Sally's cheek free of phlegm.
They watched with smiles as she cooed and giggled,
then she lifted her arms, squirmed and wriggled.
Tammy: "That is a sign to pick her up,
and hold her gently with arms as a cup.
For she is the mingling of our fluids,
not alien born or made by druids.
Not meant for spaceships or crucified lord,
but blessed by a shaman's Lakota word."
Charles lifted his daughter and as she rose,
he noticed something strange under her nose.
Charles: "Why, at first I thought she had a rash,
but now I see she grows a small mustache.
Will she be furry like a forest beast,
or is the milk she gets a steroid feast?"
Tammy: "The food is clean, she would rather
be a changeling and look like her father.
Her chemical make-up always alters
to those she bonds with, and never falters.
That is why I had a difficult time
giving her a name that sings with a chime.
Then I chose Sally Monica for her.
When I first called her that she gave a purr."
Sara came back and said the two could leave,
and not to return, if so they would grieve,
for several members of the street gang
were hospitalized and vowed they would hang
Manny and Charles from the nearest phone pole
to warn and scare others of the gangs' toll.

8

Corporate Gang Graffiti

No one had died in the gangsters' attack,
but Charles alertly protected his back,
aware that they had revenge on their mind
and desire for a blood-score made them blind.
Camille had lost interest in debate,
though she followed the news of Clinton's mate,
who tried to reform the health care network
with a system that made people berserk.
She garnered such scorn Camille felt pity
for her attempts to change the greed-city,
and the good old boy base of corruptions,
greeting the First Lady with eruptions
of contempt and hate for her disruptions.
Camille turned to painting and decided
that was where her future hopes abided.
She began by imitating portraits,
'til she developed her own unique traits.
At first her work made Bernard feel disdain,
then he saw he had a jealousy stain
for Camille's talent and ability,
and also her sense of humility.
Though she knew she was the best in the town,
she took praises with a quizzical frown.
Nor did she like the comic book about

the Jew hero who fought history's bout,
so Charles would not draw a second issue
of gory mayhem and splattered tissue.
Her critique made Bernard fume in his heart,
but knew it was entertainment, not art.
Charles began painting with sincere resolve
to keep his mind active and not to solve
the mysteries which kept him in wonder,
as if a detective hired to ponder
and track the source of evil inherent
in eloquent words or incoherent,
that tempt humans and have them justify
at their Last Judgment when they testify.
Charles had a Mohandas Gandhi painted,
defending Dick Nixon, and the sainted
lawyer seemed confused by the looping trails
of his tricky client's campaigning sales,
laundering cash to fund a covert deed,
with Enemy Lists of those who should bleed.
Camille encouraged Charles to continue
his craft and search for a buyers' venue.
Perhaps do Native paintings for a store
which specialized in that kind of art lore.
Yet Charles was caught between the old romance
of people who dressed for a Pow-Wow dance,
and the life he saw on reservations
of the poor and squalid Native nations.
The dichotomy weighed heavy on him,
yet he knew 'twas not just the people's whim.
Other races were likewise divided
social classes that rarely invited
the poor in to see what they will achieve
from hard work and what the right god can weave.
Charles and Camille came closer together,
which twined Bernard in a jealous tether.
He analyzed his abandonment fear

with a bong of marijuana to steer
him through his psyche to find the right course,
and laid the blame on his parents' divorce.
He watched the replay of the Twin Towers
in Manhattan bombed by Muslim powers.
Paranoia seized hold like a dark mist,
and he could feel his mind begin to list
overburdened by senses' stimulus,
that threatened his mind's ship with a surplus,
leaving parts of consciousness at some point
in Nether regions, detached at a joint
by fear; stranded as if on an isle reef
collecting washed-up horrors to spur grief
at a weakened state in Bernard's future,
unless he could find a means to nurture
himself intact to the third-dimension,
and not play with drugs for mind's ascension.
He telephoned Reuben and they agreed
they would go to the fair and not drink mead.
Reuben: "I have been around my farm peers,
drinking and doping, and feel made of beers.
If I do not get away from that crowd,
my parents will drape me with a death shroud.
I cannot recall driving home last night,
through vague recollections of a fistfight.
When done milking, I will drive to your place,
to give our hormones a healthy skirt-chase."
While Bernard played with a computer game,
trying to distract himself from the shame
of free will's loss, adrift in Samsara,
unable to return to the terra,
Charles and Camille walked to the county fair,
and like a freak-show exhibit, the pair
received odd looks of intense bafflement,
as if they had heads of an elephant.
Her first thought was to take Charles by the hand,

acting contrary to the common banned
unspoken rule of white women's scandal
as partner for a Native to handle.
Yet she could sense Charles' anxiety rise,
and a brewing fight would be no surprise.
Romance with Charles made her ambivalent,
but she enjoyed how Charles looked, and his scent
from sweat-lodges was sweet: the poisons drained
from his body like thunder-gods had rained.
They went on all the machines' whiplash rides,
as if in an undertow by the tides.
They sank to the Earth, then were spun around,
and launched into the Heavens from the ground.
She told Charles her bones felt an awful wrench,
so they sat to recover on a bench.
Charles: "I have mixed thoughts on the churning scenes
that inter-phase through infernal machines.
We are not all equal in what we say,
and contrary actions often betray
our real intention, unless we just sit
in front of a screen-world as forces knit
our fates to looms, all held by the same wire,
faithful to a democratic empire."
Camille: "So we sell it to the nations
to globalize the gasoline stations.
Cars are now extensions of living rooms,
chatting on phones and doing what consumes
energy to expand our private lives
in vast honeycomb dwellings like beehives.
Every perspective is put on a screen,
and we try to be a part of each scene,
impressing others with our monkey-tricks,
that we imitate with fanciful shticks.
Only our government is still secret;
their shenanigans do not make us fret,
so long as we have distractions galore,

thinking we are Muses of action's lore.
Ideologies are fine as notions,
but not all have the same thoughts and motions."
Charles: "So you too feel caught between this world,
and being on that joyride where we twirled
through Heaven, connected by cogs and bolts,
and the false reality of screen volts,
where people get lost, uncaring of plights,
dazed into a stupor by satellites."
Camille: "We have expanded dominions
where people try to spread their opinions
on every aspect of society,
whether decadent or proud piety.
Some claim environments are their battle,
others against mistreatment of cattle.
Each coin has two sides, so some want to drill
for oil in pristine lands to get their fill.
Like charlatans selling poisoned snake oil,
politicians devastate the Earth's soil.
Deus ex machina runs on fossil fuels,
and we are greased cogs, used as working tools."
Charles: "Perhaps the new Administration
will not feel compelled to prove our nation
is tough since the Soviet Union fell,
and we aid them to avoid a death knell,
as the Cold War is done, like a bad dream.
Enough of this. Shall we get some ice cream?"
As they strolled through the dusty milling crowd,
a man with beer deliberately plowed
into Charles, spilling the cups on his shirt,
then menacingly asked if Charles was hurt,
and compensation for the two spilled drinks,
giving his three companions smiling winks.
Charles calmly stepped to the man's barrel chest.
An audience gathered, hoping the best
fight they had seen in a while would occur,

and Charles would be broken like a whipped cur.
But Camille was anxious to stop a brawl,
and taking Charles by his hand gave a call:
"We can go for a spin, let the air dry
your shirt on a ride, then taste cherry pie.
If he tells you to go back to the rez,
and take me with you, who cares what he says?
It proves nothing to defeat this lummox,
who wants to be the king of stupid ox."
Charles nodded and walked away with the lass.
Behind them rang a shout she had no class,
a whore unable to get a white man,
only a savage who cowered and ran.
When they had reached the ice cream concession,
she smiled and said with no condescension:
"I am glad you did not follow your urge
to combat that thug for a culling purge
of another idiot and his sin,
because when you fight, you do it to win."
Charles: "I want to keep my teeth in my head,
because they are useful when I am fed.
I am getting too old to fight with glee,
the blows hurt more in a swinging melee."
She forced a laugh that showed her still nervous.
Charles shrugged, stoically impervious.
An older man with a lady approached,
and a quiet conversation broached:
"You took care of that problem well, young sir.
'Twas good not to see a flying of fur.
This is America and you have rights
that should not have to end in bloody fights.
If that oaf gives you any more trouble
look for me and we will burst his bubble."
He held forth his hand and called himself Ben.
Charles shook it, hoping for a good omen.
The lady smiled at Camille, cocked her head,

and touching her husband's shoulder she said:
"This is the young painter I told you of.
One can see her passion inspired by love.
We are the Statens, dear, and it is nice
to meet the artist who paints so precise.
I have some quilt-work as part of the show,
but cannot compete with your lovely glow."
Camille: "I appreciate your comments,
and will look for your work amid the tents.
Charles paints too, and though I hate to say it,
in some ways is better, when he can fit
all his ideas onto a small frame,
but does not have showings, which is a shame."
Ben: "Have you recently seen your father?
I do not wish to be rude or bother,
but we have not seen him at our vets' club,
where we try to keep him from Taylor's Pub.
Sometimes it seems one takes all the darkness
so the rest of us can find happiness."
Charles: "I have not seen him for many weeks,
and you are right 'tis despair that he seeks
for more misery, as if to capture
some sort of Hellish chaotic rapture.
Perhaps usurp Satan and take his place
on Hades' throne as the King of disgrace.
Were you also in the Vietnam War,
and when a car backfires leap to the floor?"
Ben: "I no longer have awful flashbacks
of firefights and sudden jungle attacks.
I go to sweat lodges on occasions
to free myself from turmoil with Asians.
It helps me feel whole, and not torn in half."
His wife interrupted with a small laugh:
"Of course his medications also work,
so he does not go totally berserk."
Ben: "That is so, but why say it aloud?

I am grateful for what God has endowed,
even for you, woman, who goes too far
in diminishing the light from my star."
She put her arm through his with a slight smile,
then held his hand and said with a dame's style:
"See? Here is proof that the pills do their job.
He is not even upset that I rob
him of sanity, saying he needs them
to prevent an action of crazed mayhem."
Ben: "Okay, missy, what you say is true,
but likely I need pills to deal with you.
Meeting you both was a sincere pleasure,
now we must see if she won a treasure
for her quilt-work, like Athena might weave
if drunk on gods' nectar. So we shall leave."
They departed and Camille was impressed,
saying as she took Charles' hand and caressed:
"There goes a happy couple who appease
love gods, laughing at their flaws while they tease.
I hope I am that way when I get old,
and for security will not have sold
myself into a bland loveless marriage
as a trophy pushing a baby carriage."
Charles: "You do not need to worry of that,
I doubt you will be anyone's doormat.
In your soul, Camille, you have a quick fire
and fierce independence, which I admire.
How many white women would come with me,
or teach how to mix paints and charge no fee?
I think you are too good for a college
as a bland teacher with a tenure pledge."
Camille: "I do not want to go hungry,
Though you make my *hubris* quick to agree.
The time of free agent artists has waned
for people grew weary, though they complained
of commercialism in the fine arts,

by the search through the mob of open marts.
So the college system became the source
of marketing art through corporate course.
They replaced the patron aristocrats
for art produced by college bureaucrats.
Perhaps that too will change with computers,
as art is wed to satellite suitors.
The screens of the gods call all to be picked
with sublime ad-codes to hook and addict."
Charles: "It does seem a time of rapid change,
as the rural young leave home on the grange.
The only jobs left in this wealthy town
is being forced to wear a cardboard crown
to feed dining tourists, or at hotels,
which are church-like steeples, though lacking bells."
They went on some rides as it became dark,
and multi-colored lights lit the fair's park.
They watched carnival workers pocket coins
that fell from riders, like a fox purloins
from a hen-house, then returns to its lair,
feeding young vixens with a banquet share.
Camille: "I have come to hate what drugs do.
Carnies are one step from a skid-row crew,
and each level of users thinks they are
invulnerable as a glowing star.
'Tis easy to be broken at the seams
when one stays in perpetual pipe-dreams."
Charles: "Despite what our so-called artists say,
it is not romantic to live that way.
The voice of the Beatniks lived with his mom,
his body hemorrhaging like a bomb.
Humans are naturally nomadic,
and with travel easier we can pick
faraway places to experience
the dope of the realm, using lire or pence."
Camille: "Now it seems so homogenous,

and anyone can be called a genius.
Perhaps it is best we become the same,
and anyone different is to blame
for the cogs of the machine being wrenched,
and as a player in life's game, is benched."
Charles: "Each believes he or she is special,
airwaves swarm with their tireless commercial.
Self-exploitation of meager talent
is toilsome to discern as they are blent
with each other as grotesque tapestries
in magazines not worth the death of trees."
Camille: "The Overman's will to power
was by an addict to poppy flower.
It seems all art can be mimicked and aped,
like Hitler's Reich had Nietzsche's craft reshaped."
Charles: "To disengage from society
and create art without false piety
can destabilize one's mind into night,
thinking one has inspiration's insight.
'Tis not easy making art relevant,
as world scenes quickly change with each event."
Camille: "An artist must be like a plow,
for our frenetic pace does not allow
the time needed to craft a modern piece,
warring with friends whom we were once at peace."
So they conversed, pleased with the words they spun,
when Manny approached, reeling on the run.
Charles: "You look like Hell, Manny. What is wrong?
You shoved through crowds, making an angry throng.
The last we spoke you said sobriety
was your future, regardless of the fee."
Manny shook his head and signaled with hands
to indicate his arm's newly scarred brands.
Charles: "What are you saying? Are they here now,
seeking to fulfill a revenge-feast vow?"
Manny was grateful to be understood,

like a safe haven for flotsam driftwood.
Charles, made aware, gazed round the fairground's mall,
while telling Camille of the gangsters' brawl.
She became scared, and Charles tried to soothe her,
saying he was made of peaceful matter,
and did not wish to become embattled
with the outlaws, but her nerves were rattled.
Charles: "We have to leave quick to stay alive.
How did you get here, Manny? Did you drive?
They are on the hunt, we dare not walk home.
Perhaps we can find a ride if we roam
through the crowds, meeting some people we know.
For now we are safe amidst the fair's show."
Manny shook his head that he had no car,
and Charles knew his cousin could not walk far,
staggering round, and to Camille's surprise,
Manny laughed as he wiped tears from his eyes.
As they stood talking about what was best,
a crow flew over, cawing to its nest.
Charles: "Straighten up, Manny. Things are not fine,
for I take that bird as a wicked sign."
Camille touched Charles' shoulder and pointed at
a table where Bernard and Reuben sat.
The threesome sped over and were greeted
by the two who ate while staying seated.
Charles: "We are tracked by a sinister group.
I do not seek to use you as a dupe,
but we need rides as soon as you finish,
or our life spans will surely diminish."
Bernard: "Why this hurry? We just got here,
and the three of you look stricken with fear."
Charles: "This is my cousin. We are targets
of a gang we fought to their own regrets.
He says they are here in a numbered force,
and we do not have rides for a safe course."
Reuben smeared his fingers on his bib-jeans,

wiping crumbs from a taco filled with beans.
He looked at Manny, and Reuben's brow creased,
noting the helpless state of a drunk-feast.
Reuben: "I will get you out of the muck,
but do not want him puking in my truck.
The cab cannot hold too large of a pack,
and he would fall to his doom from the back.
What could I say to police and my folks
of how a drunk fool's head broke like egg yolks?"
Manny threw his hands up in bleak despair,
and Charles desperately said to the pair:
"Do you not see he is helpless and weak?
He has no escape from a bloody leak.
I will give you ten dollars for a fee,
and sit in back, holding him beside me."
Reuben: "I am sorry but I refuse
to mix up with someone so drunk on booze."
Camille: "You do it for friends on brew,
and his safety and life depends on you."
Reuben: "That is my point. I know them well,
and up to now none have smashed to death's knell.
We have been friends for years, as we all grew.
This person I do not know, nor wish to.
I shall drive you and Charles, if you desire,
but not him, and my truck is not for hire."
Manny gave a cry and began to run,
feeling humiliated and undone.
Charles moved to go after him, but Camille
grabbed Charles' arm, and split in two he could feel
loyalty to his family's station,
yet also needing self-preservation.
So Charles stayed with them, though called for Manny,
who vanished, and Charles felt their lives' canny
metaphysical contact dissipate,
a connection torn by rancorous hate.
Charles arrived home, and told no one the tale,

but next morning he woke to a loud wail.
In the kitchen, Clara was on the floor,
crying aloud, hands lifted to implore
Heavens that what she had heard was not true:
the short life of her sister's son was through.
She could not speak, though Charles and Beatrice
repeatedly asked her what was amiss.
They led Clara to a living-room couch,
and she took sage from her medicine pouch,
which she burned, praying in their native tongue,
and Beatrice cried too as Clara sung.
Though Betty knew the Lakota language,
learning from Elders at a childhood age,
Charles was ignorant, except for curse words,
and simple ones like buffalo and birds.
Exasperated, he got some water,
and gave it to Clara and her daughter,
then he asked: "What the Hell is going on?
Why do you have a mourning guise to don?
Let me know, and use English when you speak.
Why this terrible emotion so bleak?"
Clara rocked back and forth, hiding her face,
and Charles felt locked-out from the Native race.
He turned to Beatrice and grabbed her arm,
giving it a twist, but wishing no harm.
She cried: "Manny is dead, killed in a fight.
His body was burned and found at daylight."
Charles was shocked and ran fingers through his hair,
feeling removed from women's love laid bare.
He paced a moment, then went to his room,
wiped tears away and forced himself from gloom.
He grabbed his duffle bag and packed some clothes,
and in between prayers and dark stormy oaths,
set his mind quickly, with no time to mull,
that he would join the touring carnival.
It seemed best his family did not know

that on the road he was taking his show;
they need not lie to the court-hall's office,
just saying he disappeared could be bliss.
Perhaps his family's fortune might change
for the better if they could rearrange
their minds and spirits without being stuck
in what seemed his perpetual bad luck.
He failed in avenging his brother's death,
nor stopped Manny from drawing his last breath.
Charles felt as though he lacked manhood mettle,
good only for shaping fair-rides' metal.
The time painting with Camille seemed a waste:
art is subjective to everyone's taste,
is neither good nor bad, simply pictures
designed to escape life with mixed tinctures.
He was of no value to his daughter,
and felt useless as if storm wind's water
flooded his psyche, flaying him open,
and life was scripted by a moron's pen,
a cosmic prank, which had gone the distance
to loom an evil web of monstrous chance.

9

Fueling the Revenge Machine

Friends and family feared the worst had come
to Charles due to the gangsters' hate venom.
While he toured the Western states with the fair,
Bernard went to college with a new flair
of predicting a point would soon be reached
corporate votes had governments impeached.
Stan re-enlisted in the Special Ops.
Like a ball in a game that never stops,
he traveled the world using all his skills,
no longer in refuge of booze and pills,
assuring America's finance dues
were allotted by covert agents' ruse.
Making deals with rebels or dictators,
sometimes both, depending on the caters'
banquet demands for weapons, drugs, or oil
his country intrigued for in ceaseless toil.
When Bill Clinton reduced army spending,
espionage groups began defending
global corporate stocks using intrigue
to bind the world's wealthy into one league.
Bernard took to drinking several beers,
discussing current trends with college peers.
Christian faith was one of his favorites,
and how a dead Jew was the crux that knits

teaching a terrible duality,
that can be judged by its poor quality:
"He said that beasts and birds do not worry,
and neither should we, nor try to curry
favor from the world's highest echelon,
for we inherit a new age's dawn.
Then he tells us to pick up our crosses,
and follow him to the Boss of Bosses.
I must say, that makes me a bit leery,
and has me fret, not being world weary.
To force unconditional surrender
upon our opponents has them render
their souls to whatever god they believe
wants suicide attacks to make us grieve.
The all or nothing stance proved to be so
by the new Waco Kid, Janet Reno,
who, to free the children in the compound
of a religious nut group, made a mound
of ashes and charred bodies, watched on-screen
by Yanks who judged the zealots' guide obscene.
The Jews at Masada had their own schemes,
but the oppressors won, and so it seems
diversity is only a good thing
when we think alike with one song to sing."
So Bernard passed his freshman college nights,
discussing America's evil blights,
while residing in a Kansas haven,
undisturbed by the wicked or craven.
He had not yet selected a degree,
but college set his inhibitions free,
thus considered being a professor,
spending his life with books in which to soar
throughout his consciousness, to find nuggets
of truth and beauty, with no long regrets
for detaching from the chaos of life,
and perhaps have a co-ed be his wife.

In Colorado Camille went to school
to major in art. Though she found the pool
of talent among fellow students keen,
she excelled at painting an obscure scene,
following the Impressionistic styles,
crafting illusions with all of her wiles.
She tried not to dwell long on Charles' grim fate,
inspiration helped shove him from her state.
While Reuben learned the trade of his dad's farm,
Stan was instructed that no kind of harm
was to be done to leaders of nations
in South/Central American stations
if they supported a trade agreement.
Instead, to re-direct the peoples' pent
anger towards any kind of schism
that could be considered Socialism.
No one had plans as the immigrants poured
from their lands to avoid a corporate lord,
who brought industries gringos once worked at,
now judged as an expensive, whiney brat.
Profits were higher South of the borders,
where regimes obeyed syndicate orders.
Hispanics could not live on those wages,
so fled to America's New Ages.
With the fall of the Soviet Union,
the servile states peeling like an onion,
quick cash could be made on army hardware
to the highest-bid for an ordnance share.
Baal Clinton took the usual stance
when Yanks must learn the steps to a new dance:
he threw money at Russia for bail-outs,
much of which disappeared to gangster louts.
So some peace was purchased for a few years,
and Stan was sent to strong-arm Hussein's peers,
for they were reluctant to accept loss
of control to an unbeliever boss,

at least not while Hussein berated them,
speaking so rabidly his mouth soared phlegm.
He would often shut-down petrol drilling
than serve the arms' inspectors for filling
the guts of Hussein's hungry civilians,
paying oil for food, which seemed a villain's
means of keeping the people of Iraq
pinned and dissected by oil business tack.
Though Stan had contempt for Baal Clinton,
who seemed a five-pound bag filled with a ton
of sheep manure, at least he was not scared
to drop bombs if Hussein talked tough and dared
to prevent inspectors from any site
where they sought to find weapons of his might.
Yet to Stan it was more than a career,
formatting to put revenge plans in gear.
Frightened for his life, Al-Shailah had gone
to corporate chiefs, begging as a pawn,
that retribution for his betrayal
of Stan's squad be paid for by oil stock-sale.
The oil companies agreed on a price,
and commanded the troops, with words precise,
that Al-Shailah was to be protected,
but from this order Stanley defected.
Unlike Hamlet, by a great dramatist,
Stanley kept to one goal so that no mist
of doubt or anger clouded his purpose,
malingering like an open wound's pus.
Al-Shailah was granted a guard convoy
of United Nations' troops, so Stan's ploy
took time for fruition, as he wanted
Al-Shailah to know he had been haunted,
and not all Americans could be bought,
for many had higher aims, which they sought.
Stan was not bitter for honor bestowed
on Al-Shailah, for it was a mere code

of business conduct, which Stan accepted.
He believed it would not be disrupted
by the murder of a conniving wretch,
as more could be trained, like a dog to fetch,
to take Al-Shailah's current position,
corrupt and sold to a proposition.
Stan bided his time, surveying his foe,
learning the routine of Al-Shailah's show.
A certain hotel catered to elite
diplomats and those on governments' seat,
where whores from round the world were provided
to various tastes for those excited
by exotic flavors with catamites
or the embrace of true hermaphrodites,
brought in to entertain the wealthy class.
Al-Shailah's darling was a pre-teen lass
of Euro-Asian descent, trained for sex
performances both austere and complex.
Stan needed money to further his scheme,
which was granted by his Special Op's team.
He was approached one morning by Lou Pock,
Stan's squad leader, who asked if he owned stock.
Stan replied he had no money for that,
nor was he a conniving bureaucrat.
Lou: "We have a chance to make some money
for when age has us retire to sunny
Florida to relax and not regret
the sins of our youth, easy to forget.
We fight for the capitalist system,
doing the foul work of blood and mayhem.
As such we deserve more of the profits,
combating the faith of Allah's prophets,
or helping them, as is often the case,
depending on whose sheik-king we embrace.
But before I tell you of our intrigue,
I need to know if you shall join our league."

Stanley pondered a moment, then agreed,
and Lou spoke of the plan, grown from a seed
when a group of Russians queried to buy
munitions for Chechnya on the sly.
A Muslim faction desired their own state
from Russia, which continued to deflate,
but still held Chechnya within its grasp,
as the Soviet bloc breathed its last gasp.
So the rebels bargained for munitions,
and Lou said American traditions
aided freedom fighters' heroism.
Though Stanley knew it was terrorism
the weapons would be used for, he resigned
himself that a devil's deal must be signed.
World capitalism dictated trade
towards common currency one is paid,
and Stan had been raised to hate Soviets,
as well as Muslim Sunni and Shiites.
So let them kill each other, who would care
if war-profiteering earned Stan his share?
At base-camp a computer technician
worked at the controls like a magician.
A consignment of weapons disappeared
from the budget's catalogue, which he sheared
off as if they had never existed.
When screens are real then we have listed,
like a wounded ship adrift on the sea,
from the third-dimension, locked with a key
into scenes of even worse illusions
of Samsara's ongoing confusions.
Stan's squad met with the Chechnya rebels
in the desert, away from the oil wells.
Hand-held rocket-launchers, the highest-grades
of machine-guns, and boxes of grenades.
They brought, too, a money scanner that fit
the cash to be sure 'twas not counterfeit.

The task done, Stan formed a discreet disguise
of blonde hair, a pot-belly, and blue eyes.
He used his intrigue's wealth to make a deal
to have the identity seem real.
Chalmers, the computer professional,
joked Stan would go to the confessional
in a guise because his sins were so great
the priest would damn him to a lowly state.
With forged documents and needed supplies,
Stan went to the hotel in his new guise,
saying he had a special guest that night,
who wanted an off-street room, out of sight.
Once there, he put on gloves to not be marked,
and had done the same with rental cars parked
in the valet lot of the grand hotel,
three more in the city, scattered pell-mell.
He took a moment to sit and ponder,
but when he felt his mind slip and wander,
he went into action and dressed in black
to put in motion his revenge attack.
He was on the top-floor and gained the roof,
avoiding surveillance cameras' proof
that a conspiracy was unfolding,
as the hook-cinch bit in cement molding.
He memorized the outer decorum,
and felt the pulsing adrenalin's strum.
He lined up with Al-Shaliah's balcony
and with practiced speed slid down the stony
wall, with the cinch-machine softly whirring.
He pressed to the draped glass door, not stirring,
awaiting the girl, whose common routine
was a cigarette after the sex-scene.
She went to the balcony and lit one,
at peace now that her evening's work was done.
Stan stabbed a dose of morphine in her neck,
and she quickly collapsed, a fleshly wreck.

Not caring if she was dead, Jacob crept
into the dark room where Al-Shailah slept.
Stan moved to the bed with a strap of tape
he wrapped on the mouth; there was no escape
for Shailah, whose bloated form Stan straddled
like a broken horse easily saddled.
Plastic cuffs were bound to his feet and wrists,
and a dose of morphine brought hazy mists.
Aware of body-guards outside the door,
Stan quietly dragged him across the floor.
On the balcony Stan cinched the rope tight
around Al-Shailah, who put up no fight.
Then Stan climbed the line and once at the top,
raised Al-Shailah, hoping he did not drop.
They crossed the roof and went to Jacob's room,
where he changed Al-Shailah's clothes as a groom
might dress his master with distinguished flair,
smoothing out the seams in distinctive care.
He was a bit large for the business suit,
for Stan had guessed at the size of the brute,
but it was close enough for safe passage
through the hotel, past the clerk and bell-page.
Stan turned to Al-Shailah's stringy black beard,
and with clippers and razor it was sheared.
White paint was mixed in his hair for speckles,
and Stan removed the confining shackles.
He poured some bourbon on Al-Shailah's face,
so that he would seem drunk and lost in space.
Stan cleaned the room, placed the gear in luggage,
which the valet pushed out on a carriage.
Stan guided Al-Shailah through the lobby,
as if booze was his favorite hobby,
and that other Muslims should not be mad
for breaking the taboo of Mohammed.
Al-Shailah sagged, his head lolling with drool,
as Stan feigned embarrassment for the fool.

He turned in the pass card to the desk clerk,
who observed Al-Shailah with a small smirk.
Stan: "I am sure you have seen this before.
He is the dealer for my petrol store,
but is not yet used to our Western way
of mixing business with alcohol play."
And here Stan gave a sly wink and a smile,
as if he just thought of something worthwhile:
"Like the Native chiefs of my own nation,
who had whiskey, and filled with elation,
signed away their land and its resources,
so you will be slave to greater forces."
The desk clerk grinned, not knowing what to think,
stared close, then gave a deferential blink.
Stan: "Well, this is no time for me to brag,
and because he is married to a hag,
we shall go elsewhere so he can dry out,
and come to as if he received a clout.
'Tis a shame we have to use the front door,
when he is about to puke on the floor.
All his countrymen will see him behave
as a drunken clown and unrighteous knave.
Too bad for him. Let that be a lesson
to not make deals with America's son.
Is my car ready? Then we shall depart.
Chatting with you eased my sinister heart."
Stan guided Al-Shailah to the parked car,
jesting about Iraq's ill-fated star.
A valet helped stuff him in the backseat,
who like a lost kid sighed a feeble bleat.
Stan laughed: "There is the brightest of your men,
which bodes well for Iraq as an omen.
I hope you are not chief of a clan's brood,
he would have them starve than sell oil for food.
Rather, spend the money on world-class whores,
but such is Babylon in mythic lores.

At least you have work, such as it might be,
serving heathens for a substandard fee."
With that, Stan gave the man a wad of cash
liberated from his foe's pocket stash.
While the valet searched for a place to hid
the money from his boss, whom he belied
in sharing tips, which was a requisite
to be a servant for those who visit,
Stan drove leisurely to the other site,
where a garage held a car out of sight.
He put the plastic handcuffs back in place,
as tears rolled down Al-Shailah's pumpkin face.
Steering through Baghdad, Stan watched for trackers.
Al-Shailah pled he was among backers
for the new United Nations' mandates,
and if he were kidnapped would pay high rates,
for he was much loved, that he could assert.
Stan switched cars twice and drove to the desert,
ignoring anxious pleas, face a grim mask,
as if on his way to a baroque masque
to dance with death as a good companion,
who reigned on Earth, fruit of each champion.
Stan knew which byways were guarded by troops,
circumventing them by driving in loops.
He went to a pipeline which was to start
pumping oil that morning to the world's mart,
who had put out Hussein's retreating flare.
Stanley yanked Al-Shailah out by his hair
and dragged him to a valve, which Stan opened.
He yodeled down it, and as echoes send
messages across mountains that glisten,
so Stan smiled and cocked his head to listen.
He turned to Al-Shailah, sweating in dread,
soon to be a corpse on which maggots fed.
Stan: "I rehearsed no words to explain this,
yet now I feel there is something amiss.

Not that you care. All you want is your life,
and I have killed others in battle's strife
whom I respected more than such as you,
nor gave them the reasons for what I do.
Being warriors they needed no words
from me, but went to the realms of their herds.
Yet you are a big player in this show,
who helped set the fires in Mid-East aglow.
Not that you lit them yourself, by no means,
for you are a talker who merely gleans
what others want and try to serve each side,
winnowing wealth upon which to abide."
Al-Shailah: "I have wealth enough to share
with a reasonable man who can bear
it away from this misunderstanding.
Let us work together in my handing
ransom in riches over to yourself.
I spare no item from my well-stocked shelf."
Stan: "There was a crusader, Vlad Dracul,
who fought Muslim kings and was quite cruel.
Known as the Son of the Dragon he led
his land to freedom, and on corpses fed
in The Garden of Impalement Sorrows,
destroying Muslims with bloody harrows.
Yet his faith taught Christian kingdoms were not
of this Earth, and his nation fell to rot."
Al-Shailah: "That was many years ago.
We are more enlightened about our foe.
You see I am not a devil or want
my god forced upon you, as spirits haunt.
All that I have is yours if you spare me;
you can even have my Swiss account key."
Stan: "Our religions teach that god uses
men to exact revenge on abuses.
The open market began with a bribe
to god in hopes blessings would lift their tribe.

Or perhaps with the urge for a favor,
an ape gave a female fruit to savor.
We evolved from faiths that were pastoral,
'tis man's nature to be unnatural.
Your nation is having a quick fire-sale,
like old Babylon of the *Bible*'s tale.
We got drunk from the filth in your chalice.
Like corrupt knights, went insane with malice.
The military commercials I watch
do not show how badly our leaders botch.
Nor do they reveal our country for sale,
rather, make it seem a quest for the Grail.
The Communion we partake of is oil,
and that is why we invaded your soil."
Al-Shailah: "If you want I shall become
a Christian and forsake Allah's kingdom."
Stan sighed as if at the stupidity
of forcing his foe's feigned humility.
Stan: "I see this conversation lacks worth
in the furnace fires of this desert hearth.
What I expected, I am uncertain,
but 'tis time to draw the final curtain.
Life can seem a mere shifting illusion
of atoms' and molecules' collusion,
but I learned to laugh again at their prank,
and give the revenge machine a last crank."
Al-Shailah felt life's slim cord being reamed;
he crawled to Stan, holding his knees and screamed:
"We have American troops held in jails.
Surely you could trade me for bargain sales.
They are hidden in secret, and tortured.
My life will buy many of the captured."
Stan was interested for a moment,
and questioned Al-Shailah on what he meant:
"Are there any soldiers left from the plot
you betrayed at your house where I was shot?"

Al-Shailah's eyes widened and he thought quick
and wary like a hen guarding her chick:
"Perhaps there are prisoners left from that,
but I am only a mere bureaucrat.
I do not have a part in such details,
though I promise you 'tis no fairy tales."
Stan looked at the coming dawn and pondered,
trying to stay alert as mind wandered.
Did he have a true opportunity
to free soldiers from Iraq's punity?
Would greater good be served trusting agents
to free the troops, forsaking Stan's vengeance?
Stan: "You are like a Frankenstein monster
we have created from a Hellish stir
of mixed potions and brew to fill our need
to rule the world and satiate vast greed.
You turned on us, as monsters often do,
and we sink to the level of your crew.
Perhaps if you told me where the men are
you may yet live to see the Morning Star."
Al-Shailah decided craft suited him,
seeing hopes ascend where they had been dim:
"I would like to do as you have bidden,
but I do not know where they are hidden.
My nephew knows who has them moved around,
blindfolded and gagged so they make no sound."
Stan: "The day may come when computer logs
track soldiers' movements as if we are dogs,
but even well-trained mutts can go feral,
roaming the wastelands, howling a carol.
Our masters are like trainers for dog-fights,
but I am obedient to the heights,
not chained to the political systems
that bless with one hand, the other condemns.
Especially not a president hound
controlled by bitches who lead him around.

Enough of this philosophical thought.
We are all owned by the things we have bought,
and you, my friend, do not have a good price,
nor will I be gulled by your intrigue twice.
This pipe-line is akin a dragon's coil,
for whom we endlessly work in hard toil.
I heard a legend of a god who danced
on a many-headed serpent and lanced
the twisting python wrapped around the Earth,
restoring dignified freedom and mirth."
Stan anointed Al-Shailah from an urn,
and he shrieked in terror that he would burn
from the gasoline he had been doused with,
calling for a ransom from god and kith.
Stan tightened the cuffs and began to lug
Al-Shailah to the opened pipe-line plug.
He was stuffed down the hole, the lid shut tight,
and Stan felt no remorseful cringe's bite.
Yet neither was there joy for his success,
as he hoped there might be from the redress.
He returned to Baghdad and left the car
with no trace behind which could dim his star.
He arrived early at his squadron's base,
took a shower, erasing his foe's face
from his memory, which was not daunting.
His psyche free from Al-Shailah's haunting,
Stan slept soundly until his team's sector
went in search with the weapons' inspector.

10

God's Real Estate

Al-Shailah's crushed body blocked the oil stream,
and the analysis by Hussein's team
laid the blame on a man of ambition,
who helped Saddam run the war-torn nation.
Despite mild ambience Shaklur was fierce,
his wrathful gaze could discern truth and pierce.
He was the head of human resources,
but secretly ran Iraq's spy forces.
Saddam feared his cohort, and had no qualms
in having people recite verse-like psalms
the intrigue against Al-Shailah, who met
death loyal to Hussein, with no regret.
Shaklur vehemently denied a role,
but the courtroom was beyond his control.
Terrified of the Blood Guard's allegiance
to Shaklur, as well as other regents
hoping to rise if Hussein was usurped,
Saddam trained witnesses who sang and chirped
like birds reciting doggerel and tune,
and Shaklur fled from impending ruin.
Using bribes he escaped from his jail cell,
and drove to the border, but his death-knell
could not be avoided, and he was caught
in the trunk of a car, plans gone for naught.

Hussein then used a technique oft-employed,
announcing if Shaklur was not embroiled
in the scheme to kill Al-Shailah, then why
did he run from a just court that would try
him fairly, not persecute innocence;
for the latter, Saddam had abhorrence.
Shaklur was hung as a foe of the state,
and all his wealth went to Saddam's estate.
The trial's farce did not fool one keen man,
Mustafa, a son of Al-Shailah's clan,
who had been abroad, hunting those who fled
Iraq with treasures, as foreign boots tread
the soil of their country, and hide at ease.
Mustafa's job was to kill them or seize
the riches they had taken to retire
from the wreckage of Saddam's crushed empire.
Mustafa quickly returned to Baghdad,
and at his uncle's funeral went mad:
tearing his hair and ripping at his beard,
he screamed his soul was abandoned and seared.
Al-Shailah had treated him as a son,
for his father's short life had been undone
during the long feud with Shiite Iran,
when America helped Iraq's war-plan.
For two days Mustafa mourned in fury,
then broke his fast and ate rice with curry.
He went to the trial and sensed falsehood,
for his mind detected, as all minds should,
the truth from lies in their dual schism,
naivete replaced with cynicism.
When he asked to be part of the inquest
he was quickly denied, and so a quest
began to discover what had occurred,
the court being a show of the absurd.
He went to his mother to comfort her,
a widow again, who could barely stir

from the laments for the second husband
who was also taken by Allah's hand:
a pair of brothers who were kind-hearted,
life was misery since they departed.
Mustafa held his mother as she wept,
with words of solace as revenge thoughts crept:
"We must suffer through a terrible loss,
but only Heaven is all brilliant gloss.
Both my fathers will be there, I am sure,
for they dared not have Allah's wrath occur.
Al-Shailah had flaws, with women mostly,
and he paid a dear price, which was costly.
My dad was too proud to turn from the fight
with Iran, and saved us from a dark plight.
Yes, they had character faults which doomed them,
surrounded by war and all its mayhem."
His mother, Ashia, sobbed in his arms;
then catching her breath spoke of further harms:
"Ah, my son! I feel both much cursed and blest
with four small children and you are eldest.
What shall I do? Where am I to go now?
My fortune has ebbed since the marriage vow.
Better if I had stayed poor in my hut,
squalid poverty with no door to shut
against the elements and raging storm,
where your father found me, loving my form.
Though I was a young girl, knowing little,
he brought me to this mansion to settle.
Now his relatives threaten to evict
us from our home with a judge's edict."
He gently wiped tears from Ashia's cheek,
waiting for her to calm from tempest's peak.
Realizing she was beyond his aid,
gave her a sedative and called a maid.
He carried Ashia to her bedroom,
placing her on pillows like a bridegroom.

He first thought to confront the relatives,
but acting on an impulse only gives
energy to chaos, which would betray
hopes of saving his mother from the fray.
He sat quietly, releasing grudges,
and thought it was best to bribe the judges.
Obviously kinfolk had done the same,
so he would defeat them at their own game.
Despite laws of the *Koran* ensuring
widows' pensions, 'twas not an enduring
idealism from Mohammed's day.
To maintain high-status one had to pay,
like throwing meat to a starving huge beast,
it kept the system's cogs whirring and greased.
He would not tell Ashia of his plan
to add to the corruption of their clan,
for she strove to be honest and believed
others did too, for god to be achieved.
She had not the wherewithal to survive
in their war-torn land, where greed was the drive
for those running the demented drama,
their mouths inhaling like a Black Hole maw.
Mustafa spent hours at his uncle's desk,
counting the sums wasted on his burlesque.
When Mustafa had accounts in order,
he went to Ashia's room. At the door
her servant said his mother was at rest,
not to be woke except for dire behest.
Mustafa exhaled a sigh of relief
that for now she escaped from a dark grief.
Visiting his siblings he laughed aloud
at the childish antics Allah endowed.
The youngest, Ibrahim, toddled to him,
the boy's face changing to be hard and grim,
with a toy gun Mustafa had hidden,
since Ashia made weapons forbidden.

Ibrahim crawled onto Mustafa's knees,
lisping constantly like a gentle breeze:
"Will momma be all right or will she die?
All we have done lately is mourn and cry.
I want something fun, not people buried.
Find a woman so you can get married,
then we will dance as the two of you merge,
and we shall move on from poppa's sad dirge.
Then I will grow-up strong and join your squad
to smash Americans with a steel rod.
We shall win Iraqis' love and become
the heroes of Allah's righteous kingdom.
Our people will not feel hunger or hate,
and none steal from us to fuel their state."
Mustafa: "Your mind makes tremendous bounds,
as you prattle of love with hateful sounds.
'Tis far better to stay with your first choice
to be a teacher using a guide's voice
to lead our country to prosperity,
with war obsolete, and serenity
takes its place when fighting burns out its stars,
and Allah's merciful love mates with ours."
Ibrahim pinched his brother on the cheek,
then laughed aloud and continued to speak:
"You see there are always affronts in life,
and Allah said prepare ourselves for strife.
Mother teaches love, but 'tis a dull net,
because I want to fly a storming jet."
Mustafa: "Patriotism is not
in an open mart to be sold or bought.
It is like an extended family,
of villains or those with a homily.
We believe we descend from Ishmael,
and perform our duties with filial
loyalty to Allah, who must come first,
regardless of how revenge makes us thirst.

Our enemies are crazy with vast greed,
ravenous for oil and drunk on strong mead,
which Muhammad made taboo in our laws,
and they kill our civilians with no cause.
We must rise above them and the devil
that whips them on, not sink to their level."
Ibrahim: "Is it the devil that drives
them so that good does not flourish nor thrives?"
Mustafa: "They lost their identities
of tribal roots, and divine entities
are now a face of their machinery
reflecting their vacuous penury.
We should not feel hate that they have so slipped
from the love of Allah. Yet they have gripped
the world to drag us with them to Hell's hole,
tempting us in bargains to sell our soul."
The child: "I will void that sale's procession,
as from hate stems demonic possession."
Mustafa: "Well said, my little brother.
You should listen closely to our mother.
Now I must go and tend to some duties,
but am grateful for seeing you beauties."
Mustafa felt his mind mix in a twist,
like preparing to have a devil kissed.
Can corruption help protect innocence,
or does evil suffuse a guarded fence?
His loved one's bliss had to be protected
by fiends whose deals Mustafa selected.
He gathered a large sum of currency
with plans to win the judge's leniency,
and thus Ashia could keep the estate.
'Tis easier now to purchase good fate
using bribery and gear-driving lies.
In former eras 'twas harder to rise
above one's berth and appointed station,
but that has changed with globalization.

The system has become precarious,
one worldly market to buy and sell us.
We are poisoned by our own appetites,
and the waste products give us savage bites.
Mustafa considered such awful things
that bought justice as hypocrisy sings,
and how his people fell from *Koran* laws,
while Americans laughed with great applause,
as widows, orphans who should be cared for
went homeless and starved despite scriptures' lore.
Dark shadows flitted through his mind like bats,
and his skin itched as if covered by gnats.
He looked to the Heavens for a good sign
and saw three American jets align
for their routine fly-over of Baghdad,
and in an instant Mustafa went mad.
He quivered and raised his fist to shake it,
but wisely did not have a public fit
where it might be recorded by someone,
so silently thought: Allah's will be done.
He had an auto at his disposal,
but if the judge saw it the proposal
might have to be raised to a high bribing,
not just wet his beak with an imbibing.
In case someone attempted robbery,
choosing Mustafa as a ripe berry,
he carried a pistol and stayed alert,
and interlopers knew they would be hurt
if they dared to cross into neighborhoods
where the rich sold oil meant to purchase goods,
but instead used it for their luxuries,
so that international charities
did much of the labor to feed the poor,
supplies diverted for the rich to store,
then selling the global charities' food
at an increased price to the roiling brood.

Faced with such difficulties in his land,
Mustafa had no qualms of what he planned.
If the situation was different,
and his family could afford some rent
to live in a small place on his wages,
then he would accept the lower stages
that fortune had spun through Allah's great will.
But it was Mustafa's duty to kill
whoever robbed Al-Shailah of essence,
and that meant taking a leave of absence.
The war had upturned his Blood Guard's system,
and Mustafa was sure he could get them
to grant him a year for sabbatical.
Though their best agent, was not radical
in spouting beliefs of the party-line
as if breaking taboo and drunk on wine.
A police car approached him as he walked;
with the window down, the officer talked:
"Mustafa! My friend, I am glad we meet.
I will give you a ride, just take a seat."
Mustafa saw his childhood friend, Abdul,
from a wealthy clan, though he failed at school,
despite his father's stern admonitions,
to chase girls and pursue low ambitions.
Abdul's new job had given him a lease
to bide time 'til made the chief of police.
Mustafa sat before the paneled dash,
and he felt dizzy from the smell of Hash.
Abdul: "Sorry about that contact high.
I caught some teenagers making a buy,
so thought: What the Hell, and gave it a try.
I can always say I did not inhale,
as Americans do when up for sale.
It was the most intriguing thing to do
this week, usually I just sit and stew.
Now I have a note for the Police Log

more thrilling than when I shot a stray dog."
Mustafa: "'Tis good you enjoy your job,
and 'tis easier than trying to lob
a hand-grenade you know will not explode,
bought from America by the ton-load."
Abdul: "They like to sell defective arms,
perhaps believing if they cause no harms
it will be a bloodless war and the blame
cannot be laid on their doorstep with shame.
Yet your father was killed, and hate abides
that Yanks sold weapons to both of our sides
during our long jihad against Iran,
so the Mid-East burned like meat in a pan.
They kill us off by stirring-up friction.
Are you staying in my jurisdiction?
I have been warned many times not to leave
the post, despite my testosterone heave.
I need great craft for the designs I hurl;
in this neighborhood, choose a servant girl."
Mustafa: "I go to Judge Kashan's place
for the matter of an important case."
Abdul giggled freely: "I hope you brought
plenty of cash for justice to be bought.
Ah, yes, I heard of your family's woe.
The law system is a pageantry show,
where one bids to be cast in a star's role,
with the poor as weak as a new-born foal.
Do not allow that to become of you,
though selling your soul for devils to chew
is not recommended by holy men,
they rarely reside in a squalid den."
Mustafa: "They are great at complaining
of how people's faith and light are waning,
and spur us on against the decadence
of the Western hemisphere's influence.
We are told to follow Allah's great will,

then we are stuck paying debits and bill."
Abdul: "Yes, my friend, we face a schism
of holy men and capitalism,
who both encourage 'tis for our own good
we support their lifestyles as a mule would.
One forces us on with carrot and stick,
the other with Heaven's dream rhetoric,
then both wonder why we have a deep grudge.
Well, we have arrived. Good luck with the judge.
Say hello to Liskiaha for me,
the judge's cute maid, who spurns my love plea."
The judge was in his study, taking ease
after an oil-food deal was his to seize.
Mustafa was shown in, and bowed with grace,
with no insincerity on his face.
They exchanged greetings and somber blessing.
The judge said, with paternal addressing:
"Your father's loss was a terrible waste,
but we caught the villain with all due haste.
He roasts in damnation where he belongs,
and your father, with virgins, hears their songs."
The judge gave a quick smile and a sly wink,
and patience for the fool began to shrink,
so Mustafa said: "The dead are beyond
human aid, whether burning in Hell's pond,
or risen to heights of Allah's abode.
I have seen my country slowly erode,
and done my job as no mercenary,
as loved ones become corpses to bury.
Now I find my family has no home,
treated like vagabonds driven to roam,
as our fathers were by Christians and Jews,
with whips at our backs, lashed until we bruise."
The judge nodded mournfully, wiped a tear,
then as if his morose thoughts became clear,
said: "Surely you have access to money

from your father's will. Now it seems funny
we somehow did not think of it before,
perhaps we were distracted by the war.
But if you give me a large enough sum,
it will feed them like sharks in bloody chum.
The hunt will end, and your kin find the way
for Allah's light to shine a golden ray."
Mustafa nodded: "Yes, such are my hopes
to satiate the greedy hand that gropes,
like a monkey whose paw is in a box
to grasp fruit, but cannot undo the locks.
He refuses to let go of the treat
that holds him captive, and starves in defeat."
The judge frowned, showing he did not care for
Mustafa's elaborate metaphor:
"We all have our flaws, which fellows condemn,
but only Allah relieves us of them.
Are you planning to do anything rash?
You sound as though kin should receive the lash.
According to laws, they are in the right,
and you cannot possibly win this fight."
Mustafa stepped forward as if to dash
in the brains of the judge, but gave him cash.
He had recoiled at Mustafa's movement,
seeing him wild-eyed with bloody intent.
Counting the bills the judge released a laugh,
and pushed a buzzer for one of his staff
to show Mustafa out, with great relief
for a happy ending rather than grief.
He saw Mustafa was in no hurry,
and annoyed, the judge asked with a flurry:
"What is your trouble now? We are done here.
Your kinfolk will accept this, do not fear."
Mustafa: "Your honor is like a cure,
you help keep our system austere and pure.
Why, just walking down the street one can tell

that you and our leaders save us from Hell.
'Tis not my intent to be a bother,
but I have questions of my step-father."
The judge was anxious to burrow the cash
with his other bribes in a safe-box stash.
He had no time for a soldier of war,
who was meant to be used like a cheap whore.
The judge drew himself up with dignity
used to cow the accused. With clarity
said: "What causes this unwarranted need?
His killer was tried and hung with due speed."
Mustafa: "But the security tapes
were not used in court to discern the shapes
of those involved with the well-planned intrigue,
and I do not believe Shaklur would league
himself against my step-father, and then,
despite such plotting, be caught like a wren.
Why would Shaklur risk losing his command?
The witnesses looked shaken on the stand-"
The judge interrupted with a fierce rage,
his bully tactics displayed as courage:
"Tell me quick, what do you know of the law?
You cast your imperfections as my flaw.
I sat on the bench at Shaklur's trial,
now you preach evidence to make me rile.
You can watch the videos of that court,
but the truth stands firm with Allah's support.
I have business to tend to and will not
suffer fools to speak of justice's rot."
Mustafa's hand twitched with angry impulse,
adrenalin pumped with an eager pulse.
An urge swept through him, as if cleared from fog:
free the world from the burden of this dog.
Choke the life from him and feel true justice,
but Mustafa would lose his kinfolk's bliss.
He said: "I am sorry if I offend,

and offer apologies to amend.
I also have duties to take care of.
May you always have Allah's grace and love."
The judge waved dismissively with a sneer,
and as the door closed Mustafa could hear
a short barking chortle, filled with delight,
sounding like a madman howling at night.
Mustafa thought: We ridicule the Jews
for their love of wealth and how it accrues
through usury and fraud, yet my leaders
are thieving from charitable feeders.
He knew he was no thinker, but dark mood
settled like a sand storm, making him brood.
Fortune would change its angry arrows' slings,
so he went home and played with his siblings.
He decided not to act on a whim,
nor was it his role to be a victim.
Far too long the West had issued decrees
that sank his nation to the low degrees.
He must act against his own country's laws,
for their comfort had replaced Allah's cause.
His mind became lucid and seminal,
and though he would be judged a criminal,
he saw destiny rise in the faces
of children that no power erases.
For Allah may be god, and no other,
but human love is first bound to mother.
At this he felt a sudden urge to breed,
and it usurped his thirsty revenge need.
He put aside the childish games and went
to his mother with wedding plan's intent.
She stirred from her sedative inspired dreams,
with lost love and poverty as the themes.
Mustafa quietly told her the judge
would reverse his decision so the grudge
held by their relatives would be dismissed.

She wept heartily and had his cheeks kissed.
He made no mention of the graft involved,
so she thought by true justice it was solved.
Ashia: "I am a pathetic thing
that I weep for money when I should sing
mournful hymns for your father, who is lost,
and cannot be returned at any cost.
But at least he is free now from his cares,
and I will pray hard for how his soul fares.
Today I shall begin a mourning fast,
for the money problem is in the past,
and I did not devote my attention
while fretting about a living pension."
Mustafa: "You had too much in your head.
Life goes on though we are ringed by the dead.
Perhaps it is time for us to rejoice,
and I want your approval for my choice
of wife, Sofia, as I gave it thought
after your mentioning she should be sought."
Ashia carefully looked at her son.
Was he serious or just having fun?
They held each others' gaze; she stroked his cheek.
She saw his bearing and began to speak:
"You would take as your first bride a widow?
You shall be fulfilled in Heaven's meadow.
Too often men only want young virgins,
and widows are cast aside as bad jinns,
which our book says is unacceptable,
if the widows are good and capable.
There are many things now set in motions,
have you been making daily devotions
while busy abroad, fulfilling your work?
Be honest now, and tell me if you shirk."
Mustafa laughed and said: "Allah bless you!
Your world falls apart but god keeps us true.
In my mind I rave about unkind fate,

and how to get revenge on those I hate.
I think I have spun a curse of dark clouds
that I wish wrapped our enemies in shrouds.
And you are here, suffering from their tolls,
and probably praying for their damned souls.
We work at cross-purposes, sad to say:
me for their endless night, you for bright day."
Ashia: "Why do you shun an answer?
You skip from the question like a dancer.
I do not judge your hate, 'tis in god's care,
though I think 'tis a load you should not bear.
Now be honest and tell if you practice
the proper way to achieve Allah's bliss."
Mustafa: "I am ashamed to admit
that my work for the state overcame wit.
I have failed to be a devout person,
and hope you will forgive your first-born son.
Perhaps my hate stems from not believing
that Allah exists as all-perceiving.
I shut myself off to tend to my job,
and devils crept in to pillage and rob.
Now I am called to a higher order
than money, which begets only murder."
He left her in charge of the wedding plans
for families to join as beloved clans.
Before requesting an absence of leave
from his job, Mustafa began to weave
threads for revenge, which could not be undone,
though he became an outcast people shun.
He went first to the hotel clerk's abode,
feigning a mild, ambient, peaceful mode.
The clerk, Makya, was restless and annoyed,
distressed with worries of staying employed,
and he also knew his life was at stake
as an ante for the games, false and fake.
Makya: "I told all I know in the court.

It was left to them to sift through and sort
the evidence and execute decrees
that the attorneys do for legal fees."
Mustafa: "According to my own source
you told another tale to the Guard force.
I do not care if you lied on the stand
so as not to be buried in the sand,
but it matters if you tell the truth now,
more than when you took a grave courtroom vow.
Such secrets eat away at a man's skull,
and what was once bright and clear becomes dull.
I shall not bribe you, for you seem honest,
but out with the truth now, and do your best."
Makya gazed at him, then wept in shivers,
and Mustafa understood the quivers,
and gently held the clerk in an embrace,
'til Makya felt his inquisitor's grace.
Makya: "I steered a guilt-free man to doom,
to keep my wretched life that cannot bloom.
Perhaps it is foolish for me to care
how the rich plot to steal each others' fare,
but to bear false witness in Allah's eyes
brings sure death, despite earthly enterprise
that may save the body from destruction,
though it drains the soul into Hell's suction."
Mustafa: "Do not worry over it.
I am after the number one culprit.
What you did was wicked, there is no doubt,
but we are trapped in a survival bout.
Our religion offers us homilies,
yet we cannot take care of families.
Western devils are blamed as the reason,
and honesty is branded as treason.
I do not pursue the accessories,
whose loyalty sways with directions' breeze
like poppies in a field that pollinate,

and lost in pipe-dreams they hallucinate
that they are granted to judge life and death,
while we gag on burning petrol fume's breath.
We must not be caught in their illusion,
such energy is bad jinns' collusion."
Makya sighed and said: "We are of one mind.
You cleared my path like a worker who mined
the dungeons I keep within my locked soul,
chained-up, though I present a happy role.
The truth is not something to buy and sell.
I freely give events at the hotel."
So Mustafa received information
of the young American's migration
to Iraq to incorporate plunder,
so rich and poor were driven asunder,
and was told Stanley's disguised description.
Despite the security inscription,
Mustafa linked to world-wide computers
to view lists of American looters
still stationed in Iraq with inspectors,
guarding them while on weapon-finding tours.
He searched the troops' names in the special force,
and after the computer ran its course,
Mustafa thought it was a good omen
that the oracle screen showed a few men
had been a part of the Coalition,
and still abided in Iraq's nation.
He felt his mind do a wild dervish dance,
recalling memories of Paris, France,
where his parents had sent him to avoid
the United Nations' wrath and great Void.
Mustafa had spent the time carousing
with willing women who were arousing.
He returned and found the house in damage
from the Americans' insane rampage.
Al-Shailah said a stray bomb had landed,

a gift from above by heavy-handed
Coalition forces, who were akin
angels released from Hell like harpy jinn.
Mustafa saw no hole in the house roof,
and with the computer's and Makya's proof,
he wondered if the bomb had been a plot
to reduce his father to a blood clot,
and when that intrigue had failed to do so,
other means were employed to inflict woe.
He did not know what to do with the names
Mustafa learned from espionage games,
so he waited for a more proper time
to seek revenge against the bloody crime.
He took a leave of absence from his job,
and at the wedding his heart gave a throb.
Ashia had worried that the dowry
would be depleted from the injury
Sofia's first husband had suffered from
during the war, stricken, mangled and dumb.
Sofia had spent all their resources,
but 'twas not enough: fate ran its courses.
Mustafa had no care of her status,
so Ashia stayed quiet with no fuss.
The wedding was simple, yet filled with grace,
and the children ran playing round the place,
ecstatic to have Sofia's first-born,
a vigorous girl, no longer forlorn,
who led them in songs and invented rhymes,
replacing their dirges with happy times.
That evening in the honeymoon bower
Mustafa gently used his groom's power,
undressing Sofia to gaze in full,
but could not take the head-dress from her skull.
Mustafa: "Surely you do not think me
a man gone insane. Let your hair fall free,
for 'tis not a wild aphrodisiac.

We unveil selves and show what we lack
and what we have to share in abundance,
mingling our bodies to create one sense."
Sofia demurred, and a teardrop fell,
saying she feared divorce and bitter Hell.
He snatched off her veil, he was too enthralled,
and laughed when he saw she was going bald.

11

Onan's Seeds

Bernard moved off-campus sophomore year,
boarding with a computer major peer
who was eight-years older. Clyde had returned
to school, which during his youth he had spurned.
He was part Cuban, black, and a bit white,
who preferred a debate than a fistfight.
Like Bernard, he was oft superfluous,
as his lingo changed from East Saint Louis
inflections of what he called ghetto-talk,
and joked he had to relearn how to walk
after years of strutting like a peacock,
imitating gangsters' genetic stock.
Bernard and Clyde built a monster machine
with all the current hardware they could glean.
Pooling their resources, the computer
was an owl of wisdom as a tutor.
Bernard asked Clyde who would get the rare gem
when graduation separated them.
Clyde said: "By then it will be out-dated,
so shall cannibalize what is rated
the highest in value, or sell the thing
to one of us for what the used parts bring."
Clyde was on the sofa, watching football,
when insight seemed to beckon him to call:

"I love the safety of my college life.
What to put on-screen is the biggest strife.
I have no problems with the outer-world,
like the flag-banners Bosnia unfurled,
as Christians and Muslims slaughter for gods,
with techno-death reaping them like seed pods.
Yet despite that, there seems something missing.
As if an ignored voice is addressing
a smooth temptation to my former state,
where I abandoned my friends to their fate.
I chose dimensions over human-berth,
as if I can make plans to reshape Earth.
Where does this information highway lead?
Vessels for a consumer nation's seed.
Education has failed because teachers
have become the popular cults' preachers.
I can learn on the streets the vapid songs,
or sit in front of a screen, smoking bongs,
rather than pay to be taught the lyrics
of trained jesters bragging about their tricks.
For years blacks took the high-road and declared
we were above oppressors. Now ensnared
in the vacuum of a level play-field,
we built a system to which we have kneeled.
The liberal arts have become a joke
of transient greedy mirrors and smoke."
Bernard: "Of course we want a good career,
and each era pukes up its own Shakespeare.
In former lives they entertained patrons,
who freed them from Bedlam to become pawns
singing nonsense, biting heads off live rats,
smearing dung on their faces, doing prats.
When royalty wearied of the crass show,
they would hire a true artist to bestow
verses and music, or a painted scene,
sublime and powerful, but not obscene.

The court-jesters would be locked-up again,
to practice their talent among madmen.
So they did their time, and karma pays off:
billions of eyes follow their every cough,
wondering if the star has a disease
from all the desires he cannot appease.
Hamlet's soliloquies no longer click
for the audience that applauds Yorick.
So biting the heads off of live rodents
is our art shared for defining moments.
Global democracy is insipid,
making everyone equally stupid."
Clyde: "But when did it get out of control?
Can we blame someone or are we one soul?
I have met real morons in college,
too dumb to even take the army's pledge.
Does our society have to cater
to the low common denominator?"
Bernard: "Schools changed their curriculums' pool
while Ronald Reagan slept in his own drool.
There were law-suits and hearings in Congress,
where each voice was equal in their address,
bashing white males and hurling out like discs
Homer, Dante, and other great Classics.
To be a true free-thinker one must not
blame the scape-goaters for the system's rot.
Though they practice slinging arrows of fault,
and such becomes a business of assault,
I will not sink to their level of shame,
seeking to scapegoat the pointers of blame.
It shifts from person to person the stain,
'tis like whining about those who complain."
Clyde: "We want to pluck specks from others' eyes,
but timber in ours is the Lord of Flies.
This new Golden Age will bring about doom.
Embodied to eternally consume

the Milky Way like malnourished infants,
lacking the memory of elephants.
Despite evolved consciousness we forget
through corporate distractions that target
our minds, scattered in devouring way,
defeated by those who live day-to-day."
Bernard: "Our Edens are not meant to last,
which we might learn with an atomic blast.
We are parts of orbiting satellites
acting as if Fate looming depths and heights.
There are those without mechanized routine.
From insular worlds, we judge them as mean
and jealous of our pursuit of freedoms
as self-proclaimed pharaohs of great kingdoms
in screen-worlds of brain-washing dimension,
for which our foes' chiefs lack comprehension
in our attempts at grand global markets,
selling cultures and brands of narcotics.
Our deep discussions are of rock-and-roll,
which became machine music with no soul.
There is more meaning in nursery rhymes
as subversive politics for their times."
Clyde: "I agree with what you have to say.
Though folks in my old neighborhood would bray
and talk trash, they also had common sense
to see the system is fragile nonsense.
But they also had wars over rap-songs,
which people died for as if to right wrongs.
At least no one here dies for a tune's lines
a contrary judge deems rotten designs.
Satellite dishes have become our ears,
screens, our eyes to provoke laughter or tears,
the sense to smell has become choked with smog,
and tongues are artificial flavors' cog.
We have become a bionic human,
applauding ourselves as our biggest fan.

Though we criticize the way that things are,
we chase dreams like ships led by the North Star,
pursuing new worlds of variety,
which we will destroy with insanity.
The spoilers are eternally at work
within each person where the shadows lurk.
We may try to heighten our consciousness
with chemicals that bring only duress.
Sitting here stewing I feel half-alive.
Why not call Sheila and go for a drive?"
Bernard: "Because she is a flirt and tease,
who coyly spurns my love-play's wordy pleas.
Cynical though it is, I have urges
to free myself with sexual purges."
Clyde: "Is freedom making more of yourself?
Is that what the books say upon your shelf?"
Bernard: "This school term I have yet to look
at or even lift any kind of book.
Which is strange as I used to read often,
and was a mimicker, wielding my pen.
But to answer your question, yes, 'tis true
I gain freedom when my images spew
across the world, reflecting my desire,
outnumbering you with the clan I sire.
Once there were sex temples at harvest time,
and not to pay homage was a great crime.
Judah made through his daughter-in-law's heist
a direct patriarch of Jesus Christ,
who fought with Herod, a distant cousin,
over whose kingdom was blessed without sin.
Jesus chose Heaven, King Herod the Earth,
to multiply and rule by fruitful birth.
Herod made plans to build the West Wall
that Jews worship at to heed Yaweh's call.
Christ's buildings were of ethereal clouds,
which forms minds into anti-matter shrouds.

To gain a lofty pie-in-the-sky wish
I can smoke grass, besides, I am Jewish.
We can turn Earth into Hell if we want,
where liars reign and human shadows haunt.
Some pray it happens to fulfill prophets,
and while they are at it, gain large profits.
But I have no moral obligations
to follow leaders or support nations.
The Greeks used to blame the goddess of love,
whose steel fist was concealed in a silk glove,
for stirring their madness and wild passion.
Now a porno palace is the fashion.
Has love got anything to do with it?
Some say abstaining frees one from the pit.
Love, sex, and hate are closer together
than ambivalence to a bound tether.
The new fertility corporations
have temple harlot infatuations,
who men spill their seed to by video,
not staying around to see what will grow.
'Tis good capitalism to market
the children produced and kept a secret,
yet to warp it while a stem-embryo,
in research for a gene's patent rich glow,
is considered murder of a human,
and an attempt at playing with god's plan.
The ancient harvest rituals are now
done by Hispanic field-workers who vow
that the Catholic clergy are correct
in banning contraceptives to their sect.
The corporate farmers treat them poorly,
just as in Upton Sinclair's morally
told tale of the meat-packing industry,
in the early Twentieth-Century.
So I do not mind being outnumbered
by Hispanics who migrate like a bird,

for they have paid their dues and are fertile,
and we mix together for god's cull-style.
Even King Gilgamesh and Enkidu
were plucked from life's orchard, placed in death's stew."
Clyde: "So you say you are free of Baal,
and your own ethnic group of Israel."
Bernard: "Free will supersedes religion,
just as the hawk soars over the pigeon.
If it does not then we simply cast blame
on those who suckered us into their game.
Israel should not exist at all cost
because of bloodshed in the Holocaust,
which is a word originally meant
as sacrifice to know Yaweh's intent.
What kind of god wants six million Jews dead
as sacrifice to regain their homestead?"
Clyde: "I often wonder about their fate,
but god does not barter in real estate.
Come on, I have had enough of this talk.
Why not go for a ride or take a walk?"
Disengaged from the computer, Bernard
felt like his stomach was a tub of lard.
He ate junk-food packaged in a large size,
and could not recall his last exercise.
He telephoned Sheila, she was at home,
and agreed to an aimless driving roam
through the wheat-fields of the Kansas landscape,
where the highways wind like ribbons that drape.
Bernard's car had a sun-roof, but the breeze
swept in pollen swirls and made Sheila sneeze,
so the top was closed against sun and sky,
and the air-conditioner turned on high.
They drove by pastures, turning gold from green,
the reaping near, like an old harvest scene.
Clyde: "I heard the crops will be good this year,
though most will be fed to castrated steer,

and other animals we dine upon,
whose manure pollutes rivers and lawn."
Sheila: "All I care about is the feast.
Farming is never big news in the East.
It is all they talk of in this hick state,
on and on they go with a drawling prate."
Bernard: "What would you eat if not for them?
Be more cautious about whom you condemn.
You believe New York is the world-shaper,
but you cannot live on a newspaper,
despite how sophisticated it is
with song video reviews by a wiz.
Farming takes more faith than the blind belief
in celebrities and the current chief
of economics and status reform,
who claim they can guide us through any storm.
There are weather problems all of the time,
farmers must slog through the droughts and flood slime.
They may be too far right-wing for my taste,
and as Clyde said, fertilizers lay waste.
They are easy to ignore when we dine,
but counter-balance the ornate and fine."
The rows of wheat, beans, and corn seemed endless,
weaving together like looms for a dress.
Clyde: "Each system sets up a sacrifice
so others can progress through artifice.
It is now time for family farmers
to be removed in the name of commerce.
Over-priced organic food is a trend,
but like all fads it will come to an end.
A few years of twisters and dusty bowls
shall be all we have to fill our ka souls.
We cannot decide if we are forming
greenhouse gases that raise global warming.
One side pays scientists to research, 'No,
'tis not humans' fault, just part of the show.'

Others travel the world in hot pursuit
of how we should live by giving them loot.
Throwing money at the problem at hand
will not stop the soil from turning to sand."
Sheila: "Yes, but greed helps span the schism
between the groups with capitalism.
'Tis no secret that role models get paid,
whether a shining light or a dark shade.
Even porno actresses have their cults.
We all reach for the stars with catapults."
Clyde: "Icons of fertility spill seeds
in sterile endeavors that plant thick weeds.
Are we tied to land in morality,
all linked to one fate by causality?"
Sheila: "So preach the screen evangelists,
busy preparing their enemy lists.
Not many people willingly release
comforts and conveniences for a lease
on a simple life, nor can they be found
through satellites, full of fury and sound."
Bernard thought of the last few books he read,
or at least summaries of them, and said:
"The best examples are those to live by,
not chasing after the new ways to die.
What good comes of aping a dead martyr,
being victims of a world-wide slaughter?
Females understand that better than men,
protecting their young like chicks by a hen.
They have taken a place in our work-force,
so relationships have altered their course.
Sexual liberation now means males
can be friends with women, and that entails
being screw-buddies with casual sex,
not plotting lineage to breed a *Rex*.
Females now control a portion of wealth,
no longer behind a curtain of stealth.

The Church of England made a Virgin Queen
to take the place of Mary Mother's scene,
a product of several divorces,
who embodied virtue, say the sources.
Caliban, from Shakespeare's play *The Tempest,*
was a metaphor of Irish unrest,
savages who cannibalized their god
in drunk rituals, 'til struck by a rod.
Setebos' magic could not compete with
the Faerie Queene in propaganda's myth.
'Twas also a parable not to breed
with Irish animals and their cursed seed.
Women are free now to mate as they will,
so men also let them pay their own bill.
God speed in finding a man you can keep,
who does not bail-out when going is steep.
No longer protectors or bread-winners,
just sex mules, not traditional sinners."
Clyde: "Art is created through violence.
Victors sing, the oppressed kept in silence,
'til tables are turned and art is reformed
by wrath's force as if a volcano stormed.
I had to get out of my neighborhood,
I felt adrift in the infernal wood.
Women were misused, some of them were white.
I fathomed the rage, but it was not right.
We went from being thought of as noble
hard-hit victims, not upwardly mobile,
yet given a chance the past few decades
to rise above, we choose to be thug shades.
Perhaps because white women call their males
demons to increase feminist art sales
you white men secretly want blacks to hurt
your fair gender and grind them into dirt."
Bernard laughed: "Keep all the uppity folks
together, and their spawn will bear our yokes."

Sheila: "I am not enjoying this ride.
You have hearts of stone gone to the dark side.
You try to ascertain what karma bought,
but fail to understand subconscious thought.
I only want my own work and a life
beyond being a servant and housewife.
You fix on details with a hated glare,
reading motives and thoughts that are not there.
Dostoevsky went a criminal rote,
yet a seminal patriot who wrote:
'The coin of each nation is liberty.'
And I want to earn my own entrance fee,
which you would deny females, out of spite,
with family values to guard your might.
You speak as twice divorced Republicans,
issuing a contract with levied bans."
Bernard said: "They craft public images
of guarding philosophies as sages,
quoting Aristotle's state as a bliss:
slaves are property, thus earn no justice.
The knowledge of the ancients' was passed down
to people who readily cheer a clown
hopelessly inept at discerning thought,
thinking culture, like products, can be bought."
Clyde: "Products define personalities,
as good consumers sway with every breeze.
The once ruling class is quick to change gears
of philosophies' beliefs with new seers
shaping at the base of the pyramid
a religion that will rise up, amid
the oppression and despair, to become
the policies that spread through a kingdom.
So it was when Romans held down the Greeks,
but their pantheon reached the highest peaks."
Bernard: "Changing faith is sloughing-off skins
for crafting traits to adapt to new sins.

I once considered myself a Hindu,
went as far as I could, now am a Jew.
'Tis no surprise Greeks were first to embrace
Christ's slave beliefs after leaving its base
in Israel, for the Greeks liked the shrouds
of having their heads in Heavenly clouds,
and their shafts up young men's tight derrieres,
so priests spread the Word to cross-carriers.
The same is true for the conservative
Republican closet-cases, who live
in a perpetual state of angst-fear
of being found out as a raving queer,
then hypocritically bash those life-styles,
while hunting state page-boys like pedophiles.
As Greeks in old days, they adopt young sons
to play hide the hot dog in toasty buns.
Homer would be censored by Socrates,
which happens now with new philosophies
that sprout each semester as passing trends:
transvestite lessons on how gender bends.
Their foes work as guards of the Republic,
and they hate Bill Clinton for being slick.
He prefers women, which churns their stomachs.
Treacherous men who betray them like schmucks
for females is a terrible disgrace,
preferring power of perverted grace."
Clyde: "Like the gangster thugs who sacrifice
the next generation on prisons' vice."
Sheila: "So history repeats itself,
and one can follow it from a bookshelf.
Perhaps there exists reincarnation
so we can experience each station.
No one is worthy of eternal Hell
after a few short years on Earth, nor dwell
in Heaven with god's immutable glow.
We can barely take in the conscious flow

of the senses' stimuli on this globe,
which bombards us with continuous probe.
Playing harps was once thought our just desserts,
which evolved into rock and roll concerts."
Bernard: "So humans' songs regress or grow
at whims of the music god, Apollo.
Beethoven and Mozart have been consigned
as background props for ads seared in our mind
through use of subliminal messages
for junk food that burns through our passages."
Sheila: "And yet you spend all day in front
of a screen in distracted, fruitless hunt,
endeavoring to find a new great height
from the gods of this age, the satellite."
Bernard: "I try my wings like Icarus,
and as the globe warms I hope all of us
do not melt and plummet into the sea,
amoebas again who could once fly free.
Ambition has changed, but not the high cost,
something drives us on to sell souls like Faust.
Some folks do it with wide-eyed innocence,
but I am a cynic with keener sense.
All views are subjective, subject to change,
loving the familiar, hating the strange.
Idol-makers tell me to worship oil
and that Israel is god's holy soil.
A few gold calves picked up along the way
is giving another view its due pay.
So satellites guide us to paradise,
jealous for our beliefs, with their own vice.
I could not be a soldier in this age,
where covert deeds create what seems a stage
for pontificating old fools to scream
of foes destroying our ideal dream."
Clyde: "I read my horoscope yesterday.
We all consult oracles for the way

to rewards and future occurrences:
the weather news or stock inferences.
We have become fixated on the cult
of knowing everything through the occult
of modern *deus ex machinas'* magic,
and I predict it will become tragic."
Sheila: "I have faith in a happy end.
Without rancor all the people will blend
to make comedy and romance our songs,
keeping hate in the past where it belongs."
In the backseat Clyde smiled at her belief,
with stirred sensations for her like a leaf
in autumn, aloft with wind that teases,
churning adrift by hard and soft breezes.
Clyde did not know where such thoughts might take him,
or if chances with her were good or slim.
Sheila's sleek body, with fine flaring hips,
seemed made for a two-backed beast with hand-grips.
Her green eyes were shielded by sunglasses.
Though Russian, had skin like Irish lasses.
Bernard could smell the testosterone charge.
Uncowed, though his competitor was large,
he said: "Did you drop your science class, Clyde?
The worm turned on you like a rising tide.
I never saw anyone fail like that,
not fathoming a millimeter stat."
Bernard turned to Sheila and said with glee
at that which had sent Clyde on a drunk spree:
"The whole world uses the metric system,
but to Clyde it seems chaotic mayhem.
We drove forty klicks, say the car dials.
How far is that, Clyde, converted to miles?"
Clyde brooded sullenly, then shook his head
grinning resolutely, looked up and said:
"You know, back home those would be fighting words,
but for now I will not give them two turds.

A hitchhiker goes in our direction,
so answer his prayers of genuflection."
Bernard saw a glimpse of the hiker's face:
long black hair and stern mouth hinting no trace
that expected compassion from drivers,
seeming to disdain them as contrivers
of artificial life, in delusions
they can control the worlds of illusions.
Bernard was excited: "I may know him,
though he has altered to be fierce and grim.
Of course, a few days' hitchhiking will change
anyone following the highway range."
He steered the auto beside the pavement,
and when Sheila realized his intent,
said: "Are you insane? He could kill us all.
I will get out and use my phone to call
Trisha to drive here and give me a ride
if you let bad stupidity abide."
Bernard watched the mirror as the man neared,
like a ghost of the past had reappeared.
Bernard flicked the button of the trunk switch,
and told her she would be found in a ditch
if she called Trisha and stood there to wait,
as Sheila would be obvious rape-bait.
Clyde calmed the paranoia, telling her
he was on guard if evil should occur.
The man placed his luggage in the car's trunk,
and Bernard wondered at how Charles had sunk.
For it was him, and he looked full of bile,
watching Sheila with a sardonic smile,
as if enjoying he was capable
of making her feel so uncomfortable.
At the coincidence of their meeting,
Bernard tried good cheer and laughed a greeting.
Charles sat next to Clyde and patted Bernard
on the shoulder; then his grip became hard,

causing Bernie to twist free with a yelp,
like the cry of a playful cougar whelp
bitten in games by an older brother,
then runs for asylum to his mother.
Bernard pulled the car back onto the lane,
with a list of questions as a refrain.
Charles merely looked out the window with sighs,
his face draining from cruel-lidded eyes.
He nodded to Sheila and shook Clyde's hand,
as Bernard turned off the radio band.
Charles murmured: "Relationships are poison.
God was capricious with his only son,
so if it is true in Heaven above,
why should we not hurt the ones we most love?"
Bernard: "Since when do you drink what Christ bleeds
from the Christians harvesting their sowed seeds?
That religion puts me on high-alert.
Did some Mormons convince you to convert?"
Charles: "We never lived in an enclosed space,
now need to adapt to stay with the pace
as interaction with nature narrows.
Reuben was right: 'tis the time of pharaohs.
The government controls the food supply,
getting corporate farm bribes on the sly
through taxpayer subsidies, and the greed
buys gene-technicians for a hybrid seed.
As the land is ruined, they invent crops,
controlling the market and franchise shops."
Bernard: "Jesus Christ, Charles, thanks for that bomb.
You are still a rebel like Absalom.
He died when his hair got caught in a tree,
his donkey ran off at Yaweh's decree."
Clyde: "'Tis a common theme in a Jew tale
of tree-beams, donkeys, and rebels who fail."
Charles: "Such fruit on a tree has no flavor,
nor the immortality I savor,

just manufactured food under controls
of the corporate branch dealing in souls."
Sheila stayed quiet, thinking Charles a grouse,
and Bernard drove to her apartment house.
She left without a farewell, slammed the door,
angry acrimony filling her core.
Charles watched her performance, eyes bright and keen,
laughing when Clyde called her a drama queen.
Bernard shrugged and Charles asked about Camille,
and the reply was she had no appeal,
but Bernard had found a porno web site
that was better than most of the sick blight.
On it there was a woman who appeared
to be Camille's twin-self, and Bernard leered:
"I thought she was Camille, and had a fit,
and this chick humps like she really means it.
She will do anything, and is foxy.
I felt three times removed by sex proxy,
which is safe in this age of diseases.
We can experience that which pleases
our primordial brain, still un-evolved,
with machines that have all our problems solved."
Clyde: "There no longer is forbidden fruit.
We throw seeds of desire and they take root
with countless morons at computer screens,
who may invent drama like Shakespeare's scenes."
They reached the apartment complex as rain,
like pellets, fell as if to cleanse a stain.
They rushed in and sat down, Clyde deep in thought
upon a quandary which had him caught.
Bernard mixed strong drinks of juice and liquor,
as Charles drank his eyes began to flicker.
Clyde: "It seems like Heaven has sprung a leak.
Come to my room, Bernie, we have to speak."
Charles nodded, knowing he was the subject
of discussion as if a mere object.

Clyde's room was tidy, though not too spacious;
his mind was at work for something loquacious.
Too often he reverted to slang-talk
and labeled a goon, so he seemed to balk.
Finally he sat down at his desk chair,
and ran his hands through his clipped Afro hair.
Clyde: "Why are you taking in a hard-case,
and how long will he abide at our place?
You told me stories of him and his deeds,
and you follow every dance move he leads.
What if one of my homies showed up here?
Would you welcome him with an ice cold beer?"
Bernard: "I just want to know his story.
He is one who sinks low, yet has glory.
I have not seen him for quite a time-span,
and will discover if he has a plan.
Allow some time to bring him back to Earth.
We may receive gifts that are of high worth."
Clyde shook his head glumly, they left the room,
wondering what vindictive fate would loom.
The computer captured Charles' attention,
and seeing that caused Bernard to mention:
"What do you think of our begotten child,
fabricated while you were running wild?
'Tis cleaner to manage than small infants,
with better memories than elephants."
Charles: "I wonder how much I would be paid
for pawning your first-born to a thin shade."
Clyde glared at him, then took a step forward,
Charles stood up, arms cocked as a beveled board.
Bernard: "Stop it, you two. Keep your heads straight.
Clyde does not understand your laughing trait.
You are my guest, Charles, and you are welcome,
but you do not have keys to my kingdom.
I dislike setting terms and conditions,
but 'tis better than the homeless missions.

First, you stay away from the computer,
though I trust you are not a crass looter.
Clyde does not know you as well as I do,
so stay out of his room, that is rule two."
Charles sat down: "Blame the pawn joke on my clan.
I am just another drunk Indian."
Bernard: "Why linger so long in your pit
when you are more than that and you know it?
My mom is a doctor, I watched her work
on hopeless cases where the demons lurk.
Perhaps I adopted some of her faith
in bringing to Earth a wandering wraith,
though she believes more in medications
to stop madness through inoculations."
Charles felt something trickling down his flushed cheek,
thinking it sweat, then found it hard to speak.
He glowered in shame that he could not hide
tears that betrayed his idea of pride.
Bernard: "Could we have a few hours alone,
Clyde, so I can know the cause of his moan?"
Charles sniffed and wiped his eyes with fingertips
composing himself, then said through pursed lips:
"He can stay if he wants to hear my tale,
I want to tell it with no sobbing wail.
This is his place, too, and he has the right
to know who shows up like a gremlin-blight."
They arranged themselves on the furniture,
no longer heeding the rain of nature.
Charles: "My cousin, Manny, was killed last year.
When we were young he was my brother's peer,
and went with my uncle on hunting trips.
They competed, but never came to grips.
They were best buddies, inseparable,
and this is not a liquor parable,
but one day, quite by chance, you understand,
a bottle of booze came to Manny's hand.

He drank it with Maddox for a quick thrill,
hiding in bushes on Dinosaur Hill.
They regressed to a primordial rage,
no grace from the pipe or blessing of sage.
What they fought over, they could not recall,
but Maddox beat him senseless in a brawl,
and left him there to return to our place,
with blood all over him and torn up face.
We found Manny near dead, a tree branch stuck
through his left arm, covered in gory muck.
They drank together again the same week:
no change in results from what they might seek.
Well, they are dead and I went on the lam
to avoid being a sacrifice lamb
on altars of protected convenience,
granted to us by powers of science.
I have some mechanical aptitude,
and fit in well with my bad attitude
among the carnival workers on tour,
traveling to the East and Western shore,
a grumbling, drunk bad lot who did not care
if bolts were missing from rides at the fair.
I did the best I could but when I saw
my diligence was taken as a flaw
and a personal insult to comrades,
I gave up and became one of the lads.
There was no honor in getting punched-out
for doing my job, so I went the route
of companions, watching riders herded.
'Tis hard to believe no one was murdered.
Running machines while doped, drunk to the gills,
and folks lined up for death-defying thrills.
Would they have done it if they knew our states,
twisted on drugs, echoes bouncing vile traits?
They knew from our looks we had a grim past,
yet trusted their lives to a lower-caste.

So it was with the carnies around me,
and for a while it was easy and free.
I was brought into a circle of friends,
feeling my wounds heal, as time always mends.
Due to probation I assumed the guise
of Maddox, and began to realize
that what I did was how his life might be
had Stanley not leveled out death's decree.
At first it was good, feeling his spirit
was happy as Heaven had it so writ.
Then he demanded I do my job well,
if I did not, my head ran like Hell's bell.
To make him happy and keep the pain mute,
I became professional and astute.
I shared a trailer with six other men,
most of them just freed from a prison pen.
They got drunk one night about a week back,
and roughly yanked me out of slumber's sack.
Saying I was not true part of the staff,
they beat me up and I heard Maddox laugh.
I felt strength subside with an awful wane,
on all sides I was afflicted by pain.
Had Maddox lured me there for a beating,
jealous I lived, his own life so fleeting?
Or is he trying to drive me with whips
to kill Stan to face his apocalypse?
I do not know, for my mind is hazy.
The Furies' blood-thirst can drive one crazy.
The consciousness a person has in links
with those about him helps form what he thinks
as part of a gathered mentality
to fit in one's place for stability.
As family and tribal life changes,
so a person's psyche rearranges.
It can seem like chaos, going so fast:
progress chugs on, leaving some in the past.

The next day I was drained of energy,
towards fate I felt only lethargy.
I took a lunch break from selling tickets,
and thought of laying to die in thickets
in the park where we had set up our site,
but knew the attempt would be a mere trite,
when an old man approached me at a tent,
introduced himself and spoke his intent."

12

Feldon's Story

'We can sit down and have a small picnic.
I am Feldon, and I am Hispanic,
though I have blue eyes from an Irish dad,
as well as this cheek scar when he was mad
that I burned down our henhouse to stay warm
when he locked me out during a snow storm.
I was sixteen when I left the terror,
for god had not killed him to heed my prayer.
I went on the lam for forty long years,
to escape cruelty that laughed at tears.
Soon I learned to suppress crying in vain,
except on a bad drunk and half-insane,
then I become a sentimental goof,
but I will not drink now to give you proof.
You shall have to take me upon my words,
any beer and I will sing with the birds.
What I want to tell you is a story
from last year about my fallen glory.
Though it might be good in a song-bird's voice,
I will use English as my second choice.
I appreciate how the languages
adapt and evolve with human changes,
but I think our minds are becoming weak
with the involvement of computer-speak.

I have an Indian friend whose fine talk
has our babble seem a babe's learning to walk.
He could soon be running entire nations,
as we mangle essence from our stations.
While I do not believe the Word was god,
we seem stuck in performing prayers that laude
machines and ourselves to be fused as one,
and human stories are lost or undone.
I believed in the holy trinity:
me, myself, and I for infinity.
If there was something greater, I cared not,
as that is for the faithful to unknot.
I was born unto this planet at odds
with every religion and their false gods.
It affected various states of mood,
'til I developed the bad attitude:
spare me the lectures of your belief's myth,
just hit me and get your job over with.
Yet a spark of humanity remained,
despite how I tried to keep myself stained.
I had been out of prison for two years,
where I avoided gangs and shrugged-off queers,
then I was captured for driving while drunk.
I took care of it and fled with my trunk
because the heat was coming down on me,
both literal and figuratively.
I left Florida with a carnival,
angry and stung like a tormented bull.
In a Georgia city things fell apart,
and I had a glimpse of my darkened heart.
Some of my fellow carnies, black and white,
picked up a stray and kept her out of sight.
At most she was fifteen, though likely less,
and I saw her one day in her soiled dress.
They had been selling her for coupling turns,
like a ride, and I could see cigar burns

on her arms, hands, and legs as she tottered,
and I could tell she would soon be slaughtered.
I cursed the fates that brought me to these lows,
and thought to break the code of my fellows,
and become an outcast even from them,
another society to condemn
me to a life of wandering like Cain.
So these things revolved in my aching brain.
I do not have much of a family,
and disregard a holy homily,
but she might have people who loved her still,
and I did not want my life to be nil.
I walked up to the girl and said, 'Come on.'
She gazed at me like a blinking young fawn,
and began to stumble to the trailers,
where they kept her confined as her jailers.
I said: 'Damn it, I am not after sex.
I need to save you, so please do not vex
my good intentions and get me murdered
by having your vile rapists alerted.'
I could not tell if there was anything
left in her soul that was worth redeeming.
She had gone so far in calamity,
all that remained was stunned insanity.
I hid her behind a tree while I went
to the manager for my last payment.
He had seen me with the girl and said so,
adding he had grown weary of her show,
and I would become a casualty
because I could not face reality.
He said: 'I do not know why you bother.
We are meant to prey on one another.
After years of living the way you did,
you cannot suddenly put on a lid
and expect everything to turn out right.
At best you can stay ahead of the blight

by running and keeping from a groove-set.
Not on the move, you will be a target.'
Those were prophetic words I failed to heed,
being her savior on a charger steed.
I believed I could get away intact,
but for doing good things I had no tact.
I could not escape freely from my past,
it caught up to me with a lightning blast.
She had no footwear so I gave her mine,
and though I was thirsty for some cheap wine,
I kept us on-track to a gas station
where I phoned a cab, filled with elation
that I was a decent human being,
no longer a scoundrel, always fleeing.
It had not been easy to make her trudge
and guide her while I carried my luggage,
but it was now finished, or so I thought:
peace of mind and happiness had been bought.
She was so beaten she ran out of fumes,
and collapsed in the cab, muttering dooms
for herself if she did not make it back
to their trailer for their nightly attack.
I patted her hand but hit a fresh burn.
She moaned in pain, making the driver turn
his head and ask if I had done her dirt.
I turned seething mad and yet also hurt,
telling him he took money for a ride,
not for the innuendo he implied.
I felt like I rode into a new life.
I even thought of binding to a wife,
and having children who would be a part
of society at the local mart.
I would have steady work and pay taxes
to a gentle government that waxes
full and bright, never waning like the moon.
Yes, I would have it all and get it soon.

The cabbie followed us to the front desk,
and though I told him to scram as a pesk,
he stayed with us through the entire ordeal
of the police spinning my fortune's wheel.
The future-tellers at the carnival
could have told me it would be so awful.
Though they are false, I would believe their pitch
if warned police have contempt for a snitch,
unless it is a wealthy citizen,
who monopolizes the city's Zen.
I traveled enough to witness such webs,
and each town has its own eddies and ebbs.
My Hindu friend agrees; his theory is
every town spouts growth, which soon becomes fizz,
and the era of colonization
is replaced by corporatization.
Cheap labor arrives with the immigrants,
and global markets force the governments
to ensure there is a flow of workers,
and jails fill with the savage berserkers.
North America's Free Trade Agreement
has us pretend cultures are bought and blent.
If it remains a good economy,
everyone can taste the potent foamy
brew, if only by the television.
But contraction follows each expansion,
and the greedy elite have their own mobs,
and need not worry of losing their jobs.
They succeeded in building a system,
which they say cannot afford to lose them.
Everyone else becomes expendable,
regardless of how wise and capable.
That is what my Indian friend told me,
and trust his knowledge of a caste country.
I gave the police an edited tale
of how I found the young girl up for sale.

When questioned who had done this wrong to her,
I hedged my bets and said I was not sure.
Perhaps other carnies, not of my crew,
had warped and destroyed the girl through and through.
The cabbie spoke his piece, quite malicious,
saying I acted very suspicious.
A policewoman took the girl away,
and though I hoped she had something to say
on my behalf as her great rescuer,
or at least not as a rapist-skewer,
she was too shell-shocked to say anything,
and I began to feel bad fortune's sting.
Detective's took me to a private room,
and I felt the system start to consume.
In my mind I heard the prisoners' bell,
and as the heat grew I began to yell,
which only made their inquiries more fierce,
seeking a means to upset me and pierce
my story with lies and contradictions.
Like any criminal, I tell fictions,
but since I do not write or uphold laws,
like Bill Clinton and his cronies, whose cause
is to imprison all competitors,
acting as hypocrite legislators
who sing: 'Three crimes and you are in prison,
meanwhile, we sex-predators have risen
to enforce the legal forms of conduct,
and you are so stupid, you have been shucked
of your human value, paying our fee
for guessing wrong which shell covers the pea.'
I asked the police why I would bring her
to them if I had been a tormentor.
One of them replied, a bullying lout,
that that was what they wanted to find out,
and if I had nothing to hide, and cared
for the young girl, then I should not be scared.

'Tis a standard statement of officials,
acting as priest-confessors with missals.
I said: 'Every one has something to hide,
but upon this subject I have not lied.
This is no talk-show to bare my lost soul.
I have played many parts and know my role.
If you proceed to ask the wrong questions,
you will get answers that make suggestions
I have a sordid life, which might be true,
but with this police case 'tis not a clue.
It seems to me you take the simple way,
not arresting those who used her as prey.
I have had my battles with dope and booze,
and I will look bad on the evening news
when you release it to the media
with me as a suspect, and a Shiia
Muslim terrorist will be their next tale
after ads put better lives up for sale.'
The detectives did not like that too much,
and since they had me firmly in their clutch,
could do with me whatever they felt like,
as I was a threat to their peaceful dike.
Their job is to hold back the massive hordes,
and keep humans tied to electric cords.
Once in the satellite, one cannot stray
without punishment from their godlike sway.
I told you of my old drunk-driving charge,
I thought it was done and I was at large
to roam about without any warrants
for my arrest acting as deterrents.
I had been forced to see a counselor
of alcohol, who was like a solar
god, telling me all the rotten effects
booze would cause to my personal defects.
I listened to hours of how the disease
would become something I could not appease.

Resentments kill, he told me, glad to share,
but hated me because I did not care.
He was but another whose true intent
was selling an attitude adjustment.
I have often met such founts of knowledge
trying to gain support to take their pledge.
He lectured how the disease would progress,
then sent my papers to the wrong address.
The police in Georgia checked my records,
and I was bound again in handcuff cords.
I told them the warrant was a mistake,
to call my counselor and he would make
the justice folks in Florida aware
that I finished my treatment program there.
Such work did not interest the police,
they were happy to be able to fleece
the public that a hardened criminal
was behind bars and my freedom was null.
Three weeks later, Florida cops arrived,
and their contempt for me had been derived
for ratting-out thugs from the carnie crews,
who went free while I had no pair of shoes.
I was taken to Florida and held
with the worst criminals, with whom I meld.
I do not know what became of the girl
whose life was a ride through a Hellish swirl.
I think they kept me in jail 'til she told
them I saved her from being bought and sold.
I spent another three weeks behind bars,
resuming my habits because it mars
the mind if one continually dwells
on the outer world of no lockdown bells.
And of course while there one has time to think,
and I consciously watched my conscience shrink.
I was soon blaming the girl for my woes,
and men's justice for its pageantry shows.

I had been force-fed Christianity,
and seeing my life was insanity,
I imaged myself as an innocent
for scoundrels to misuse as a hate-vent,
just like the rapists had destroyed the girl
so their evil progeny could unfurl
from its embryo state and take control,
issuing contracts for a starring role
in Satan's war against god's white peace-dove.
I then thought of unconditional love,
and how I demanded it from others.
No matter what I did, I thought mothers
and fathers, who are in every person,
should love me forever as a good son.
I hated god for making me this way,
and his stupid stories that held such sway.
What god would enforce on humans the cuss
like those tribal laws of *Leviticus*?
Yaweh was lord of many insane laws,
then killed by his own system for just cause.
I also thought goodness might be designed,
and a darkened veil dropped from my dim mind.
I did not need to be a sacrifice
for my own or others' appetite vice.
This strange spiritual experience
was very personal and quite intense.
Most of my life I lived in a bottle
like a genie who appears full-throttle,
wishing to be free, but crazy on juice,
to serve a master who heaps on abuse
to destroy his rivals and be made king,
forcing all the angels to laude and sing.
That is the way the lower-class survive,
feeding on each other while the rich thrive.
I saw it before, during Reagan's reign,
the trickle-down theory poured acid rain.

Co-worker intrigue at low-wage work sites
were typical to avoid homeless plights.
Yet here I was again, waiting in jail,
around addicts talking of dope for sale.
What good was I doing except to learn
criminal acts for my mind to discern?
Why would I adopt such lessons from them?
They were failures caught in the jail system.
To learn successful illicit knowledge,
be a Business major at a college.
My mind became the poor versus the rich,
but I had to find myself a safe niche
to practice the experience I gained
from that which was not a scapegoat nor stained.
I had sown my seeds across the Midwest,
where 'tis said fertility is the best.
I decided to contact those women
like ports in a typhoon for lost seamen.
I had money from my work and would buy
a one-way bus ticket and say goodbye
to the correctional facilities
where I stayed when not roaming as I please.
I heard someone say we will all soon speak
as television actors, whom we seek
to become, and emulate their language,
one mass of consciousness on a screen-stage.
I laid on my mattress on the jail floor,
crowded together, jammed against the door,
and watched the people on television
debate their quest for a public vision
guiding the nation to a higher realm,
with their hands, of course, to steady the helm.
New words and phrases would make us better,
and give fresh spirit to the law's letter.
Both political parties bashed their foes
for being paid shills of groups who oppose

true American values and ideals
for the progressive growth of cogs and wheels.
The inmates of jail have their own language,
which is hard to keep up with as I age.
We are released with a different tongue,
and like Job sitting on a pile of dung,
we wonder about fate and destiny
that has driven us down to bended knee,
then in a moment of revolution,
commit heinous crimes of devolution.
At my court-hearing the judge released me,
but kept most of my paycheck as a fee
for my time in jail and for their bad food,
which put a damper on my heightened mood.
Since I could not afford a bus ticket,
I bought vodka and went to a thicket.
I decided to get drunk in earnest,
like a hatchling shoved too young from the nest,
fluttering with wild chirps, then crashing hard,
like a fallen angel sung by a bard.
With music on my stereo head-set
I sung aloud and danced with no regret.
Wobbly drunk and barefoot, with little form,
as I ignored the brewing thunderstorm.
I felt free, dancing, at least for a while,
listening to music gone out of style,
which reminded me of how transient
life is, and to enjoy every moment.
All we take along with us when we die
is karmic flow that has us laugh or cry.
When I began to get drenched by the rain,
I took my luggage to a culvert drain.
The river flowed some ten yards beneath me,
and I was happily drunk, dry, and free.
I wanted to buy a pair of good shoes,
and I could not afford to spend or lose

any more money, so I tucked it in
my knapsack, then turned towards Heaven's din.
Fabulous lightning flashed across the sky,
and I felt like an elemental guy.
The same atoms that make me what I am
run through nature without causeway or dam.
I felt confident I would rise again
to establish my kingdom among men.
I would set things right and rule at leisure,
for the fates owed me a wealthy treasure,
something substantial, not just a rainbow,
that would center the world around my show.
In previous eras it would be called
faith in self-grandeur, which people forestalled.
But we live in a screen-world up for sale,
antics from The White House and county jail
are placed between ads for a new image,
the same stuff in a different package.
The Cyclop's glaring eye is everywhere,
and I would make the monster dole my share.
Why should I not be the one to bombard
the audience with my song as their bard?
The written languages have run their course
as folks demand an immediate source
of sounds and images for distraction
from this strange world of cause and reaction.
The irony is, the more we retreat,
the worse the world gets, and suffer defeat
at the hands of those who control the gears,
and I wanted to be the one who steers
us all into the divine programming
of god's bliss or Hell's eternal damning.
In that moment of knowledge so complete,
I saw a trickle between my bare-feet,
then I felt a rush of cold air move by,
as if the culvert had let loose a sigh.

I paid no mind until a sudden wave
of water blasted me out of my cave.
I shot like an enema from the drain
into the river, and flushed from my brain
were thoughts of achieving honor and fame,
which history writes as being the same.
Even defenders of the infamous,
who rise to the top and conquer the less,
know that history can take any shape
when words and rituals are used to drape
actions in well-known guise for consumption,
but that was washed clear by the eruption.
My stereo, knapsack, and luggage sank
as I struggled drunkenly to the bank.
I retched polluted water laying there
in the mud, gasping violently for air.
I crawled like an animal to high-ground,
scared I would lose consciousness and be drowned.
'Twas a good thing, too, for the river rose,
when I woke up it was lapping my toes.
I was too weak to even curse the sky,
I just laid in the mud, wanting to die.
Everything I owned had been flushed away,
another would-be king with feet of clay.
I staggered up the bank and through the trees,
noticing the clouds shifted with the breeze
to reveal the sun, which seemed to delight
in the woes I had been through in my plight.
Even the weather was set against me,
and with that thought I fell under a tree.
A stick placed there by a capricious god
pierced my Achilles tendon like a rod.
I did not have the strength to pull it out,
so I crawled as blood spurted like a gout.
I slithered toward the civilization
that I had damned as a ruined nation,

like a crazed prophet who lives on honey,
with nothing to lose, so curses money.
I could not conform to the standard mode,
nor did I fit with the criminals' code.
Both have a façade of honor's esteem,
grouping fans' energy like a sport's team.
Yet I believed they would all face my wrath,
as I somehow made it to a bike-path.
I would bring the world down to my level,
feeling I was miscast as a devil,
but also knew I was in need of help,
as I crawled like a cougar's new-born whelp.
I gave one more chance to society,
and their false images of piety.
I passed out on a park-bench and woke up
to drink from a Christian man's loving cup.
He came across me as I retched and bled,
and a hospital put me in a bed.
Of course I had no kind of insurance,
and I thought the Christian man rather dense.
He said he would pay the hospital bills,
and also buy antibiotic pills
that my wound required to prevent gangrene.
He had no faith's lecture, or pose and preen,
but paid a week's rent at a hotel room,
where I could recover and try to groom
myself back into the world I had spurned,
and it seemed this time my fortune had turned,
for inexorable time holds no grudge,
'tis my own actions that act as my judge.
I felt better and thought I would get drunk,
when the Christian man appeared with a trunk,
which he had filled with cheap but new garments,
and tears came to my eyes as in laments.
Whatever fury I had in me died,
he patted my hand while I sobbed and cried.

He put me on a bus to Omaha,
and my feelings were so intense and raw
that the image will never leave my skull,
though the Christian was uncomfortable
to have me weep and hang on his shoulder
with passion that continues to smolder.
I arrived to find my family left
the town long ago, so I was bereft.
But jobs came my way and I made some friends,
with life still to come, that other part ends.'
It was a story worth listening to,
ancient heroes had their tragic flaws too.
He seemed a man who could have won some rank,
but fate decreed his esteem to be blank.
A pirate does not always gain honor,
and great minds can slumber in a dark snore,
waiting their turn in another life's game
to win ill-gotten booty and bright fame,
and push the old heroes out of their place
by rewriting tales with a muse's grace.
Odysseus has been consigned to be
a drunken Irish Jew on a bad spree.
Modern day trivia becomes epic,
and commercials replace the main topic.
Choosing pointless tales in which to invest,
because like magpies we garnish our nest.
Such crazed consumption is easy to herd,
believing we have tales which must be heard.
Feldon's Hindu friend called him Ravana,
a savage shape-shifter who fought Rama.
To me, he was the wandering sinner
in *The Rime of the Ancient Mariner,*
which you used to quote, Bernard, as a tale
of Jews roaming Samsara, up for sale
to the high-bidder who bought their stories
of Chosen People and their god's glories,

and run the entertainment industry,
expelling artists who do not agree,
but steal their stories and reform the face
to the blessed ones of their god's special race."
Bernard interrupted, shaking his head,
and looking at Charles he quietly said:
"I am not that way, as I have foregone
my beliefs in the Hindu pantheon.
It was mere adolescent rebellion
that had me put faith in Kalki's stallion.
Perhaps this world is just an illusion,
but without comforts it is confusion.
Though it may be at another's expense,
I have come to believe in convenience.
It is human to gratify each sense,
and when 'tis my turn to suffer the stain
for another's pleasure, I will complain,
as it is also human to do that,
when a crushed victim, listed as a stat.
Such is the fortune for each monarchy,
and it is better than sheer anarchy.
I put little faith in conformity
to the open-minded diversity
that people insist I should partake of.
I choose for myself what I hate and love."
Charles: "Yes, suffering seems to wax and wane.
'Tis not our duty to feel others' pain.
Feldon's story convinced me I was done
with life as a carnie-geek on the run.
Maddox's spirit could not be appeased,
demanding that my body's shell be seized.
We are all possessed by the things we own,
and by our past actions of what is sown.
I told Feldon I refused to go back
to my home town, for my courage was slack.
I had broke probation, Manny was dead,

and Maddox still controlled parts of my head.
Feldon told me he had a Hindu friend
who could help me put my life on the mend,
a computer-whiz, tracking the world round
like a new pedigree of a bloodhound.
He could locate you, Bernard, or my folks,
to help relieve the burden of my yokes.
Then, perhaps, I can face up to my sins,
and commit new ones as fresh life begins.
Money is a factor in such a start,
and a homeless manger is not a part
of the script or role I attempt to play,
I had enough of returning to clay.
I got my last paycheck and rode along
with Feldon as he sang a country song
about the beauty of America,
with a blunt 'love it or leave it' mantra.
I felt no patriotic urge to join,
having little faith in liberty's coin.
'Tis but a tool, but somehow defines us,
for we rarely have enough in surplus.
The fellow from India was brilliant,
his wife was beautiful and salient,
without vanity or guile's pretension,
so courteous that I felt no tension
in being amid a host of strangers,
nor was I on-guard for sudden dangers.
Feldon was a janitor of a firm
the Hindu worked at as a hacker-worm,
engineering computer viruses
like a composer writing bad verses.
He was to infiltrate foes' satellites
and conjure against them destructive blights
he auctioned to other national teams
that wanted control of the nightmare dreams.
He said the temptation was hard to bear,

so I do not blame him nor do I care.
Annihilation by screen seems peaceful
compared to driving one's spear through a skull.
'Tis hard to stay loyal in a screen world
that alters like mercury being swirled
by vast temperature change, hot and cold,
and overnight millionaires quickly fold,
poor again as quickly as they got rich,
with no regulations on the sale's pitch.
I entrust no one with my destiny,
though I am driven to a bended knee.
Fur will fly, bodies shall be dismembered,
the old ways will rise and be remembered.
The Hindu man had an odd moral core,
saying when he reached America's shore
he sought to gain a desire in his heart:
have sex with a busty, blonde, blue-eyed tart.
His family had arranged a marriage,
and fearing she had the hump-backed carriage
of a camel's soul reincarnated,
he came here to avoid being mated
for life with a woman he had not seen,
to where his parents could not intervene.
His friends, however, sent him a picture
of his betrothed, and her graceful allure
stunned him so much he contacted the lass.
In school, she was at the top of her class,
and her electronic-mail showed her style,
with quick wit and humor that made him smile.
He was suspicious, as it seemed too good,
happiness surrounding him like a wood
of dancing people at a festival,
drinking and eating until they are full.
He thought his father was trying a trick
to have him convinced she was a great pick
by switching photos of the real one,

the most hideous thing under the sun,
with pictures of a beautiful female,
deceiving him through electronic-mail.
He hacked into the administration
of India's identification
department and found official pictures,
and was elated to see they were hers.
He hurried to India overnight,
married her, and came back on the next flight.
He looked you up, Bernard, by a web site,
and got your address like an oracle.
I am here, chained to my karmic shackle.
I thought there would be freedom on the road,
and there was, but 'tis no longer bestowed."

13

A Fair Split

Charles stayed for a week with Bernard and Clyde,
then returned to his hometown to be tried
for breaking the rules of his probation,
which earned six months' jail for violation.
He had turned himself in and his lawyer's
explanation that there had been spoilers
who killed Charles' cousin, causing Charles to flee
for safety's sake, worked in the bargain-plea.
Upon his release, Clara was joyful,
and they spoke when the party had a lull.
Charles: "We should quit having celebrations
when I am free of incarcerations.
Other families have parties for life
achievements, like marrying a new wife,
or becoming part of a religion.
We rejoice because I am a pigeon,
who was suckered into the losing game
of spinning jail doors and media's shame."
Clara: "Well then, follow my remedy,
stay off the booze and you can live with me.
Betty and I have been sober a year.
I remember well my last bout with beer,
I was so hung-over I could not move,
and the television would only prove

that I was powerless. All I could do
was watch ten hours of smarmy white brats spew
scripted lines of unfunny dialogue,
feeling my brain whimpering like a dog.
I suppose it was a version of Hell,
though to Christians the show is a church bell,
tuning in daily so they might perceive
ways of life they should prepare to receive."
Charles: "You and Betty deserve a kind fate,
and are examples I should emulate.
I must steer my life from the prison path,
because according to the odds of math
that is where my destiny is going,
as if fates conspire a loom with sewing."
Clara: "You do not have to live in gloom,
nor be fixed on perpetual doom.
I also felt each day was a new death,
and purposely sought out the lowest depth.
Glimmers of light were drowned in alcohol,
I laughed a fool's glee at my steady fall.
While life is not perfect now, far from it,
I do not feel my destruction is writ."
Charles: "You have a job now and seem happy,
but emotions are making me sappy.
I will go for a walk before I burst
into tears that shall create a beer thirst."
Clara sighed: "My son, do not retard love,
for it is a gift beyond a white dove.
The cosmos is full of symbols we choose
to represent our feelings and amuse
ourselves with what they mean within our mind,
taking them apart for what lies behind.
Love is the ultimate reality,
and it alone deserves our fealty.
Distracted by the superstitious signs,
we plunge in for gold and fame through the mines,

believing our instincts cannot be wrong,
yet what have we achieved with such a song?
The land is wasted and becomes sterile.
Within search for status lies our peril."
Charles: "You have become a philosopher,
speaking in clarity without a blur.
Perhaps hate is driving me to the end,
so captured in snares I will never mend.
Yet I also seek a noble purpose,
not merely for myself but all of us.
A cause to fit my own ideal image,
and lift us beyond our mechanized stage.
Instead I have only unfocused rage."
Clara: "Such wrath makes it easy to sink,
but I know your heart better than you think.
You still want revenge on Stanley Jacob,
and by his demise you hope to wake up
to a life that will bring honor and peace.
I shall not deny my hatred will cease
if you should succeed in murdering him,
for Maddox' death was like losing a limb.
Yet that part of my life has concluded,
and Stan would be happy to make you dead.
To release the past is one of the fees
I pay for my new life's philosophies."
They sat on the porch-swing in mild silence,
no longer dwelling on past violence.
Clara rubbed Charles' back while he hung his head,
pondering the gentle words she had said.
He felt weary and blasted through his soul,
which made him angry at the assumed role
he thought was forced upon him by the world
in its idiotic scripts as it swirled,
which preached and taught a mad duality:
embracing foes like Christians' quality,
and competition to be the fittest,

procreating to prove self is the best.
When Clara suggested a ritual
to purify Charles' mind and free his skull,
he shrugged and replied: "What would be the point?
The medicine man would sing and anoint,
then I would go right back to booze and drugs,
as one of the many Lakota thugs.
Since I despise the Christian hypocrites,
and how they condemn us to fiery pits,
I would be as bad as them to partake
in rites my contrary actions forsake."
Clara: "One of your youthful ambitions
was to help by performing ablutions.
You saw each day as a journey to light,
an eternal vision quest to take flight
and collect our souls from the furthest star,
to reveal to us what we truly are."
Charles closed his eyes, and laughing nervously,
replied he had just been acting squirrely.
What could one expect from someone so young?
He tested each voice to see which had sung
the best and fullest of all the cosmos,
and in return he received a large dose
of the knowledge that one should disengage,
for every voice can lead to a bad page
of scripted hate promising miracles
that chain souls to terrible oracles.
Dark matter and light contribute to verse:
the former dominates the universe,
and light is only a small percentage,
which we try to shape to a godly pledge.
Clara: "You sound like a contradiction.
Life is not a tale of science fiction.
I have to avoid my own dear sister
because she acts like a stormy twister,
and thinks I betrayed her insane lifestyle,

judging her like god at her Last Trial.
She has spent her short time on Earth that way,
believing alcohol will somehow pay
grand dividends for her life's investment,
and things are as should be with god's intent.
I hope you do not follow in her wake,
but if you do I will invest no stake.
'Tis too heartbreaking and miserable,
and I doubt I am fully capable
of nurturing you through drunken binges,
because my own serenity hinges
on what you said about disengaging,
and 'tis not my duty of arranging
the lives and happiness of everyone,
like the solar system orbits the sun."
Charles: "I am jealous of you for finding
escape from the eternal re-winding
of the ongoing rerun we contrive
to make ourselves fit in and feel alive.
We create a system we recognize,
and society shapes us to a size.
We cling to the roles, hoping for rewards
that will launch us to the satellite lords."
Clara: "A new paradise is within
each of us, no matter how bad the sin.
Why not return to your detailed art-work?
Put your fiends at bay wherever they lurk."
Charles: "That, too, is a source of depression,
and I will give you my new impression.
We so invest in our entertainments
that we call them art in fools' arguments,
insisting they are not mere distractions,
because that would reveal stupid actions.
The big literary question last year
was who should play a vampire and appear
in a flick as a blonde or with black hair:

an important topic for those who care,
and were weary of a famed sport's figure
accused of killing his wife with vigor,
which also spawned mass-produced books and shows,
and art is left reeling in its death-throes
with vapid renditions of Othellos.
We are still pack animals following
Alpha mates' violent domineering.
Do we have a culture worth fighting for?
If the world is merely a franchise store,
mass-producing items to be consumed,
with democracy as a guise assumed
to cloak our ignorance of real art,
for desire of convenience in our heart,
we will dumb ourselves down to a bland stage
as partakers of a new Golden Age.
Computer graphic effects will detail
humans' pathetic screen-lives up for sale."
Clara: "You have a well-voiced opinion,
so do not surrender your dominion.
Artists will rise and make stupid scenes burst,
if booze and dope do not murder them first."
Charles: "I have a morbid self-interest,
as if I pit my will against a test
to see if I can rise through the despair
and trap my enemies in their own snare.
Once I thought I did it for everyone,
that people were like shades cast by the sun,
and I could lead them to know who they are,
with a vision path not fueled by a car.
Now I see we are designed to consume,
and meander herd-ways to our own doom.
Some folks call it free will, but they are trapped
in ancient scriptures that have long been mapped
to keep us chained to animal instinct
that disappears when we become extinct,

and are raised to Heaven in pure glory
to sing a vapid hymn of our story."
Clara: "It does not have to be that way.
The animal nations will have their say.
Predators shall always need sustenance,
and we will keep our pipe and the sun dance.
Not everyone strives for more than their shares,
we just get distracted by machines' fares.
You are not alone in perceiving hate
and jealousy tie us to a blind fate.
We may be, for now, mere cannon fodder,
bound to the empire like metal solder
and spinning cogs within the whites' machine,
who act as gods trying to make us wean
ourselves from clean land, good food, and water
to prime us for a Biblical slaughter.
The blacks have long lost their tribal cultures,
and feed on the leftovers like vultures.
When I was young I felt pity for them,
now they also want to run the system,
which is so corrupt they cannot withstand
the temptation to pollute sacred land.
One who was made a Supreme Court Justice
has revealed how far things have gone amiss.
He wrote the legal ruling on soy seeds,
warped through genetics by corporate deeds,
for whom he once worked as an attorney.
Now small farmers are forced to pay a fee
to plant the bean each season, and are sued
in expensive, long-running legal feud
if the farmer has his own seeds to plant,
and are doomed by ritual legal cant.
He also often sex-harassed Miss Hill,
now rapes the Earth with monopolized till."
Charles: "You sound like Reuben, whose prophecies
predict corporate farming subsidies

will grant food control to a ruling few,
and pharaohs shall rise with their corrupt crew."
Clara: "It seems more likely than space-ships
arriving to take us on distant trips.
Which is beside the point of what I say,
blacks lost integrity with money's sway."
Charles: "Yes, and it happened to our nations
when the greed-crazy seized reservations.
Whether they are dupes of the white empire,
the fact is they forced the good to retire.
We are no better than the other folks
in forcing our own people to pull yokes
of oppression to satiate vast greed,
like mules to plow land for a poisoned seed.
I had enough of this depressing talk.
I will clear my head and go for a walk."
Clara: "Though it hurts me to see you fall,
do not come here if you drink alcohol.
I have gained a reprieve and a new lease,
which I hope does not involve the police,
so stay clean or I will call them on you,
even if you have but a single brew."
Charles nodded but made no vocal promise,
wondering how life revealed so much bliss,
but he could not make the images fit
into one. Instead, they scattered and split
before realizing their potential,
and great wits became focused on the dull.
Humans seemed caught in a bi-polar tale:
The Unified Theory was doomed to fail,
no matter how hard Einstein worked to prove
one power behind the scenes made things move.
Charles was weary of draining adventures,
but it was all he knew to keep the blurs
of his past at bay with a sudden change,
learning new bizarre lingoes and the strange.

Bernard had taught Charles some computer-speak,
and on-line be aggressive with the weak,
for the yin and yang are always at odds,
and rule from the satellites as young gods.
So women had to scream in a cell-phone,
if they went outside after dark alone,
to warn away attackers and assaults,
which is one of America's great faults
that is ignored, yet they preach to Muslims
not to treat their females with cruel whims.
Thinking of this, Charles felt mean and shady
as he approached a lone, drunken lady.
To avoid the woman he crossed the street,
but she made his gesture a humbling feat
by calling out, "Are you some kind of fag?
Take yourself to a queer bar dressed in drag."
Stunned for a moment, Charles did not reply,
then mustered his wits and let forth a cry:
"The last girl who insulted me that way
ended up with a child from our love-play.
There are many things I would rather do
than invest my genetic stock in you,
for I have already purchased a share
in the system of government welfare.
I will not further human resources
that Clinton denies enlightened courses,
cutting the money for social programs
while sending great wealth to Russian flimflams.
Then he deregulates all oversight
of global high-finances, and they write
the laws of our nation to benefit
themselves as we sink in a Hellish pit.
I will not buy into a bankrupt firm,
though Clinton will oblige you with his worm."
Charles had carried vile hate so long it spilled
as toxic oil that was carelessly tilled,

spreading forth from a gaping wound on Earth,
which poisoned life like a phantom of Dearth.
In search of rich rewards, instead was found,
released from the dirt, a rabid Hell hound.
Do all tasks give birth to unwanted spoils,
which set out to raze the favorite toils
of laboring love, in which we take pride?
Such was the notion that Charles felt abide.
Meanwhile, Stan Jacob had become certain
he must cease the actions his dream curtain
unveiled to him several years before,
when he was the serpent of *Bible* lore,
corrupting order in a foreign land,
a garden for a tyrant's elite band.
So he set out to spread tranquility
to further Iraqis' ability
to guide themselves separate from Hussein
and the oil companies' ongoing drain
of Iraq's resource, and thus destitute,
their land was like Babylon's prostitute.
Still a devout Catholic, Stanley went
to a native chapel the government
allowed Baghdad's Christians to worship at.
Alone in a pew, Stanley did not chat
with fellow believers, who looked at him
in great surprise or suspiciously grim.
The priest offered up the body and blood
of Jesus, begotten, not made of mud,
unlike Stan's ancestors formed in Eden,
which he thought a metaphor of man's pen,
carefully composed by clairvoyant scribes
to understand the power that describes
the need for order and obedience
in the world and each human being's sense.
Stan partook of the godly sacrifice
he did not want to think as artifice.

He ate the fleshly bread, then took the stein
and drank the blood of Christ transformed from wine.
He thought: Do I believe in such magic
while surrounded by scenes that are tragic?
Around them their world is put to the torch,
yet believe 'tis god's love fueling the scorch.
I could not live so humbly while oppressed,
with jet-bombs killing the cursed and the blessed.
We undermine our own work, building hate,
running the business of a corrupt state,
failing to make harmony generate.
Then blame it all on Hussein's fraudulence,
which average people know is nonsense.
We play the Sunnis off of the Shiites,
hoping they kill each other in their fights.
So Stan thought as he digested his god,
the peace from above who ruled with a rod.
When service ended, Stan went to the door,
his combat boots ringing on the tiled floor.
He was stopped at the steps by four old men,
who thought his appearance a good omen.
They introduced themselves with Christian names
as Philip, Thomas, Matthias, and James.
In faltering English they queried Stan
about his faith and lineage's clan.
At first he was oblique as he answered,
but when they continued he felt assured
they did not attempt to divine secrets
of scheduled bombs from American jets.
They would not talk of the occupations
of their country by franchise gas-stations.
Instead, they were considerate and kind,
and Stanley felt harmony in his mind.
They made no derisive comments towards
their Muslim countrymen and jihad swords.
They invited him to a near café

to have a discussion on how to pray.
Stan was uneasy of being kidnapped,
and their peaceful demeanor had him trapped.
He did not want to be boorish and rude,
so for a moment he appeared to brood.
Matthias realized Stan's thought-process,
and turning to Philip made an address
in Arabic, which Philip replied in
so harshly it caused the others to spin
and berate the fellow with angry cries,
until he gave in with lachrymose sighs.
He pulled a pistol from under his coat,
and while the other three smiled to emote
satisfaction at their comrade's display,
Stan knew he was not their intended prey.
It was an old revolver that Stan checked
the cogs of, making sure it was not wrecked.
The gun was oiled, all of its parts clicked well,
a much doted on weapon, Stan could tell.
Philip: "I am unarmed and in the lurch,
which I truly hate, even while at church.
Though it is illegal to have a gun,
'til now I surrendered it to no one."
He hung his head and muttered a regret,
while Stan hid the pistol in his jacket.
James patted Philip's arm, and cheerfully
said Stan could now join them to have coffee.
He nodded and walked with them to the place,
enjoying the talk of god's given grace,
and Thomas's own ideology,
which was a patch-work of theology.
The café was habited by Christians,
and Philip waved off their many questions
about Stan, who they were curious of,
as if an appearance by a white dove.
Philip: "It is his first time here, my friends,

let us work him in slowly so he blends,
or you will scare him off with your queries.
We shall tell you all when he is at ease."
They took their coffee to the outdoor seats,
Stan watching the passers-by on the streets,
his back to the wall of the café shop,
so no one could stand behind him and lop
off his head, and relay the filmed image
around the world on screens, with the dire pledge
that Americans shall die in such ways,
and jihads will bring about better days.
Thomas, however, was quite unconcerned,
for he had a new audience, not spurned
or belittled, as his friends often did,
though feelings of isolation were hid.
He talked of the necessary schism
in the forces of Manicheism:
that god is untouched by good and evil,
which have the same strength, though different will,
and because Christ was part human, they mixed
in him so that all things can not be fixed
by eternal good that takes human form,
evil is also present to deform.
Thomas went on as his friends released sighs,
shifting in their chairs and rolling their eyes.
They were used to such talk, and thus were bored
to hear Thomas's version of the lord.
Uranus the god gobbled his children
so they could not compete for faith of men.
Then Cronus was born, who gelded and ate
his father, ending the old reign of hate,
and began what was thought a Golden Age
of strict peace with only one god onstage.
Cronus also performed infanticide,
'til Zeus killed him, aware of patricide.
Zeus ruled, forming the incestuous clans,

and confused breeding-programs with humans.
A pantheon of gods creates chaos,
as they compete for their own gain and loss.
Now to reach the enlightenment of one,
Christians devour the all-father's son.
So Thomas spoke of the dualities
of twin-some evil and good qualities
that Christ represented and relinquished
without telling how evil is vanquished,
except by death, which is no pleasant means
for those who enjoy life and its good scenes.
When James saw the sagging of Stanley's head,
he interrupted Thomas' speech and said:
"Though our friend speaks of impossible tricks,
he is one of our best-liked heretics.
Please give us a rest for a while, Thomas,
we will converse when Stan leaves, I promise."
Stan nodded, affirming he had his fill
of nature's essence and Heavenly will.
Though Thomas was ready for more debates,
they discussed Stan's wife, at home in the States.
Her name was Trisha, and she taught grade-school.
Two children had emerged from their gene-pool.
One was Ted, the other Stan called Dolly,
though her name was Peg, he thought the Dalai
Lama had her kind of serenity
of contemplation on infinity.
His companions liked Stan's family tales,
and encouraged him for further details.
He talked, forgetting his problems and woes,
though aware he was with potential foes.
On the street an argument erupted,
and noticing two opponents, James said:
"We had best go inside the coffee shop,
for violence brews and it will not stop
until one of them is dead for the theft

of your country's aid, leaving us bereft.
Do not get involved, my Christian brother.
The Ba'athist guard lets them kill each other,
then makes deals with the survivors for food,
to be sold to us at a price quite shrewd.
The gangsters recruit people for the strife,
who are weary of a malnourished life."
They went in the café, and Philip spoke,
as if he had furies he could invoke:
"The medicine we buy is watered down,
for I know a man in a nearby town
whose daughter was sick, and the medicine
was rotten stuff, and like a berserk jinn,
who steals souls to consolidate power
and control elements in wrath's glower,
it corrupted her body and she died,
so her father joined one of the gang's side."
Philip looked at Stan with accusing guilt,
though his voice contained a resigned, sad lilt.
Stan: "Maybe it was no fault of the cure,
but the doctors' equipment was impure."
Thomas: "There are international groups,
not protected by Coalition troops,
who try to get us the needed supplies,
and so far have told us no insane lies.
One tested the batch which destroyed the girl,
a victim of intrigue's chaotic swirl."
They sat quietly and heard the gunfire
on the streets, as Stanley sunk into mire.
His soldier ideals, which pulled him aloft,
had him wondering if he had gone soft.
Self-image did not match reality.
Had money bought his nation's loyalty
to Hussein, who did not want people fed?
The words of Stan's captain ran through his head:
'Better to deal with the devil you know,

than an unknown demon running the show.'
He nodded slowly, then shrugged his shoulders.
The politicians always use soldiers
to strew corpses for picking by vultures,
done in the guise to defend their cultures.
Philip patted Stan's hand, James weakly smiled,
but what he spoke had demeanor beguiled:
"You are a good lot in many a way,
but get distracted with the games you play,
and they need energy, which we supply
through extortion and the ongoing lie
we earn mistreatment because we support
a cruel tyrant and his corrupt court.
I understand you must make good wages
to pass your lifestyle on through the ages,
yet it cannot last, something has to give.
We will share the terror in which we live.
Our young generations never know peace,
they have nothing to lose as hopes decrease.
They shall be exploited, just as you are.
Their Heaven is not a satellite's star,
but a promise that if jihad succeeds
the bliss of Allah is won for their deeds."
Stan: "We put our consciousness in machines,
jihadists place theirs in fantasy scenes.
I will not judge which of them is better,
they both have laws of spirit and letter,
chaining faithful to an insane fetter.
I have killed for tranquility, and bled.
I am expendable, not exploited."
Philip: "Our country is older than yours,
and we too have belief in mythic lores.
You say contrary things, as if you knew
you must say such lines and hope it is true.
We have to justify what we have done,
saying it is for peace we wield a gun.

I have not used mine yet, but a quick thrill
shoots through my mind when I think of a kill,
and I am not a soldier like you are,
though my war is close, while yours is afar.
You have a secure life, and can go home
to peace and comfort, tasting the top foam,
while we drink the dregs of a bitter cask,
accepting our own Herculean task.
Heroes will arise, though with tragic flaws,
and they shall not abide by corrupt laws."
Stan: "Yes, we make martyrs for the jihad,
'tis easy to call them soul-less and mad.
Our war is the business of a lifestyle.
Muslims think Allah gives them a trial,
and rewards follow great tribulations
if they conquer the united nations
pushing Muslims face-first down into mud,
draining their resources of oil for blood.
The firefight has ended and I must go.
If we shall meet again, I do not know.
I will call the bomb-squad and have them come,
as I could be blown into bloody chum
if my jeep was rigged with bombs while I sat
here with you, learning lessons from our chat.
I understand how you want me to be,
but war is a pervasive industry.
'Tis said necessity breeds invention,
but comfort-products hold our attention.
Here is your pistol, Philip, hide it well.
It may save you from a looming death-knell."
His comrades stood and shook hands, then he left,
as Philip tested his revolver's heft.
He was not yet accustomed to its weight,
and admired Stan Jacob's warrior trait.
Ambulances arrived, as did police,
to take away corpses and enforce peace.

Stan edged his way through the gathering crowds,
which rumbled in discontent like storm clouds.
Sectarian violence of Sunnis
and Shiites had Stan think them all loonies:
They seem to require the order we brought
to convince them better lives can be bought.
We need to find the words that are precise
to achieve the goal of their selling price.
A young Shiite grabbed Stanley by his arm,
and turned to others, shouting an alarm.
Stan did not comprehend the fellow's words,
but a throng of people gathered like birds
who sense an intruder near their region;
alone, they are helpless, but a legion
of them collects as a force to attack
from the air and drive the invader back.
Stan felt their grips trying to pull him down,
as if hatred embodied the whole town,
and singled him out for the sacrifice
demanded by god for freedom from vice.
He lashed out and heard their shattering bones,
and cries of malice turned to painful moans.
But there were too many hemming him in,
and it was a battle he could not win.
His martial art's training was of no use,
they would drag him through the streets with a noose,
as done in Somalia when a war
over oil sent troops to Africa's shore.
An arm wrapped around Stanley's neck and squeezed,
and more Iraqis approached as he wheezed.
He flipped the man behind him to the front,
smashing his foe's face, who died with a grunt.
They drove at his legs to bring him under,
shredding Stanley's uniform asunder.
One of the Iraqis kept Stan's medal
of success, displaying the bright metal

to visitors of the Iraqi's house,
describing how he alone killed a louse
of an American soldier, who wept
for mercy and his fighting was inept.
At other times the Iraqi would tell
how he sent a courageous man to Hell,
and kept the trophy to give to his son,
but the false stories would soon be undone.
The fates planned his glory to quickly fade,
his family was killed in an air-raid.
The story closed, the medal became char,
'tis easy to brag of death from afar.
Stan knew if he did not keep to his feet
he would be dragged down and crushed in the street.
Gunfire began to rage about the scene,
and it struck one foe, exploding his spleen.
The crowd parted like waves on a breaker,
as troops delivered souls to their maker.
The city's guard chased them, shouting war-cries.
Only one was left, groping at Stan's eyes,
who saw through the mist Philip standing near,
pointing his pistol with tremors of fear.
Stanley grabbed his attacker by the hair,
and yanked his head back as if Stan would tear
the scalp away from the man's living flesh.
Philip saw them cling in a hatred mesh,
as if to release all the anger pent
within each, now having an opponent
to tear fingernails at snarling faces,
and all their humanity erases
from their spirits, leaving dark vacant cores,
which Philip thought as beastly metaphors.
Young civilizations laude such a thing
to be proudly displayed, and bards would sing
how humans evolved with their gods' input,
and like them violence was at the root.

We killed our animal competitors,
and have become our own chief predators.
With a veneer of domestication,
a wired button can destroy a nation.
Stunned, Philip watched the atavistic brawl,
as they tore and rent like animals maul.
The human guises seemed to fall away,
each was absorbed in destroying his prey.
There was no artistry or bright finesse,
drawing each other's pulp like a wine press.
Bodies and blood mingled in communion,
becoming exhausted from the union.
Stanley head-butted his foe like a ram,
then crunched his knee into the diaphragm.
The Iraqi curled up, gasping for breath,
and Stan decided to level-out death.
He turned to Philip, demanding his gun,
who trembled in fear and started to run.
Stanley did not give pursuit after him,
but landed a final blow on a whim
to his enemy, who went in a faint,
dreaming he had become a martyred saint.
Stan walked away, feeling dizzy and glum,
planning to drink a full bottle of rum.
His desire to mingle with Iraqis
sorely failed, for they had different keys
to open their minds for Allah's Heaven.
Like all creatures, were forcibly driven
to obtain their order through dominance,
as enforced peace follows from violence.

14

Job Security

The commander told Stanley to report
the incident to the tribunal's court,
and warned Stanley not to go out alone,
for Iraqis were like a single clone
responding with hatred to everything
which did not match *Koran* verses they sing.
Stanley replied he had met decent men
who changed his mind of the communal pen
the Iraqis had become trapped within,
as they paid for some past karmic debt's sin.
Stanley: "Most will not surrender Islam
and buy into our capitalism,
where images of screen-gods promise wealth
and fame if we support the screen-gods' health
with our faith and money to help them grow,
and bless us with their entertainments' show.
As this country becomes a huge prison
our greatest efforts are quickly undone.
KLike Malcolm X became a Black Muslim
while a convict, to beat the jihad drum,
the Islamic faith has severe strictures
against their god's and his prophet's pictures.
We are so at odds on many levels:
we think them savage, they call us devils.

Only by working with the populace
can we create a communal address.
If we force upon them our techno-lords
they will despise us and our screen-god hordes.
The men I met with can help us begin
to clear the airwaves of our greedy jinn."
Stanley was dismissed, as if he told lies,
and that his new friends were probably spies.
Three weeks later a mission was assigned
to car-bomb the café where Christians dined.
Stanley's squadron was to assassinate
an oil diplomat from the Chinese state,
who was embezzling funds from Iraq,
and China did not wish to call him back
to a trial, for he was popular,
and the government would split in polar
sides of his innocence or accused guilt,
wasting time as the evidence was built.
He also went to the Christian chapel,
near the shop where Stan fought in a grapple,
which was not sponsored by China's nation,
another cause to end the man's station.
For each religion in China's country
branched out from the government like a tree,
and no one was to taste forbidden fruit
of knowledge that might make one more astute.
And as China grew with technology,
the government judged the theology
of good and evil's computer ration
with the censorship of information.
The oil diplomat had not played his part,
so he was to be killed for a fresh start,
and China teamed with American troops
to keep each other complicit in groups.
Stanley was to make the car-bomb seem crude,
and thus his squad could easily elude

suspicion for the act, and blame would fall
on Shiite rebels heeding jihad's call.
Hussein would enforce oppressive levies,
and oil companies could split the divvies.
To Stan, the work seemed to get more sordid
as he rose in rank with the jobs he did.
Should he look after his own interest,
or caution Thomas, Philip, and the rest
of Stan's new friends to avoid the café
when the intrigue occurred on a Sunday?
He questioned himself in hazy turmoil,
feeling his mind wrapped in a knotted coil.
The reason for his military tours
was to abet the weapons' inspectors,
not to commit egregious murders
on a foreign oil company's orders.
War can seem ambiguous and brutal,
laced with adrenalin or glum and dull.
Chaos is unleashed but the point remains
a new order rises as the old wanes,
and it is achieved by following rank
and file orders that have the machine crank.
Yet if those running it chase only greed
the lower-class will imitate the seed
planted in their minds that they too deserve
all the rewards promised by those they serve.
Had Stan deceived himself that leaders knew
how to form order, and falsehood from true?
He came from a lineage of soldiers,
and was not used to questioning orders.
He had such a keen and aware insight,
his squad would follow him in a fire-fight.
Should Stanley risk their lives when he had doubts
of the new commands from oil-greedy louts?
He knew not to go to the squad chaplain,
who would report it to Stanley's captain

in the hierarchy of bureaucrats,
that Stan did not wish to kill diplomats.
As he pondered his various options,
Mustafa completed the adoptions
of four children whose parents had been killed
when America wanted to rebuild
Iraq's economy for a profit,
with the television as a prophet,
which told a self-fulfilling oracle
with cheap gasoline as a miracle.
'Twas better news than Timothy McVeigh
bombing a government building to slay
federal workers as a revenge act,
after learning the military tact
as a soldier honorably discharged.
He saw children murdered when troopers barged
into a well-armed religion's compound,
who spanked their children, and thus their home-ground
was turned into a television screen,
and Americans judged them as obscene.
A few of the children escaped the scene,
but McVeigh was on the run and would not
consider taking a child to adopt.
Revenge haunted him, so he bombed a site,
for the lesser evil is always right,
or so it seemed to him, as he maintained
the federal government was bloodstained.
Mustafa's devotion to god was lax,
but having children inspired faith to wax.
They were a source of continuous joy:
two teenage girls, a baby, and a boy
who would imitate all Mustafa did,
but also heeded what Sofia bid.
She had a child by Mustafa, a son,
who Mustafa tried not to dote upon
at the expense of his other children,

for he wanted no jealousy hidden
that might come out in a secret attack,
like Joseph faced his brothers' angry pack.
Mustafa had told no one of his plan
to achieve sweet revenge against the man
who had plotted and carried out in full
the deadly scheme on Mustafa's uncle.
Sofia knew her husband was bothered,
for while he was kind to those he fathered,
at night he spent long hours in seclusion,
as if to conjure forth an illusion
that would tell him what course he was to take,
and aid with decisions he had to make.
So she asked him if she could be of help,
and he pinched her arm, causing her to yelp.
He apologized and hung down his head,
mournfully shaking it, and with sighs said:
"Why do I hurt the one I love the most?
Too long have I been talking to a ghost,
who drives me to pull down the blessed structure
of our family to gain a rapture
that I doubt is Heavenly connected.
But I must do it to stay respected
at least to myself, if not to others
who accept that America smothers
our way of living with their corruption,
and we face continual disruption
of core needs, while they brag of lenience
to us, as they live in convenience.
Women are not meant to fight against that,
having the heart for a rumor-spread spat."
Sofia: "You seem to be in a haze.
Women are stronger in different ways.
Behind the scenes we are called king-makers,
with deals among the givers and takers
to shape a sense of normalcy for men,

as we cannot do it in the open.
Out in public I play the role assigned.
In private you let me speak heart and mind,
and have I ever caused you to regret
following my opinions to abet
your decision-making in our household?
For I keep to myself what I am told.
Your mother is irked that I do not share,
and you never told her I lost my hair.
I kept my name to honor my parents,
though it is a sign of Christian nonsense.
After they died, I was quick to convert,
for Islamic faith heals all wounds that hurt.
I will stay quiet if I cannot aid,
but 'tis wiser to tell me than a shade."
They went into his den and he sat down,
while she sorted his notes from out of town,
when he had been traveling through Europe,
and written her love letters like syrup
that runs sweet and sticky with a bold taste,
dedicated to their union and chaste.
Mustafa said: "I was recently sent
news from a reliable informant
that the oil conglomerates of nations
are plotting public assassinations
at a Christian café tomorrow night,
and staged to look 'tis done by a Shiite.
I have no love for the Christian belief,
their intrigues for idols cause only grief.
They are lackeys to a crucified Jew,
and I must pull Muslims from the vile stew.
as foes play our sects off of each other,
and those left standing, enemies smother.
What is worse, I have heard that the target
is being framed by a widely cast net
through a Chinese man, who wants the dupe's job,

accusing him so the former can rob
when he acquires the business position
by destroying all his competition.
It has become so foul in our country,
that oppressors roam the streets, wild and free,
killing each other to satiate greed,
mixing together for a future breed
to continue their war on us for years,
an heirloom passed to our children and peers."
Sofia saw her husband's brow turn red,
so she kissed it gently and softly said:
"When we act from patriotic duty
against pirates pillaging our booty,
we are called criminals and terrorists,
and like mass suicide, slit our own wrists,
as life has become intolerable.
Fate is not in the stars, though the Hubble
Telescope studies their dancing movements,
which seem to giggle at our bereavements.
I accept my destiny lies on Earth,
watching my nation be ruined by dearth.
I cannot escape to other planets,
but I will not live a life of regrets
by telling you to accept our slow death,
'til we release our last lingering breath.
Allah built this world for us to enjoy
and avoid those whom the devils employ.
Yet now we are faced with their wickedness,
capricious laws ruled by fond decadence."
Mustafa: "But to risk my informant
in the Coalition Forces who sent
me the material is not worth it,
for he must get by alone on his wit.
There is no value in the Christians' lives
if he is smoked from American hives,
and cannot relay more information

of greater worth from his secret station."
Sofia: "If you sabotage their plot,
the Americans will clean out the rot,
and can you trust your agent not to tell,
if tortured, you buy what he has to sell?
As it is a job he does for money,
you cannot out-bid Americans' fee.
They spend all their resources to corrupt
nations' officials, then watch wars erupt,
and complain their puppets are not honest,
like magpies steal glitter to gild their nest.
It is your life I am concerned about,
as your agent will sell you with a shout."
Mustafa: "He put his life up for sale
in Judas' games of hate and betrayal.
After the invasion he converted
from Islam to a belief perverted
enough to pray to a human prophet,
and he did so merely for a profit.
I have seen it before: people switch faiths
like jinn alter forms from solid to wraiths.
An eternal quest for something to gain,
not caring if their souls are doomed with stain,
they change their faiths like clothes for approval,
purchasing the latest mythic fable."
Sofia: "So you know then what to do,
stay clear of the Hellish concocted brew,
where greed has people add their potion's share
to fuel hatred at a high-priced fare.
I learned from reading volumes on your shelf
that history always repeats itself.
We want things that are recognizable,
thinking it will keep us sane and stable.
Yet no one can stop ongoing changes
as the force of nature rearranges
to the will of Allah, who has no son,

and whose slightest whim cannot be undone.
For now, we are blessed and cursed with much oil,
and our land simmers to a rolling boil.
There is much to wonder on of our fate:
does god test our love with infidels' hate?
They will face their destruction like the jinn,
who committed an egregious sin
by not bowing to humans Allah formed,
casting the jinn out, despite how they stormed.
A lawless group of demons who pillage,
and to defeat them it takes a village
that adheres to the laws of the *Koran*,
accepting what comes as part of god's plan"
Mustafa: "You cover many subjects,
and I am glad you have been reading texts,
history, magic, and the books of law.
The jinn find a home in each human flaw,
planting the seeds of their ongoing war
with Allah and humans, whose fertile core
can breed and sprout such a terrible blight,
we are forced to eat the stew of our plight."
Sofia: "According to Christian faiths
vengeance is taken by angelic wraiths,
and humans are not to be violent,
'tis the angels' duty, Heavenly sent.
Perhaps 'tis why Christians have their machines
do the filthy work of wrecking our scenes.
Like Aladdin used the jinn of his lamp
to build a palace with a royal stamp,
the Christians wield their high-technology
to make slaves for a man nailed to a tree.
They are groups of sucking vampires who toil
like Nazi gangs for Romanian oil
to feed life-blood of organized scenes
of war entertainment by machines."
Mustafa: "You are correct, Sofia,

the Christians worship angel Mafia,
whose duty is to tear, rend, and plunder,
thinking each angel's voice rolls as thunder,
and death falls from the sky like acid rain,
while Christians keep their hands clean of bloodstain,
rinsing them like Pilate to avoid blame,
for Christ made human violence a shame."
Sofia: "You are not an assassin,
so do not put upon yourself that sin.
Our religion requires us to believe
that we rely on soldiers to retrieve
the traditions and laws Mohammad taught
to idol-worshippers, whose faith is naught
but a fancy for Earthly images
passed on through the superstitious ages.
The Roman Empire made statues of gods,
and on their heels the Catholic Church trods.
We grew out of that custom and are blessed,
while they honor their media's incest,
knotted together for a big fission,
preached by computer and television.
Between their actors and politicians
there is no difference in their fictions.
They will do whatever script is supplied,
selling their souls to the high-bidder's side,
and clog the airwaves with their images,
carefully constructed as false sages.
At first, Aladdin thought he needed oil
to light the lamp he found buried in soil,
and released a jinn who brought great fortune,
so Americans plunder each sand dune,
in murderous search for oil to consume.
Like Aladdin almost went to his doom,
we are tricked by technology's magic,
which quickly turns frivolous or tragic.
We worship Allah, the one and true god,

as they heed distractions like a seed pod
that opens and blows with the Northern breeze,
and the seeds fly into a land they seize,
procreating without thought, love, or laws,
genetically tuned for genies' cause."
Mustafa: "So you have already read
that great book I wanted to read in bed
with you each night to pass the time in awe
of the rich fantasies the ancients saw.
You make me feel foolish in how you soar,
using it as a modern metaphor.
I am glad we can spar wits, though I lose,
it is a battle I am glad to choose.
So you think I should let their plot unfold,
and wait for better intrigue to be sold,
like espionage on fellow Muslims,
who are part of us as one of our limbs."
Sofia: "It is not for me to say
that Christians must die and Muslims should stay
to suffer at the hands of enemies,
tied with us and driven to bended knees.
But if Americans want to murder
their fellow believers to keep order,
then it may be an act of providence
that we should accept as good common sense.
For our minds and bodies have been battered,
emotional stability shattered,
and each sense revolts, not knowing the form
they were attached to, thus cannot perform."
Mustafa: "You give me oblique advice,
perhaps that is part of a woman's vice.
They do not approach a problem head-on,
but send their men forth as a bull-like pawn
to do the deeds of filthy work and hate,
while women collect the rewards of fate
that the men have won by violent act,

and return to females who use more tact."
Sofia: "I will not argue that point.
We have worked well together as a joint
of an arm flexes and strains for reward,
which can only be granted by the lord.
Listen to my story about the Hell
we descend through that I swore not to tell
because it was so upsetting and sick,
when your brother played upon me a trick.
Last week, Ibrahim brought me a package,
a present, he said, to bind our love-pledge.
I opened it and found a severed thumb
that was turning black, and I felt so numb
I nearly fainted from the awful sight,
while he giggled as if it were a trite,
clever prank children are allowed to do,
suggesting I put it in our lunch stew."
Mustafa gritted his teeth and nodded,
then holding Sofia's mild gaze, he said:
"You have been holding onto that story,
waiting to tell me the sick and gory
details for a discussion such as this.
I knew life with you would not be all bliss,
yet your cunning exceeds our dictator's,
as you go about your housekeeping chores."
He shook his head, smiled grimly, and hugged her.
She stroked his shoulders as though a pet's fur,
and hummed in his ear a soft melody,
cooling his ire to placid harmony.
He asked where Ibrahim had found the thumb,
and she said the park was where it came from,
or so she suspected, as he played there,
and she got rid of the thumb's ugly fare.
Mustafa: "I think men want to be plied
by women's intrigue, and then mollified.
I will attempt to not be paranoid

in my dealings with your designing void,
but if I lose my temper, then my hand
may strike my beloved. Do you understand?"
She nodded and lowered her gaze downward.
His bully tactics made him feel absurd,
so he lifted her chin and kissed her cheek,
and pressing her close to him, he felt weak.
Mustafa: "We are as one in our hearts.
Tell me if he brings home stray body parts.
They seem to be littered about the town,
and he should not act as a grotesque clown.
'Tis not good to be accustomed to death
as if it were sunshine or drawing breath.
When he comes of age and still wants a role
to retrieve what the Americans stole,
then he can be a soldier and my peer,
I am sure by then they shall still be here."
Sobs distorted Sofia's pretty face,
knowing she had caused Ibrahim's disgrace
for his future that Mustafa had planned,
altered from the doom of their Motherland,
with hopes that successive generations
not be mired in endless wars with nations.
Sofia: "We are more than blood and clay,
though you speak of roles we are forced to play.
Let our enemies invest in facades,
worshipping their screen images as gods.
Our lives are real and we have spirits
that yearn to obey Allah's lawful writs,
which has grace to free your brother from sin
among the false humans and tricky jinn."
Mustafa would talk no more of the plot
to reduce the Christians to a blood clot.
She let the matter go for him to tend,
using her soft touch to make an amend.
Putting between them a fractional wedge

would only drive him further to the edge
of lost anger, and he might be so grim
that she would become his scapegoat victim.
Sofia knew that, so she used her wile,
to placate as might the Queen of the Nile.
Unlike Cleopatra, who went through males
as ships change directions with their wind-sails,
for in a man's world there can be rewards
by playing them off each other with swords,
Sofia did not want him feminized,
staying with the one whom she truly prized.
She studied history and the mistakes
women made placing bets on the wrong stakes.
She knew women could suffer from the rage
of the men they produce behind the stage,
and the global theater audience
had grown with high-technology's science.
A leader's family had been slaughtered,
claiming they were saints being martyred;
round the world people watched Romania
spill blood in a frenzy of mania,
and in each heart was the thrill of Dracul,
as ended the Soviet puppet's rule.
Sofia knew her husband's weakest spot
that can lead to tragic flaws' moral rot.
She would not work on his deepest shadows,
but tried to shore its ebb and eddy flows.
On the day of the assassination
Mustafa phoned Abdul's police station,
telling his friend there was a faint rumor
a bomb would go off at a plaza store.
Abdul disconnected without reply,
then returned the call, his voice shriek and high.
Abdul: "Are you trying to get me killed?
Suicide by cop to have my guts spilled
is not a good career move for the staff,

or what I want writ as my epitaph.
Are you on a safe phone, as I am now?
Swear it to me, friend, as a solemn vow."
Mustafa tried to calm Abdul's concern,
but his words were difficult to discern.
After long moments of hysteria,
Abdul said the main target's area
had been given to him by informants,
which was the reason for his insane rants.
For the assassins did not want Abdul
killed as an innocent-bystander fool,
because his father ran a big business,
and Americans did not want a mess
interfering with their ongoing trade
by a partner's son becoming a shade.
Then Abdul asked where Mustafa had gained
the knowledge the streets were to be bloodstained.
Mustafa grew wary and knew his friend
had become their foe's ally, who would send
all information to Americans
who needed to purge their spy-system clans,
putting at risk Mustafa's paid agent
working since the American advent.
Mustafa said: "You know how rumors start:
someone weaves a fantasy at the mart
and soon people lose their ability
to discern falsehood from reality."
Abdul: "You are like a cagey dancer
skipping from a direct question's answer.
I am aware of how a rumor flies,
soaring through the air like chirping magpies,
yet before now you did not contact me,
to do our best in common fealty."
Mustafa rolled his eyes at the mention
of shared love and honor for their nation.
Perhaps Abdul still cared for their country,

but corruption rolled in like a tide's bree,
and Mustafa knew he was not alone
in love for his land that could not be shown.
He gave Abdul the name of Judge Kashan,
hoping the judge would then be spied upon,
and perhaps be caught in one of his schemes,
gaining the bad fortune that Allah deems.
Abdul: "We wondered who your agent was,
passing secrets along like a bee's buzz.
His antennae will be plucked from his head
when we have a trial where charges are read.
You have crushed a corrupt aristocrat,
and my father will be happy with that,
for it shall save him bribe fees on a case
the judge was charging to receive his grace.
He made many enemies through his greed,
and we will hold his trial with due speed,
and find out if he likes false evidence
when it is used to ruin common sense.
The Americans shall be overjoyed
to vent on a scapegoat their paranoid
delusions that they deserve gratitude,
instead of a long-running bitter feud.
You avenged Judge Kashan's fraudulent rule,
and his fated life's string runs out of spool."
Mustafa was surprised they would proceed
in charging the judge with a covert deed,
for he had done so many awful things
it was ironic that the deadly stings
which ended the judge's terrible life
would be false accusations of a strife
he played no part in, to the spies' knowledge.
Mustafa desired to not swear a pledge
of honesty to Allah and the court
to uphold the laws he swore to support.
He refused to repeat how he had lied,

not because he cared if Judge Kashan died,
but rather due to belief in Allah,
who can help the poor and ruin a Shah.
Abdul understood the hesitation
by Mustafa to betray the nation
of laws that Allah gave to Mohammad,
and dismissing the tension, Abdul said:
"You need not worry, for at the trial
we shall say the information worthwhile
came from an agent we cannot expose,
and you will not take an oath to dispose."
They ended the telephone connection
and Mustafa felt a vaccination
was required to cleanse himself from the plague
that swept his land like a fishing net's drag,
ensnaring all and bringing forth the jinn
who had been locked and buried due to sin.
Freed by the drilling for wealthy fluid,
there was no hope of replacing the lid
with the jinn trapped inside, helpless and weak,
instead followed commands to loot and wreak.
The liquid oil becomes a ghastly gas,
and what once happened comes again to pass.
It seemed to him the foes sought to destroy
the world's past, like a child mad at a toy
that is durable but has lost its shine,
so it is broken, and with a shriek's whine,
the child demands a model up-grade,
and the parents buy one like the child prayed.
The old toy is tossed out with the garbage,
yet an urchin finds it for the next stage
of its existence. He mends the broke part,
and considers the toy a work of art.
So the past is reinvented with hope
a different future is within grope.
If life is bartered so capriciously,

then Mustafa's brother can easily
present dead body parts to Sofia,
laughing it comes from a sect of Shiia.
Mustafa prepared to watch the intrigue,
but trusted no one of his covert league.
On the evening the plot was to unfold
he wished to see the man who would explode
the Christians' café with bombs in a car,
so Mustafa went to a site not far
down the plaza from the busy café,
where he could drink honeyed tea and survey.
Stanley had been ordered to hire a man
of Iraq descent to fulfill the plan,
for an American would be noticed
on the streets of Baghdad during the tryst.
It was a hard verdict for Stan to make,
with his new Catholic friends' lives at stake,
but had they helped him battle the street crowd
he would not have them dressed in their death shroud.
Obligations set by priorities
will crucify the good people on trees.
Such was the cost of controlling the state
and the eternal sacrifice of fate.
With an effort Stan was freed from tension,
and gave no voice to inner-dissension,
which mocked his thoughts as he silently prayed
for the souls of the men on whom he preyed.
Somehow his duty had led him astray,
perhaps it was his own love for a fray.
He thought: I am addicted to combat,
and deserve what I get from bureaucrat.
Why shift the blame to the chain of command?
In the end we are equal grains of sand.
We are dark and light manifestations,
doing monkey-tricks for wealth or nations.
For my own benefit I must release

the morbid thoughts that disturb my mind's peace.
The hired man parked the car at the shop's front,
where outside customers would get the brunt
of the bomb's blast, and where the diplomat,
who turned Roman Catholic, calmly sat.
When the explosion hit and people screamed
Mustafa felt bitter that those who schemed
had once again succeeded in their tasks
of ruining his country behind masks.
As people rushed to the terrible scene,
he slowly walked away, angry and mean.
Cameras would be recording each face
of those who helped the victims at the place
where a moment ago smiles and laughter
showed camaraderie, now a slaughter.
Mustafa knew American forces
had photos of him supplied by sources
aware he worked as a covert agent,
so he had to conceal his true intent.
To be filmed at the scene would give them cause
to decree that Mustafa broke the laws
and blame him for the terrorist attack.
His trust in Abdul had a certain lack,
for he had become ambitious to rise,
just as the Chinese man whose insane lies
had gotten his work-supervisor killed
by sowing the seeds Americans' tilled.

15

Inventing a Religion

On a snowy day in February
Charles walked to Rapid City's library,
and sat in a corner, reading a book,
waiting to go to his job as a cook.
How long his time lasted in that career
revolved on how much he partook of beer.
He could stay with some friends if he supplied
them with alcohol like a rising tide.
Yet his body felt weakened and ancient
from the ongoing drunk of bad intent.
For a year and a half he had drifted
through sundry jobs and friends as he sifted
chaff from grain, searching for a banquet meal
to energize and allow him to feel
alive again from the numb darkened void.
Yet being aware made him paranoid,
for there were karmic debts still outstanding.
When he was sober, they were demanding,
so he shut them out any way he could,
with various Soma to feel like wood.
Was it the cross he was meant to carry,
subsisting on crackers and cheap sherry?
He did not wish to think of it, so read
an action-packed horror novel instead,

wherein the AIDS virus had mutated
to all humans, who could not be sated
with the medications available.
A dark prince arose who made life stable
after riots and wars for the serum,
and he treated humans like bloody chum.
Charles read of the dark prince being vicious,
and doing so, became superstitious,
as if reading might make the book come true,
for our subconscious helps form what we do.
And Charles was already filled with darkness,
nor did he desire fictional duress
since he could not sort through what was real,
with senses attacked on how he should feel.
The world's population growth had results
as old white men built fertility cults.
Baal was re-elected president,
and had women to have his urges spent.
Yet many feminists defended him,
because they controlled his vigor and vim.
Such a man is easy to lead around
on a tethered leash like an aging hound.
The loser of the presidential race
still had a powerful audience base,
so a corporation hired him to shill
an erectile aphrodisiac pill.
Fertility clinics specialized in
competing to see which of them might win
the media attention's glowing hail
for the most births given by one female.
Like a litter of puppies, babes spilled out,
and were greeted with a televised shout.
So Charles thought as he read the horror book,
and then replaced it in its proper nook.
Though he had ceased watching most films and shows,
he paused a moment by the videos.

As Charles stepped near, he saw Reuben hovered
close to a band being rediscovered.
Their songs were famous thirty years before,
and new generations made it their lore.
It is easy to pass on history
if it is a mere triviality.
With a grin, Charles chanted one of their tunes,
as if reciting ancient magic runes,
for should beloved devices ever fail,
people shall return to an oral tale.
Reuben turned and greeted Charles, shaking hands,
and talked of how they bought commercial brands.
Reuben: "I try to be discriminate,
as not everything mass-produced is meant
for me to consume, though it seems that way,
since we are all the targets every day
for the world conglomerates that sponsor
the media forums on every shore,
while we work, searching for entertainment,
daily news, or fictions they might invent."
Charles: "As a farmer can you be detached
from the espionage so often hatched?"
Reuben: "Part of my profits go to ads
by the milk industry and all their fads
of hiring celebrities for a pose
on billboards, magazines, and other shows.
They sometimes use famous people I hate,
but for now their fortune is a star's fate,
and I try not to despise them too much,
though they grab at everything with a clutch,
making more wealth for one milk-photo leer
than I do with the dirty work all year.
What about you? Have you a job and wife
and surrendered the joys of youthful strife?"
Charles: "I saw my daughter two months ago
when I hitchhiked to Rosebud through the snow.

I could not get a ride, no one would stop,
and at each painful step, felt I would drop.
I made it there, half crazy and strung-out,
and found Tammy had shacked-up with a lout.
We got in a fight and I went to jail,
thus I chase enlightenment like a snail.
Bernard would say a god built those jail walls
to slow me down from brisk, horrible falls.
'Tis safer than becoming a Jim Jones,
a preacher who built on followers' bones
in the heart of savage, dark wilderness,
pursuing life, freedom, and happiness."
Reuben: "You have always tried to spread lights,
unlike your father, enduring his blights
to tame the Lakota from wicked ways,
and form new icons from raw earthly clays,
regardless of how it tears soil and hurts.
His flaws led to alcohol, unlike Kurtz.
Marlowe found salvation in routine work,
others' duties are where the shadows lurk."
Charles: "I, too, have read Joseph Conrad's book,
and search for no visions as a fry-cook.
Humans can do without me as a guide,
and Lakotas rise with Samsara's tide."
Reuben: "To work with no hope for reward
surrenders control to the devils' lord,
who metes out prizes to the corrupt aides,
and turns the rest of us to wraith-like shades.
Yet we, too, can be slaves to luxuries,
with appetites we can never appease.
'Tis sad how the great render themselves blind
and lose vision for the comforts of mind,
or sink into the depths because the fight
corrodes the glory he wins with his might.
All that was garnered by ongoing pains
is ruined by the means, which become stains."

Charles: "According to Bernard, the Hindu
god, Krishna, said it is better to do
one's duty poorly than another's well,
for that is how to rise from the caste Hell
and be reborn to the great pedigrees,
whose job is to enslave lower degrees.
In America a similar dream
casts its shadow that we can taste the cream,
which I observed at the homeless shelter:
no matter the depth where one might swelter,
television is there to show lifestyles
of rich celebrities with marble tiles,
stone columns, and voluptuous fountains
in mansions spread over tops of mountains;
and it was a terrible thing to watch
vagrants hope some day they would fit that notch."
Reuben: "They learn not to care how they win,
by entertainment or stock-market spin.
Do you have a place to stay or just roam,
and wherever you lay your head is home?"
Charles: "Like a snowdrift I sway with the breeze,
not holding on too long with what I seize.
I prefer to think it gives me freedom,
yet I am shackled to what makes me numb.
In a bizarre way, I thank alcohol
for draping my consciousness in a shawl.
It is a reason to arise each day,
and when life gets rough 'tis easy to stray
into the nearest bottle to lose self
and become a grand wizard or an elf.
'Tis simple to love in worlds of pretend,
with various women as a girlfriend.
And you? Do you still believe that Egypt
will become the model as we are stripped
of our personal inner-resources,
as global industries control courses?"

Reuben: "We are near the start of ages
where we are compelled to buy images
that can be wrathful or benevolent,
releasing energy like Heaven-sent
commands to increase their profit margins,
and those who interfere commit grave sins.
In most of Egypt's pharaonic era,
he had to prove he could tend the terra
by shepherding cattle and other flocks.
Now Machiavellis control food stocks
with taxpayer supported subsidies,
and pose in photo-opportunities
as farmers and ranchers who work the land,
while the soil is eroding into sand.
Then rent their plantations to sharecroppers,
who work to make us all happy shoppers.
They control the food supply but do not
regulate food, which becomes high-tech rot,
making the laws that fuel our actions,
herding us to the newest distractions."
Charles: "Your father would support their antics,
and disagree with your odd politics.
I saw him still wearing his cowboy hat.
He would disown you for placing a cat
among Catholic saints, paying them heed
for killing rodents and protecting seed."
Reuben: "I thought of buying a civet
to do battle with the disease of Set,
who can wreck a harvest with deadly plagues
that spread to the cattle, like burning fags
which ignite the Black Hills, flaming each tree,
and a hard rain washes down the debris
to lower levels, polluting the land
and water as if sent by a god's hand.
Civets are known since ancient times to hunt,
and are larger than cats, who are a runt.

A lawsuit would be a lawyer's carol
if my civet went savage and feral,
and attacked someone who would blame our farm,
collecting payment for bodily harm.
So my dad said, and I agreed to that,
thus raise kittens to battle Lord Set's rat."
Charles: "You have truly gone agrarian
in a nation full of sectarian
media voices for strict obeisance
to modern technology's high science.
Christ had an audience of rural folks,
and spoke in parables of lifting yokes
from the oppressive civilized decrees
that came from emperors and Pharisees,
who claimed great lines of hybrid pedigrees,
and won by artificial selection
the high peak of a pyramid's section.
What is more artificial than belief
in civilized religions for relief
from the gene structure of our primeval
cortex that goes beyond good and evil?"
Reuben: "The mysteries and oracles
of ancient times are now the miracles
of handheld gadgets promising rewards
to those filial to the satellite lords.
The image of a preacher on a screen
is magnified to present a bright sheen.
Yet the poor keep toiling in rocks and dirt,
and their way lasts longer despite their hurt."
A slim Asian woman approached the two,
and Charles was attracted by her skin's hue.
She had glossy back hair, beautiful rings,
and a smile that meant a number of things.
Reuben introduced her as Ahn Leika,
and said she possessed his human form's ka.
Charles shook her hand, which was like small bird bones,

and her soft voice had quiet lilting tones.
Reuben: "Do not be fooled by her disguise
of delicate framework and tiny size.
Underneath it all is a firecracker,
who makes me feel like a morbid slacker."
At Reuben's praises, Ahn lowered her head,
then quickly pushed him off-balance and said:
"Do not give all of my secrets away,
for vanity bids I mold my own clay."
Reuben: "Though she calls me a lost pagan,
she self-worships as a lady-dragon.
Yet god also made the crafty serpent
and with your help, Charles, I want to invent
a new religion for the future base
of a pyramid that spans every race,
which combines and reaps, forcing us to sing
as the current structure is collapsing."
Ahn smiled, shaking her head, and walked away,
saying she would drive out later that day
to the farm and make him a fine dinner,
after praying for him as a sinner.
Charles watched her leave, his interest growing,
though he tried to keep his face from showing
the quick fondness he felt within his core,
like soft moonlit waves caressing a shore.
Reuben: "I met her at a casino
when Camille was in town a month ago,
who called me to go out gambling for fun.
She lost eighty-five dollars and I won
the gaze of Ahn, who works as a cashier,
though she also started college this year."
Charles: "Is Camille still in Colorado?
As I search for the lost El Dorado,
with gold beer to light my blundering path,
trying to stay drunk to avoid crazed wrath,
I sometimes think of Camille and her art.

They are good memories, but seem a part
of a fragmented past, long since shattered,
when craft-work with paint was all that mattered."
Reuben: "She is still there, among mountains,
not feeling the pressure of social pens.
Out there, people are allowed to be weird,
as long as one has cash, one is not feared.
Colonies of artists are built to rise
among evergreens as an enterprise
in reworking the land for urban sprawl,
which brings an occasional cougar's maul
when they want fast-food at a franchise-mall."
Charles: "She has a home now and is stable,
I am happy she is comfortable.
She can be the artisan and prophet
on the peak of a mountain who has met
the gods and goddesses of that region
you can include in your new religion."
Reuben: "Very good, Charles, you catch on fast.
You can be atop of our ship's mainmast
as we navigate the millennium,
but I cannot trust you if drunk on rum,
which you drain like a hundred-thousand sieves.
There are meeting places for the Natives
who want to have a sober, honest life,
and run the gauntlet of clearing past strife
to end the cycles of perpetual
incarceration through habitual
use of alcohol, with courts and trials
as judges of those destructive lifestyles.
One of my brothers is sober four years,
and enjoys his life without boozing peers.
He inspired me to craft a new belief,
and a benevolent god is the chief."
Charles: "If you hired me now as a spotter,
I would probably see Zeus's daughter,

and destroy your ship on barrier reefs,
where old gods are wraiths of faded beliefs,
yet still call as Sirens from histories
which we reinvent for modern stories.
Marx and Nietzsche were industry sages
at the end of agrarian ages.
Yet to keep up with machineries' pace,
Russia traded in its Communist face.
We wanted fools to capitalize on,
and Gorbachev was too much of a khan,
so Boris Yeltsin has all our support,
drunk as a sailor on leave at a port.
He squandered all of their satellite states,
and we send him money in shipment crates,
that vanish into Russian mobster hands,
true capitalists whose crimes spread through lands."
Reuben: "Yet Clinton dismantles the share
poor Americans deserve through welfare.
Job growth in this region is a career
in vacuuming carpets or selling beer
at a casino or a grand hotel.
And like Pavlov's dog hearing dinner's bell,
the paid-for politicians salivate
at the idea of a gambling state.
Loan centers with a high usury rate
are next door to pawn shops and casinos,
which makes things convenient for addicts' shows,
especially if an alcohol store
is part of the strip-mall's shining décor."
Charles: "As Bernard might say, we are involved
in ongoing Soma Wars that evolved
from China's Opium War with England
to pharmaceutical's latest pill-brand.
Soma turns to turd and fertilizes
new Soma to battle for as prizes.
What kind of elixir will you design

to be ingested to view a god's sign?"
Reuben: "I am not in dairy commerce
as a drunk samurai guarding farmers
from the bandits of global industries,
which decide what crops will grow by decrees.
Like a high-tech Jehovah with a plague,
leaving poor farmers in a land of slag,
poppy-fields are blighted for our nation's
addicts to synthetic medications.
Bill Clinton claims he did not inhale grass,
just faked it to commune with his peer-class.
Corporate health-care owns part of his soul,
demanding competitors have no role.
Faith's induced madness is the opiate
of people since before the time of Set."
Charles: "Atheists consider sanity
as consciousness without god's vanity,
but Set's diseases are inherited,
sloughing off like snakeskin to raise the dead.
The blood of life attracts a hungry wraith,
and such combat belongs in your new faith.
Following Egypt's firstborns' epitaph,
Moses placed their serpent-god on a staff,
which was then adapted to symbolize
the medical pharmacies' enterprise."
Reuben: "Jews trace their lineage to Seth,
but to Egypt he caused Osiris' death:
chopped-up, he sailed the Nile in a casket,
trailed by baby Moses in a basket,
who was adopted by Egypt's princess,
perhaps an avatar of Queen Isis.
It was a long-running family feud
over who would control the chosen brood
with stories of fratricide and incest,
yet despite the horrors, were still the best.
Osiris and Set were brothers like Cain

and Abel, who practiced fratricide pain.
One was a shepherd, the former tilled the land,
and was banished by Yaweh's smiting hand.
Descended from clay, Cain tried to sow
his grandma like Set caused his sister's woe,
and passed along inherited defects,
which deformed lines of worshipped godly sects.
Now the long lineage of Abraham
murders each other with a crazed goddamn."
Charles: "Perhaps a Beowulf will emerge,
like Horus, to purify with a surge.
Aliens arrive to destroy Grendels,
and their mothers' wombs open into Hells,
where dragons pour forth like the snake-god, Seth,
who also avenge their lineages' death.
The fuel running the dragon's fire-blast,
is oily hate and rancor of our past.
Misspent energy becomes the fumes
the oppressed use to propel masters' dooms.
'Tis human to define our destinies
against the belief of our enemies'.
Pestilence and healing are intertwined;
the War Department is a dual mind,
crafting biological diseases,
then offering a cure that appeases."
Reuben: "One discerns the mind of people
by the construction of their faith's steeple.
Some image their gods as a deal-maker,
and when things go well, is a caretaker,
yet fortune spins onward to a bad fate,
and their gods' blessings quickly turn to hate.
Or so 'tis perceived when real estate
combat turns the land into a cesspool,
and the gods allow the wicked to rule,
acting as gadflies to drive people on,
'til deities destroy the corruption,

and restore blessed order, with a new deal
penned by scribes on a scroll with their god's seal.
So Christians embrace capitalism,
since Christ paid for human and god's schism."
Charles: "New loyalties are conspired by greed,
sown in the public's psyche like a seed.
Turning on former allies, the treaties
are made and broken with the greatest ease.
The hated become allies once again
if peace ensures a great profit-margin."
Reuben: "Some keep revenge as a motive,
and survivors demand oppressors give
portions of the wealth made by slave labor,
forced to work at the point of a saber.
The Jews are filing a massive lawsuit
against German industries that stole loot,
and did not pay the Jews for their careers
in concentration camps, corralled like steers.
Perhaps you Indians should do the same.
Or does your god not want you in the game
of throwing money as a solution
to wrecking the Black Hills with pollution?"
Charles: "The Great Mystery has not yet told
us what to do about the pillaged gold.
For we have no scales to prove the whites' harm,
nor timecards from when we were forced to farm,
though we will take your guilt-money, of course,
since treaties no longer have any force.
Then the government would have to borrow
from China to grant us a Hell's harrow.
Some of us desire mass integration
to be part of the globalization
that offers a fruit's homogenous taste,
and nations can bury nuclear waste
on reservations for the correct price
to expand menus from subsidized rice."

Reuben: "Inventing a global network
creates dark energy where shadows lurk.
We have built foreign exchange stock-markets
and citizens seem to enjoy the bets,
so long as they have convenient comforts
designed for them by the corporate courts,
who make the laws to keep people stupid,
lost in entertainments which are vapid."
Charles: "Political ambition requires
international support from empires,
and the laws enforced become as arcane
as *Leviticus*, and doubly insane.
We try to outgrow our past karmic laws
through a divine communion without flaws.
People only look at defeats too late,
due to compulsions for a supreme state.
That is a lesson for your new belief,
enlightenment leads to cycles of grief.
For I suppose you will use histories
to embellish your religion's stories."
Reuben: "You are being fatalistic,
but I know my descendants will be quick
to warp my faith to weather future storms,
like the god, Proteus, altered his forms.
Or the early Christians, who used a tale
to excuse mayhem as quests for the grail.
Each of the twelve apostles is a tribe
of Jacob, and reformed Judas's bribe
from patriarch Judah, wanting to sell
his brother, Joseph, tossed in a dry well.
Even Muslim ancestors played a part,
Ishmaelites, who gave Joe a new start,
buying him for twenty silver pieces.
Christ cost more, but inflation has leases
on a life rise quicker than slave-wages,
and chasing dreams only gilds our cages."

Charles: "Yes, it is true of all the nations
that they construct temples of temptations.
Whether 'tis for a better life on Earth,
or when we die and are granted rebirth
into Heavens with virgins of pure hearts,
or a porno palace with busty tarts.
Skinny cows or fat, we chase banquet cream
while wide awake or in a famine dream.
Our machines grant us oracular charms
on ethanol exchanges from corn farms.
We do not live by supplies and demands,
markets are based on speculators' hands
typing in numbers of quantum physics
into computers built on logistics.
Subliminal messages implant seeds
which create a faith's demand for false needs.
We do not trust third-dimensional sense,
forgetting gold calves give no sustenance.
I sometimes learn from personal failures,
yet collectively we are like sailors
whipped to frenzy by iconic Ahabs,
who direct our hate at whales or Arabs.
So we proceed through histories' progress,
hoping visions will save us from duress,
adapting the past to our perspective,
thinking our screen world makes us reflective."
Reuben: "You surprise me with your insights,
and your knowledge of the Egyptians' blights.
Most people settle for a distraction
that thrills them with instant satisfaction."
Charles: "As we said, there is much one can learn
from oppressors when fortune takes a turn,
and I grow weary of my sordid life,
and want to be in shape to face the strife
when revolutions usurp monarchies.
I can live for a time with anarchies,

as I have proved to myself with drunk sprees,
yet also desire a kind of order
that relies on a natural border.
Perhaps your new faith offers what I want,
a means to escape from spectres who haunt."
Reuben: "When you are ready, let me know,
for you likely have fine kernels to sow,
and I feel a debt to you for Manny,
but I will not be your wet-drunk nanny.
I have pipestone for a mother-idol
to keep us busy and not be idle."
Charles: "I am certain your place is calmer
than boozing with a future Jeff Dahmer,
and his practice of occult communion
on young males in his sheepfold dominion,
captured by the Cyclops among his ewes,
fueling social abandonment issues.
Dahmer was catered to by the police,
like the ocean god answered his son's pleas.
Most aliens settle at a low price,
but some have agencies' divine advice,
like a psychic safari with Jim Jones
or Kurtz through graveyards of Ganesha's bones.
We chase god-hood for power, sex, and fun,
while Iraqis bow to Baal Clinton."
Reuben: "I use pipestone, not ivory,
nor issue an immolation's decree.
Though armed militias become popular,
they still worship the almighty dollar,
which they freely spend on legal cases,
claiming the laws have no worthy basis.
Civil wars brew like Macbeth's ghostly feast,
placing us in the belly of the beast.
The past returns, haunting us to relive
each moment of the horrors that we give,
multiplied tenfold if people follow

an image we create that is hollow."
Charles: "The only way to fill such a void
is to eat the faithful in paranoid
delusions of abandonment and loss,
which means being alone with ordure's dross.
Is that why you want to recruit my soul
to your new rites, and fit me to a role?"
Reuben: "I make no laws nor act as guide,
and concoct no conflicts to take a side.
You would be better off staying with me
than a menial job's feeding frenzy,
where the employers encourage intrigues
among underpaid workers to form leagues
that turn on themselves for small promotions,
and the worst bully gets the big portions.
My young brother tried those kinds of careers,
scheming and plotting with his worker-peers,
developing a sullen attitude
towards the entire hierarchy brood,
saying: 'You do not have to scheme at me
for the low standard minimum wage fee.
You all embrace the Christian ideal,
like Judas Iscariot formed a deal.
I would rather walk out than spend my time
crafting espionage, bold or sublime.'
He is sixteen-years-old and had his fill
of low-wage jobs and stealing from the till
just to ease the pain of a work-headache
that was only cured by robbing a stake."
Charles: "Since Clinton dismantled welfare rights
there is more gun-play at schools and work sites.
In this town, the tourist trade of summer
creates the intrigue when months are glummer,
and business slows down and savings are gone,
and one must crush any aspiring pawn
scheming for increased work hours with deceit,

telling tales to the boss like a lamb's bleat.
And those who become part of the lost flocks
are shepherded behind the town's jail locks,
and that place has a direct connection
toward the homeless shelter's location.
We are made in god's image, and are told
to fruitfully multiply the sheepfold,
spreading god's image with liquidity,
as It writes of human stupidity.
Now I must go get ready for the shear
to earn a day's rent and purchase cheap beer."
Reuben: "Our parts add to a greater sum
than our acts which have contrary outcome.
We identify our various traits
by what we consume that guides us to fates.
Yet what would we be without definition,
and vices to send us on a mission?"
They bid goodbyes and Charles walked through the snow
that drifted in eddies from the wind's flow.
He remembered his vow of no oil use,
and wondered if breaking it placed a noose
around his neck with no chance of escape,
doomed by pollution, as was the landscape,
which granted the means of destructive thrills
through slagging for minerals and fossils,
as well as the plants of barley and grain
to make alcohol, which Charles sought to drain.
Fighting in the hemispheres of his brain,
industrial and agrarian gods
had it seem he and humans were at odds:
everything he partook of signified
a terrible destruction's rising tide.
The sun was bleak, like a lighthouse in fog,
and the snow turned gray from acidic smog.
What had once seemed nature's vast miracle,
now portended a gruesome oracle.

The past was burned as fuel for the scenes
of modern progress and new gods' machines,
who bestowed lessons that conveniences
were better than life through the five senses.
And one could be a famous avatar
to guide others like the sailors' North Star,
and be granted their humble fealty,
suiting a pharaoh's immortality.
Redemption would come for the planet's heist,
as it did for the kind thief next to Christ.
New worlds would be found to loot and pillage,
as aliens find a peaceful village,
like Troy was wrecked by Greek tribes of Danaan,
or Danites murdered their way through Canaan.
His abstract thoughts went from one to the next,
as if spirits guided him through a text,
which divulged mysteries on a high-plane
as notes he left for himself to maintain
sanity in the material sphere,
while his soul was wandering with good cheer
through the Bardos, leaving behind letters
of instructions to be free of fetters.
Yet his focus was compelled to return
towards alcohol's insidious burn.
He had judged Christians and found them wanting,
yet he desired freedom from the haunting
by Maddox to gain his released Heaven
once Stan was killed, to which Charles was driven.
For much of his life he prayed for visions
to guide him and help make hard decisions.
Now that it was happening, he felt trapped,
as if each movement was already mapped.
He need look no further for Heaven's sign,
at his feet had been laid a grand design.
Still he fought it as an oppressive route
that would burden him with a banner's tout.

He thought of getting drunk to gain some peace,
forcing his dual nature's war to cease.
At that moment, he suddenly felt chilled,
as if his own judgment had been fulfilled.
The opened scrolls and letters disappeared,
and he sorely grieved, though it had been weird.
Charles decided to call in sick at work,
and quit if the manager went berserk.
Charles quickly reached his apartment complex,
believing he cursed himself with a hex.
Joe Bear Feet, Charles' roommate, was embattled
with Sherry, Joe's girlfriend, and he rattled
her head as he clutched her around the throat.
Charles watched sadly, not taking off his coat.
Feeling detached, he rolled a cigarette,
wondering how he could afford to let
another apartment, with sane roommates,
who would not complain of Charles' bizarre traits.
She blinded Joe and his bifocals broke,
while he called down doom with a vicious stroke.
Sherry cried to Charles with a tearful gasp,
and he went to them, releasing Joe's grasp.
Joe stepped backwards, then kicked, grazing her chin,
then calmly got a beer from the kitchen.
Charles helped her on the couch as she panted,
and Joe returned in fury and ranted:
"That damn slut gave me some kind of crotch-rot
as a love token or forget-me-not.
She better leave for good and not be here
by the time I drink the last of my beer."
Sherry: "Do not give me that crazy noise.
You play so much with your goofy butt-boys
you probably caught it from one of them,
yet I am the innocent you condemn."
Charles was happy his mind was too muddled
for sex with her, except when they cuddled.

Two nights before, she slipped into his bed,
but he had been so drunk he snored instead.
He was aware Joe had proclivities
that he practiced among Rapid City's
young male homosexuals' bands and cliques,
and Charles had grown weary of the antics.
Joe refused to keep the apartment clean,
cockroaches and lice made the place obscene.
As Joe and Sherry fought, Charles packed his gear,
rejecting Joe's offer of a truce-beer.

16

The Passion of the Buffalo

For six months Charles rented a sleeping room
so small it felt like a chamber of doom,
and neighbors encouraged him to consume
large quantities of alcohol with them,
but Charles lived a sobriety system.
He spent most of his waking hours at work,
or at cafes where it was safe to lurk
with fellow members of sober programs,
choosing the good people who used no scams.
Clara and Betty were grateful he chose
to surrender his angry drifter's pose,
and gladly accepted him in their home,
no longer wandering Samsara's loam.
Clara resided with a high school friend,
a man of Lakota and Aztec blend,
who worked for the county's social service,
and whose eyes seemed to have peered into bliss.
His name was Paul Dart, and he did two tours
of duty in Vietnam, then his chores
became an illegal kind of rampage,
which sentenced him to twelve years in a cage.
Paul stayed sober, and when he was released
his anger at society had ceased.
During his first two years of freedom's way,

even in summer, beneath the sun's ray,
Paul wore long-sleeved shirts as a sort of ruse
to hide his arms' multi-colored tattoos.
He was patient with Charles, but called him out
when Paul thought Charles was acting as a lout.
Dave Standing Horse had been gentle and kind
when not having alcohol on his mind.
Mostly he practiced a benign neglect,
for life's stage required no one to direct.
Paul had a bit of this philosophy,
and knew Charles was old enough to be free
in making his decisions and choices,
not haunted by Maddox's dire voices.
Charles' mind was slowly becoming his own,
and he made amends for the bad seeds sown.
Yet it took an effort to accept Paul
as a father-figure whom Charles could call
upon and be completely at ease with,
and not be ignored or face a grim scythe.
Charles' relationships had been divided
by fierce loyalty where hate abided
for outsiders or looming betrayal
to the doomed crusades on which he set sail.
Charles was embarrassed to see how he tried
to gather people to support his side
in the ongoing war of dark and light,
to share the burden and enforce a blight
on those deemed unworthy or a traitor
not dining on hate Charles had to cater.
Charles was accustomed to people who use
others to fortify a power ruse.
When folks replied with rage at his demands,
Charles would recruit new members to his bands,
or go off on his own and sulk with wrath,
and find a difficult means as his path.
Then return to say he found a vision

that people should follow as a mission.
When they did not, he responded with hate,
or derisive humor at their glum fate.
Charles had to learn that compassion was part
of being human with an open heart.
For years he had a fixed, solid image
of how a Lakota medicine mage
should perform austerities for a tribe,
and never falter or accept a bribe
for visions and cleansing those to be blessed
by casting out spirits of the possessed.
When young, Charles' white peers desired to become
the leaders followed by a beating drum,
who guided people to a greater wealth,
assembling kindness if it fit their stealth.
Charles' ambition was to locate a course
and set a shifting trail to the world's source
that would not destroy it with a pillage
of Mother Earth's vast natural silage.
He had failed, thus far, to pass it along
to the next generation's sacred song.
He still retained a notion of standard
that he would set, and not have it slandered.
Yet slowly he was becoming aware
all tunes change, even for the bird and bear.
For as habitats were destroyed, the stress
of living altered the voices' address.
Paul took Betty and Charles to a Pow-Wow,
where Charles did not feel holier than thou.
The drum-beaters let him practice with them,
and patiently watched him learn the rhythm.
He got a telephone number to call
from a dancer who cleansed his inner gall.
Karen Buffalo Who Mourns wore a dress
that dazed Charles with the speed she could impress.
She danced with her daughter, who also wore

a fancy garb not purchased at a store.
Karen approached Charles while he was eating,
who put the food aside at the meeting.
They introduced themselves, and attraction
was a common bond of satisfaction.
Charles: "I saw you keep time with every beat.
The judges must be blind. Please, have a seat."
Karen: "Winning is nice, yet I wonder
the merits of chasing worldly plunder.
Perhaps there is gambling on the dances,
placing bets on the odds and the chances."
Charles: "Earth's psyche becomes a casino,
hedging our bets on the polar caps' snow,
like injury reports for a sport's star,
who was driving drunk and destroyed his car.
Will he be in top form for the big game?
Is Earth burning to Hell in Satan's name?"
Karen: "Is there time to invent fuels,
or should we invest in forgetful pools?
Beer is being sold now, so we shall leave,
and miss the tribe members stagger and weave,
doing their self-induced retarded dance,
with slurred insults and curses as their chants.
Maybe the softball tourney is fixed too,
like oracles by a crucified Jew.
Here is my phone number so call me soon.
It is you or dancing that has me swoon."
Charles: "Thank you, my beauty, I feel the same,
I have passion that perhaps you can tame.
It could be fate conspired fortune's forces
by weaving together our sewn courses.
Yet the plot does not make me paranoid
of nature's work that I used to avoid."
Karen: "I had a superstitious mind
that life is arranged and badly designed
by forces that gain terrible rewards

in shaping themselves as capricious lords.
The only way out was to sink deeper
than they dared to go as a grim reaper.
In this dimension they act as spoilers,
crafting investments as tireless toilers.
Yet they fear the underworld, where I went
to escape in self-imposed banishment."
For a flashing moment, Charles held her hand,
laughing at the horrors which made them band.
Charles; "We are each alone upon the stage,
thinking we control the spotlight's image.
Yet when we go beyond it then we find
a common consciousness that has us bind.
We can help create enlightened levels
that dismays the rigging of the devils."
Karen: "Men have more practice with free will,
yet return to women to sow and till,
relying on us to create new scenes
because the old ones have too many liens.
This crumb-snatcher is my daughter, Betsy,
who is caught in our era's fantasy,
convinced she is destined to sit for hours
in front of screens that mimic the powers
which are fated to rule various things,
and give her roles to act with verse she sings."
Betsy hid her face in Karen's long dress,
and Charles felt a delight arrive to bless.
Charles: "It is strange how we choose parts to play,
yet in the end we all return to clay.
I once desired celebrity-status
as a holy man who could reform us
into a new Earth's kind of rising breed,
like sowing dragon's teeth to reap the seed.
Then I saw I would also be reshaped
in wars for dragon's oil as Earth is raped.
I would not be capable to withstand

my own tragic flaws guided by fate's hand."
Karen: "Americans sometimes embrace
fictional heroes who tumble from grace.
Screen leaders are allowed to do penance,
even if sins are terribly immense.
Their hungry spectators are always thrilled
if heroes never have innocents killed.
At Nixon's funeral Clinton spoke out
that Tricky Dick knew how to handle clout,
and history would be kind to Nixon,
writ as America's favorite son
who the media cast into the pit,
resurrected by them for a new script."
Charles: "So we go through life in pigeon-holes,
switching costumes to pretend we changed souls."
Karen: "I am not from a museum,
raising culture from a mausoleum.
Yet there is some truth in what you have said,
when around white folks, thoughts change in my head.
I am unsure if to expect the worst,
and reply by having their spirits cursed.
Or ignore me like I do not exist,
a wandering ghost in a foggy mist.
Should they be courteous, it is startling,
and my appearance shows an altering
to gladness they acknowledge that I live,
or stoically ignore what they give."
Charles: "I know what you say, 'tis so with me.
Though I feel now that I have become free,
I still switch roles with an unbidden mood,
as if a thick, tumultuous storm brewed
that patiently waits for an unveiling,
destructive typhoon as I am sailing,
sometimes adrift, on life's deathly ocean.
Yet I no longer search for a potion."
Karen: "I, too, constructed a false dam

to hold true feelings and not give a damn.
I invested in artificial means
to create emotions for awful scenes.
Little Betsy could tell you of our plight,
she is still scarred by perpetual night.
She probably remembers it better
than I, reciting it to the letter.
I quit acting the source of painful grief,
who then changes to Heavenly relief."
Charles: "Sometimes I wished to be everything
to every one, from a pauper to king.
And if they acknowledged that, they received
gifts of bounty suiting what they believed.
If their faith was fickle or my head hurt
from a hangover, then I would assert
myself to crafting capricious judgments,
and make the world pay for my punishments,
which were self-inflicted by my own flaws,
though according to my Yaweh-like laws,
I was above rules of cause-and-effect,
and demanded adherence to my sect."
Karen laughed with a lilting, hearty tone,
and Charles closed his eyes and released a groan.
Karen: "You no longer seem the Pope-type,
surrounded by sycophants and their hype
carefully forming a media-style,
with all of the trappings and intrigues' wile."
Charles: "You bring out my best, and yet remind
me of all the stuff I held in my mind.
For some reason it is easy with you
in dividing darkness and light in two.
I do not ponder my lost, wasted years
in regret that tortures my soul with fears."
She touched his shoulder and he pressed her hand
with his fingers, thinking it was as planned.
Yet his feelings were beyond oracles,

and emotions work their own miracles,
which do not have to lead to paranoid
delusions created to fill the void
that once held sorrow, anger, greed, and lust,
which Charles felt exorcised by loving trust.
Charles: "'Tis strange not to fear good attachments
to those other than siblings or parents.
I allow my feelings to go unchecked,
and you admit that you are not perfect.
I think for too long I desired to craft
a beatific vision and a raft
that would get me to a splendid harbor,
a grueling task of homecoming labor."
Karen: "A Lakota Odysseus
who would set the order right and free us.
You certainly had a high ambition,
but used alcohol as ammunition
to self-sabotage your vessel's journey,
yet you made it to our Pow-Wow's tourney."
Charles: "It can be hard to accept defeat.
A war might be won but destroys the fleet.
I am not a great hero in battle
with bullies guiding women like cattle.
The only one who I tried to impress
was my self-portrait god, wearing no dress.
In the end, my maze was worse than corrals
that lead to a charnel-house of gut smells,
fueling the insane actions of people,
who also dine on Christ at their steeple."
Karen: "We have a great common union.
Thanks for not making me your communion.
Women have more independence these days,
and we try not to wreak havoc and raze.
Betsy is nervous so we must go now.
Unlike Penelope, I spoke no vow,
so do not wait ten years to telephone

because by then I shall not be alone."
Charles: "I can learn from others' past mistakes
in gaining knowledge by advice from snakes.
There is more to the world than to shape-shift
in destroying and building a new rift
with the aid from jetfighters or a dove.
And one of the reasons we always love
our enemies is they help to define
symbols of war and peace, which we design.
We can survive our brief mortality
by evading stringent morality."
Karen: "Jesus taught the truly bad sin
is desire for wealth, like a gold calf's kin.
Temptation to know our inner-godhood
is something we partake of as we should:
we hunger for the formless that shapes forms
beyond the logic of timeless tapeworms."
Charles: "Moses' reward was viewing god's rear,
then banished from Canaan for a rock's tear.
The Jews rewrote Egypt's *Book of the Dead*
as a guided tour by what Yaweh said.
They reached our Eden and forced us to class,
teaching us new roles as snakes in the grass,
changing our name from Lakota to Sioux,
to pray at passion stations or a pew,
traveling along an oracle road,
with a prefabricated heavy load."
Karen: "Like I sew to a size that fits.
We have been leaving for twenty minutes,
and am glad for our moment which occurs,
but Betsy just ate buffalo burgers
and demands she sleeps off her gorging feast
or she will become a fierce little beast."
Charles: "I wanted to take you to a tent
or a sacred teepee for lust's intent
that would please the lords of love and romance,

but will risk a hug and kiss at this chance."
Karen: "It shall have to be on the cheek,
as Betsy is quite capable to speak
extended grandiose tales of my acts,
with a complete disregard for the facts.
To her, the full moon will rise from your hair
and I transform into a small black bear,
then we shall both hunt for berries and fish,
and she will prepare an antelope dish,
that springs to life inside of us to run,
expanding our forms until we are one
with the cosmos to shape a universe,
which she describes with her dandy free verse."
Betsy laughed, then yelled and pulled Karen's arm,
and spoke as if mad at a broken charm:
"That is my tale and you should not steal it.
I work hard to make all the people fit.
How did you know that was my grand story?
Why do you take my lightning and glory?"
Betsy cried as Karen tried not to smile,
and stroked her daughter's hair to calm her rile.
Karen: "Your stories are so vast I find
myself inside them and can see your mind.
Always at work on some fascination,
you build and destroy many a nation,
except for when you sit in front of screens,
and let others fill your head with their scenes."
Betsy: "That is how I shut off my brain,
because running my worlds is a big strain.
You said once I am not yet polluted,
and I roam free without being rooted,
but my worlds always demand a savior,
and I must escape their bad behavior."
Karen: "Well, that is one way to be free.
Many nuts fall from our family tree.
You can transport from the television

a savior to your own unique vision.
I am certain the actors will thank you
for adding hosannas to their stars' brew,
constructing cosmos around their fictions,
as Earth's audience follows the actions."
Charles: "Galileo changed star-gazers' jobs,
and now television follows heart-throbs,
which is easier than going against
a church's order that keeps us all fenced
within structures to not be curious
of hidden powers that shape all of us.
Now television and computers tell
us what to do to avoid their mean Hell.
As Shakespeare might say of how the world chars:
'The fault lies within us, not in the stars.'
Shakespeare did not know that novas exist,
and fortune gave those burnt planets a twist
due to orbiting global karmic flaws,
and their dark energy gravity laws.
Betsy, 'tis good to meet a fellow seer,
you give me much hope and a laughter's cheer."
Karen: "She fired Coyote, took his job,
and giggled when he howled his yapping sob.
Now she spreads the stars as an alphabet,
catching each of us in her language net.
As computer satellites change lingoes,
and confusing Tower of Babble grows,
she invents words that become popular,
then makes them extinct like a worn-out slur."
Betsy recited the two through ten rolls
in Lakota, to show her multiples.
When she began to add and then subtract,
her mother's patience slowly became wracked.
Karen: "She can go on like this all day,
but she must like you to perform this way.
The last fellow I introduced her to

received foul names in a Spanish storm's brew.
He was unaware what she labeled him,
signifying her fury to the brim.
Sometimes she acts as my barometer,
a rain dancer asking for a mixture,
who to feel juice with and who to avoid,
and Pow-Wows bring spirits to be employed.
I believe they want to be used for love,
but she demands rule over hawk and dove."
Charles gazed at the small astrophysicist,
who gave him a smile, and then Karen kissed
his cheek, and they walked away holding hands,
leaving Charles to wish he could join their bands.
He sat wondering on his own daughter,
conceived while mixing whiskey and water.
Should he scribble her out of his life's script,
like an ill-fated paper, torn and ripped?
Charles had often felt discarded that way,
and had helped form her spirit into clay.
To dismiss creation as a mistake
has the worlds formed by a god who is fake.
It is one thing to be a good trickster,
and stir the cosmos for a fun mixture,
but humans are more than ink on pages
to be wrote or made extinct images.
At times Charles felt pressure, as if to dance
for those seeking a command performance.
They wanted romance and bleak tragedies;
backgrounds of historical comedies
to show them where they had gone wrong, and laugh
as he became the White Buffalo Calf.
Charles realized humans adapt to roles
with a fierce resiliency in their souls.
He would rather be a woman than queer,
and imagined himself as a twin-peer
of Karen, linked closely to Mother Earth,

going through the rapture of giving birth.
Charles felt the sensation grow and then wane,
as he disengaged from sympathy pain.
Does orbiting gravity collect minds,
and looming the stardust lights are hard grinds
for those who must make others' dreams come true?
Yet enforced labor constructs nothing new
except a group consciousness that expands
until it contracts through the rape of lands.
The spirits remain, as in a ghost town,
astounded by what they built, then tore down.
Yet love wins through biodiversity,
and souls go elsewhere from the wrecked city.
Living in the now can be difficult,
with many lost in a satellite's cult.
Was it Charles' duty to arrange their thought
back to Earth than in the gadgets they bought?
Charles had his own flaws and might run away;
if people turned to him he would not stay.
He still had medicine-man ambition,
and in his own strange way craved attention.
Yet so many people before him died
through an addiction to spotlights and pride.
Lessons of history should not be lost
when the proud say they serve at a high cost.
Charles did not want a fickle audience,
nor wished to demand strict obedience,
neither a martyr for his own doomed cause,
or hallowed in a moment of time's pause.
Beatrice found him ruminating so,
and asked if he enjoyed the dancers' show.
Charles nodded and his sister scratched his back,
then gave him soda and a fry-bread snack.
Betty: "I am unused to this junk-food,
it plays havoc with my body and mood.
I have not ate it since I quit boozing,

and now regain the weight I was losing.
Fried grease and canned food are the main staples
of Lakota settlement lunch tables.
They would not know what to do with fresh fruit,
but ferment it to a full buzzing toot.
The only yield in this ecosystem
is the war element uranium.
You are quiet, Charles, and seem in deep thought.
Have you located something which you sought?"
He did not speak and she gave him a poke
with her finger, and then he softly spoke:
"I met a woman and have been smitten.
Like Pilate, what I wrote is so written.
Pontius quit scapegoating his audience,
and allowed them to get bloody vengeance
on one who reputedly took the sins
of the world to prove that good always wins.
I do not want to take another's vice
casually cast out by a device.
Nietzsche taught that compassion killed our gods.
The Industrial Age gave us death rods
to smite our foes from a detached distance,
not caring who is killed in gambling chance,
like Shiva performing his deadly dance.
The machine of the gods' possesses ghosts
who wander in search of new, unique hosts.
To form one's identity through machines
builds dispassionate and conscienceless scenes."
Betty: "When mom went on a drunk mission,
I was placed before the television
to be adopted by white role models,
with plenty of phony coos and coddles.
I learned then how to disengage from love,
and tried to tune in something far above.
Is the woman you met a Thunderbird,
soaring around while dancing with the herd?"

Charles: "Karen and her daughter are dancers,
searching for The Great Mystery's answers.
Though artists must disengage from their works,
they still want rewards, benefits, and perks.
Frustration festers when the audience
cannot comprehend visionary sense
that is timeless and spans our history,
yet encapsulates an era's story.
Disengaged, the artist might go insane,
and imbibe in Soma to ease the pain,
which detaches the artist even more,
'til he or she cannot practice their lore.
Chaotic energy fuels their hate,
like watching machines kill and masturbate,
and art is corrupted to segregate
the individuals locked in systems:
one button blesses, the other condemns."
Beatrice: "That is how I play alone
when I get bored with friends on my cell-phone.
If I push the right codes I get rewards,
like notes on a harp from angelic hordes.
A misplaced finger can summon dark wraiths,
who seek to put my image in their faiths."
Charles: "'Tis natural to be curious,
and chain love to what is superstitious.
Releasing one's vengeance is difficult,
especially if it involves a cult
of furiously driven acolytes
who seek control of universal lights."
Charles, granted the vision of holding court,
saw the means of building a faith's support.
In the struggle, some form an agency
to keep bloodstain clean like a Pharisee.
Nulling the command-chain of a Jew-priest,
Pilate had Christ flogged, nailed-up, then released.
Pilate did not follow their god's order,

having received no reward for murder.
Why do your occupied foes' work, whose tribes
want a blood-purge, yet not get any bribes?
Rather, civil and religious unrest
because the conquered believe they are blest.
Covert leagues guard and hide the command-chain,
so none are responsible for the pain
induced to settle a hierarchy
they control with the threat of anarchy
if not allowed to do their king-making
of new Manna-communion, like baking.
Pilate followed their espionage ruse
and labeled Jesus the King of the Jews,
then set him free to show the priests they lacked
power to over-influence Rome's tact.
Uriah's letter had the bearer slain,
and Dave's heirs were victims of command's chain.
People enjoy rewards their soldiers' glean,
who are sent to keep the dirty hand's clean.
Pilate went free as Yaweh's button-man:
buffered himself as a mobster Roman.
Cleansed his hands of the storyteller's blood,
both immortal through *Gospels*, though of mud.
The vision had Charles feel both cursed and blessed,
and said to Betty of what he witnessed:
"Our art inheritance goes through eons,
each generation has kings and peons.
We cast ourselves as villains or good folks,
tethered to free will and our karmic yokes.
Our tribes have spies for agencies to herd
us to be one with the Corporate Word.
'Tis an artificial continuance
of a greedy false resurrection's chance."
Betty furrowed her brow and shook her head.
'Twas too serious, so she laughed and said:
"I need ransom for my captivity,

a redeemer from my self-imagery.
I vaguely remember when I was young
how you taught the word 'Mine', and it was sung
by me each time I grabbed hold of some thing.
I am glad I found better words to sing,
for possessions come and go with their pain,
and chasing their joys makes resources wane.
Folks say they work to support their children,
who inherit a polluted burden.
Tell me of this Karen who smote your mind.
I will make a place to keep her aligned,
both within and without my boundaries,
so on a hot day she is a cool breeze."
Charles spoke of Karen with all due respect
and maturity he used to neglect.

17

Promises

Bill Clinton's sex harassment perjury
evolved to Congress' impeachment jury.
Wishing he had paid off Miss Paula Jones,
or an accident had interred her bones,
Clinton battled the crusading Ken Starr,
a leading agent for the legal bar.
He discovered Monica Lewinsky,
an intern at the White House, had a spree
of various sorts with the president,
and sperm samples made the case evident.
For years the Clintons supported the cause
of victims needing sex harassment laws.
Facing the opposite end of the gun,
he had to leave his other work undone
to marshal global and domestic groups,
thus Iraq banished arms' inspector troops.
As Clinton focused his dark energy
to stay president, and have folks agree
that young, single women are easy prey,
and god was forgiving if Bill would pray,
Hussein made use of the televised acts,
wherein every side distorted the facts.
Stan packed his gear to flee the Iraq scenes,
drinking gin and gobbling amphetamines

to stay wide awake, although in a haze,
watching his work go to ruin and raze.
He felt he was watched by audiences,
and disconnected at all five senses.
He thought of what a priest recently said
on being chosen to stand in god's stead:
'Some are selected to pass along grace,
and though humans try they can not erase
those chosen throughout history's long trails
who enlighten the big picture's details.
Folks use metaphors to associate
themselves with what they think is their right state,
and enacting the tales guides them to fate.'
Stan looked in the mirror of his barracks,
and felt as if a spoiler played some tricks.
His reflection ebbed and flowed through his skin,
which asked if only one story would win,
a conquering tale that could not be warped,
despite breeding the bastards who usurped.
Stan: "I feel an answer is owed to me.
I am locked in myself, you hold the key.
Each generation has those who promise
if we follow them we shall attain bliss.
Then others pursue to repeat the same,
the only changes are the leader's name.
All I ask for is one clear perception
to gain something from this misconception
that I was immature when I started
warring with Iraq, which I have charted
on my way through our interior depths,
where images shatter and cause true deaths."
'There is one you can call Reality,
and to it is owed your full fealty.
Follow my heeding to an area
where you can escape your hysteria.'
Stan did not know if he could trust the voice,

which seemed to him the best of a bad choice.
He walked into the warm evening desert,
feeling a cosmic trust, though quite alert.
He stopped on a sand-dune and watched the air,
as if sensing beasts emerged from a lair.
Stan suddenly felt clouted on his head
by a beam of light that could lay him dead.
He fell, and the sand skittered under him,
which then spilled over to bury each limb.
He slowly detached himself from the grave,
then laid on his back, watching the sky rave:
'That first tale was what you asked for in One,
which you cannot manage, so it is done.
There are others, though, who can show you things,
revealing your life as the chorus sings.
Some you will not understand, for you link
with others' patterns beyond what you think.'
Stan nodded and watched the spirits descent,
laughing and crying on paths they were sent.
Some hobbled with age, others twirled a dance,
looking for freedom or a fine romance,
then fight over who was the best mimic,
the most sophisticated, or rube hick.
City guardians and rebels who prowl
revealed faces or hid behind a cowl.
'Ganesha is a bastard deity,
who writes the worlds' sadness and comedy,
spawns illegitimate lineages
of artists who craft in their images,
until there is nothing left of the soul
that created the vast original.
Thus writers are wrong on stories and fame
resounding through the ages a great name:
stories become extinct or edited,
and unable to resurrect the dead.
All that is left are shallow illusions,

which fight each other in crazed delusions.
Krishna was correct about the facades
you think are real to control your gods,
investing the senses into machines
for rewards you believe are Heaven's scenes,
then to the Void, like Achilles' shade went
on his death to fulfill the god's intent,
and the machinations that only lords
deserve immortality's great rewards.
But the gods died too, and their story fades,
plunged into dim culture like mortal shades.
'Twill happen to humans who now control
the devices where you invest your soul.
Global conglomerates and their mated
subsidiaries are all related
with incestuous tangles that spur war
in consumers for the idiot lore.
As did the European royalty,
all related cousins, whose fealty
was to power and gain, hoped to be won
by sending forth soldiers for World War One.
The aristocrats wept crocodile tears
with enemy kin and royalty peers.
The men who survived the incest battle
formed corporations We now hear prattle
insane lies of how We must protect them
for the rewards by a global system.
They grant scripts by an advertisement scribe
to battle for the Soma you imbibe.
With Us, they watch as their tale disappears,
and new ones shall arise with sibling peers,
perhaps regressed to troglodytes, whose tails
have vanished with ever-changing entrails,
and draw on cavern walls the huntsmen's hope
that wooly mammoths are killed on the lope.
It will evolve from the unique, though crass,

for communions with gods shown in stained glass.
Thus the illusions are inherited,
evolving Rudra to strike bastards dead.
The light and dark are passed on to sages,
who bequeath garbled, messy messages
that promise knowledge beyond human ken,
which is built on bodies burned and broken,
who fertilize pleasant garden bowers
hanging amidst comfortable towers.
When these sage messengers bring Us their flocks,
demanding their foes be kept out with locks,
We reply that it is not Our duties
to fulfill their promised Hell and beauties.
They ask if We do not work through prophets
and messiahs who teach Heaven's profits.
But We chose freedom rather than service
to those who seek eternal Hell or bliss,
thus it should not seem some kind of surprise
We are not responsible for their lies.
They blame scapegoats for the tales going wrong,
and fit the sacrifice to a new song,
each time thinking it guides them to knowledge
that they swear upon their souls as a pledge,
until something new comes along to grab,
told by messengers who pay the bill's tab.
Distractions are the sires of invention,
and breed to reshape human attention.
Imitation does not always flatter
when great energy becomes dark matter,
that mimics their way through eternity,
until ignorant shades under the Tree
of Knowledge and Life to partake of fruits,
then going crazy to tear out the roots.
This desert you see was once paradise,
now churns out fuel for your car's device
that grants escape from the third-dimension

to where the machines make your decision.
A mass of consciousness is led to scenes
of guardian angels upon the screens,
gathering followers, excluding some,
creating Soma to make people numb.
Such is the reward for being zealous
and guarding shares, of which they are jealous.
They set an order upon a screen's slate
that they want no one else to regulate,
and promise great rewards in a god's name
to keep the primordial leashed and tame,
while insisting your fate is to consume
mass-produced amusements to avoid doom.
Work ethics are instilled, though work changes
as high-technology rearranges
patterns of life, movements, and migrations
of people searching for their own rations.
Work evolves to sitting at screen-modems,
one button blesses, another condemns.
They become too vapid to scribble scripts,
so they write in scribes for words from the lips.
Some of these scribes come from the underground,
watching shadows, hearing echoes resound.
Like the towers' heights of your bureaucrats,
they burrow as deep as fierce tunnel-rats.
Emerging from lairs for promises made,
the scribes seize hold of gifts and are well-paid
to expand the promises round the world,
chained to their masters' freedom, flags unfurled.
Even the subversive can be employed,
writing contrary scripts of peace destroyed,
and rearranging cults in images
like Robespierre and Danton as sages.
Europe's monarchs supported their French kin
so as to suppress their own rebels' din,
and France had war from without and within.

Momentary leaders arose and fell,
as if on the hour by a chiming bell.
Building power-niches, the subversive
who fought for freedom became oppressive.
Monarchs' incestuous control of states
warped to Bonaparte's family estates.
He tried to include Egypt's pyramids,
but fled, leaving his troops like bleating kids.
Dostoyevsky's nation reaped with a scythe
Napoleon's self-cultivated myth.
Russia has ever bred subversive folks.
Perhaps the weather is like bitter yokes
that they drag along in hopes to harvest
a fulfillment of what they were promised.
The land can be cold, which makes truth hard woes,
as ideals flitter in minds' shadows.
Crushed under decades of atheism
that fell, now lands are torn by a schism.
The new religious freedom brings peril
as violent packs of troops go feral
in the commission of a holy war,
with weapons purchased from the Kremlin store,
which used the sales' money, dollars and cents,
to repay yours and other governments.
The Russian Christian Church rose to power,
and the politicians deemed it the hour
to encourage their once satellite states
to purge the bad blood of vehement traits.
The Christians are armed to slaughter Muslims,
with pillage and rapine on focused whims
that loath ideologies thought as odd,
but loving the humans as taught by god.
We spoke to you before of the mess done,
it recurs in the spot of World War One.
What We show you may not fit in your skull,
but in the end it is merely fiscal.

You have been taught to hate Communism,
and admire their new capitalism
as Russia borrows to buy parts onstage
to script roles on the global power's page.
The world is full of ironies that mock,
investing in one's hypocrisy stock
keeps Us laughing at those who seek to find
weapons of destruction with both eyes blind
to the fact if any are located
it is as the free market dictated.
And if it dictates, then it guides the ink
that scripts and enacts the chromosomes' link.
We watch people sell their gene entities
to parent incorporate deities.
What is it in humans that induces
them to battle for states of psychosis?
A new door of consciousness opens up,
like the eyes of a mewling near-blind pup,
and a human thinks he alone can grasp
the door so often removed from its hasp,
that swings on hinges of revolution
to clear out the achievers' pollution,
and prepare for others, who will arrive,
each convinced that he or she can contrive
a means to bring others into the realm,
by guiding them with a hand on the helm.
As levels of consciousness open wide,
and sand-dunes are Samsara's teeming tide,
oracles are created to suit needs
of planting on rocks and good Earth the seeds
of souls' desire for spiritual quests
to be free of one's self in dire conquests.
Never mind that sooner or much later
one finds himself as a horny satyr,
and wonders how he came down to all this
from an achieved state of Somatic bliss.

The rituals of civilization
are outdated with sterilization
and the pollution of all the past ghosts,
who dubbed themselves the monarchs of the Hosts,
and tried to control the breeding forthwith
so as to shape and dictate their own myth.
The formulated state of psychosis
shudders at the brink of a void's abyss.
Mass hysteria is manufactured
as quickly as a catch-phrase or a word
denoted to shape schisms or reforms,
making foes of friends with new Eden's worms.
As Soma evolves with technology,
and fruits are seedless on a hybrid tree,
not fertilized when it comes out with dung,
old songs are reinvented by the young.
The primordial shrieks at lost senses,
but will not surrender conveniences,
and mimic those who gather acolytes,
and promise to guide them to the great lights.
They seek a script of ancient tradition,
with them on top and slaves in perdition,
though sour with their own infidelity
to the old truths of exclusivity
by breeding a lineage of bastards
with those bought and sold as the low-caste herds.
Regret at the loss as wish-fulfillers
and esteem as community pillars,
they seek through the underground for support,
and ancient laws as justice of the court,
like Minos in Dante's dread Inferno,
where the only light is a tortured glow.
Revenge is granted to the prisoners
by spilling excretion through Earth's sewers,
putrefying the system up above,
where consciousness thinks itself as True Love,

except to those 'tis directed to hate,
such as prisoners or foes of the state.
People go to stores, meek as a martyr,
to buy the demigods' bottled water,
for the madness induced by excrement
fouling waters, by an angel god sent,
is like the bitter cup you drink alone,
here at the foul breasts of old Babylon.
You call her a whore, yet desire her touch,
fueling your need for a compulsive clutch.
Perhaps take a look at yourself and peers,
and what you do as a choice of careers.
She lives within and without ancient myth:
at times, civilized, then savage Lilith.
When you cast blame on her unchaste chalice,
recall your vow to her freedom's service,
how you disarmed and disrobed for your lust,
and then blamed her when you betrayed the trust.
She casts you out to find another slut,
which you do like a Brahma bull in rut.
Combat in Bosnia can be your course,
switching sides, like costumes, to join the force
of Muslims against a Christian crusade,
while you chant Christ was begotten, not made.
Like angels guarded the nativity,
so you protect your vain naivete
with beliefs that terror must be unleashed
for a peaceful era, tamed from a beast.
If it cannot be so in the present,
would god do it for Heavenly ascent?
Will your foes be waiting there with weapons
your nation sold to them to use as pawns
in conspiracies against other foes,
with their own image of a savior's pose?
Muslims do not allow any portraits
of Mohammad's unknown face or his traits,

so Islam nations make up for the lack
of Big Brother propaganda attack
with photo-posters of current rulers,
whom you regard as jihad-crazed droolers.
Yet for years you supported Ron Reagan's
dithering Berlin Wall condemnations,
ignoring the horrors of Leningrad,
the waking nightmare of a man gone mad,
who invaded Russia, as Hitler did,
spreading mass murder to have Europe rid
of a species considered sub-humans,
to make living room for the great Germans;
and though revenge is unreasonable,
for Russians it was understandable.
Their allies helped carve up the continent
into blocs, which then had their hatred vent
at each other, of course for a profit.
It does not take an oracle prophet
to see Russia's nation, whose lands were spoiled,
wanted revenge after frozen and boiled
in a seething cauldron of staged combats
by war-profiteering chartered pirates.
America had its Vietnam War,
and through Southeast Asia it ripped and tore.
Soviets invaded Afghanistan,
and were wrecked by the tribal Taliban.
Something Russia and America lost
through technology, bought at a high cost,
which isolates people from families,
are the rites of vendetta homilies.
So you make deals and quick compromises
for high-standard of living promises
from those who say they must be protected
for making their images reflected,
like Jehovah created Adam's face,
then capriciously spurned him from the place.

Gaining knowledge made Adam's god jealous,
who got angry revenge, quick and zealous.
Massive images float around the world,
each touting a banner to be unfurled.
Some have their own images on the flags,
spreading good and evil with their gene tags.
We do not try to control the chasms
wherein people have their own orgasms.
You are all like miniature Yawehs
seeking control of Eden's drama plays.
Each has within you a Garden of Bliss,
but to gain it you must choose ignorance,
which is easy to do with a fission
to computers or a television.
If Yaweh made Adam in god's image,
then god, too, did not have the privilege
of knowing good from evil, unaware,
thus made a reflection that did not care
if he was in bliss or surrounded by
polluted waters and acid rain sky.
One can no longer see Noah's rainbow
due to the curtain's filth in Heaven's show.
You will not have an image if you fail
to keep clean water in Earth's holy grail.
You shall see a distorted reflection
that is far removed from love's perfection,
unless you wish to fulfill silly books
that demand destruction until Earth cooks.
Is your god such a narcissistic fool
that it would dirty up its mirror pool
just to make you happy your oracles
of destruction are Heaven's miracles?
We do not believe that to prove its strength
god is compelled to such a stupid length
to grant your self-fulfilling prophecies
so you can say you follow its decrees.

Even your greatest hallucinations
chase and form their own deluded nations.
Was Yaweh as ignorant as humans
forming incestuous idiot clans?
Lot and his two daughters escaped ruin,
then bred together to form the next kin,
and in a cave they achieved ignorance,
and paradise by pedigree romance.
We chose not to partake in a story
told by the imbeciles' sound and fury
passed on through generations as it warps
like a Shakespeare drama becomes a corpse
banquet to display weekly distractions,
updated to fuel hollow actions.
He wrote of royalty family fights,
which are now inbred educated blights:
movie and novel versions are on sale
as students purchase a moronic tale,
keeping them stupid and good consumers,
with Soma to control all their humours,
except for knowledge that has its own fruit
and enlightenment beyond the astute
manipulation of the human will,
which people seed in others and then till,
forming leagues and regulations, then laws,
which they promise come from the Causeless Cause,
and will bring them to a great destiny,
if folks shall but serve on a bended knee.
Leaders forget that followers become
hunters like Great White Sharks after blood-chum.
For quite a while they might be directed
at supposed enemies, so selected
for their wealth and resources or oddness
as dire threats to lifestyles and happiness.
Or have followers turn upon their own,
to cannibalize and gnaw on a bone.

Yet since the energy has been misspent,
Ahab and Jezebel monarchs are rent,
even though from a royal lineage,
the hunters purge their leaders from the stage.
Bison and the sun were painted on caves
to forecast good hunting and solar waves,
but Louis XIV, known as the Sun King,
could not predict what the future might bring
to his royal heirs, who were preyed upon
as ghastly communion for a new dawn.
Transubstantiation is a high-stake
that feeds on those who say, 'Let them eat cake.'
We have seen it all: Tsars, kings, dictators,
and emirs served like a banquet caters.
Even the strongest individual
must confront a nature that is dual,
and the seeming contrariness of life
in the scenes for control of senses' strife.
If this is true for a single person,
then how is it for a father and son
or a conglomerate community,
where polar folks gather in a city,
village, or even at a single room,
meting their versions of enlightened doom?
We showed you your Eden is ignorant,
as is your legislator's lordly cant.
Will you be sullen like Prince Achilles,
fighting in Samsara's polluted brees,
drinking from the bitter cup of dregs' woes,
accepting your lot is to battle foes?
Vengeance stirs more passion in splintered strife
than patriotic pride for mundane life.
Genghis Khan allowed his conquered their choice
of religions, but warned them that their voice
praying for deliverance from Mongols,
though fine with him, would not prevent their skulls

and females from adorning Mongol tents
if the conquered were late on their payments.
So it was better just to pay up-front
and have votives to their gods take the brunt:
a far more practical comprehension
than bribing gas-ghosts of fourth-dimension.
You know now afterlife is but a myth,
invented to use soldiers as a scythe.
Note: those in power condemned a peasant,
who taught life on Earth would be unpleasant
for those who followed him to god's kingdom,
and to accept life is a destined slum.
So he promised, and those in power work
to fulfill oracles where shadows lurk.
Buddha also taught life is misery,
which he escaped under a lotus tree.
It seems with joyful, deliberate care
people purposely destroy land and air.
On your right is an oil refinery
that burns for America's finery,
creating a Hell to doom people's soul,
while you play a vapid Heavenly role.
What have you built with all that energy,
but chains to screens in the guise you are free?
You fight for cultures influenced by jinns
who need blood transfusions to relieve sins
of promiscuity of bestial grades
inherited by a monkey with AIDS.
Like Vlad Tepes Dracul was not alone
in his Garden of Sorrows, so the tone
of tortured beasts by rock-and-roll guitars
gathers an audience for big-mouthed stars.
Finally, society abandons
them to live like Dahmer in Cyclop dens.
But the *Iliad* and the *Odyssey*
are replaced in your land by a jinn's fee

of buying souls for fame through diverse songs
that the scholars study while doing bongs.
You look deep in thought on the eternal,
nor are you the first warrior to mull.
Achilles fought for trophies and long tales
of his exploits in battle, which entails
his desire for revenge against Hector,
as they fought for breeding-rights at Troy's shore.
Hindu Arjuna asked a deity
if slaying kin is part of fealty.
The answer was one must do his duty
without hope for reward or great trophies.
The lesson was wrote in epic strophes
that to conquer and win gains Earth's glories;
lose, and one achieves a Heavenly realm,
steered through Samsara with god at the helm.
Krishna taught to kill in detached fashion,
Achilles murdered in wrathful passion.
Can you learn anything from those extremes,
when friends become foes in illusion dreams?
Trophies mean nothing, Noriega learned
when Bush gave him a medal that he earned,
then betrayed him in a dope-deal gone bad,
pounding some one small because Bush was mad.
Maybe hemorrhoids were bothering him;
the world lives at the mercy of a whim.
Ralph Ellison met white Olympians,
who played with black people like champions
at a chapel, deciding black folks' fate,
with an insane, shady afterlife state
after being expelled from a college
where White Man's Burden was taught as knowledge.
Behind ivy walls of the garden scenes,
progress toiled blacks as fodder for machines.
What do people learn? That money buys kings,
and that breeding eventually brings

monarchs to chapels where more hatred sings.
An intriguing fact of the *Iliad*
is 'tis not a ranting jeremiad:
humans at Troy did not fight over gods
needing men's defense like thorns on seed pods.
'Tis easy to demonize enemies
to rally fervor, and drive to the knees
any dissenters for a human cause
beyond sacred books writ as if god's laws.
You no longer face worthy opponents,
but finding them strange, kill from a distance.
Achilles' revenge, and blood on his hand,
is something most Yanks do not understand,
thus fail to see that primitive structures
can be invested with loving allures.
Time and money spent on mere images
mass-produces technology mages.
Hindu warriors are told to slash through
the false illusions of Samsara's brew,
killing without hate, as battles are fought,
nor to love foes, unlike what you are taught.
And thus soldiers protect a populace
who sit before a modem-screen's palace.
It is an irony worth a good laugh
a prankster could write as an epitaph:
"Here lies a soldier who fought illusions
sold on the market with the collusions
of the consumers and corporations
that build homogenous screen-world nations.
He fought to support lives of escapement
into one-dimension entertainment.
The part he played added to the small sums
of images that flicker as phantoms.
Everyone wants a tailor-made version
to spread through the air-waves with dispersion
that shepherds others to Heaven's city

to shear and slaughter a community.
Did he do great deeds? What does it matter,
if existence itself becomes flatter
than when ancients thought the world was not round,
and Atlas's shoulders had the Earth bound?
Work brings with it a contrary treasure,
so get lost in one-dimension pleasure."'
The spirits laughed at the unseemly jest,
and Stan knew victory could not be wrest
from Soma-induced hallucinations
that enjoyed freedom with great elations.
He wanted to say: 'But have I not fought
for you and freedom that cannot be bought?'
Stan felt he was in a large theater,
and American faces seemed a blur
watching as he queried the vanities
of a god who blesses or damns cities.
And worse: humans are mere karmic levers
to mete out justice that binds or severs,
altering like the flick of a channel,
going from purity to the carnal.
As that thought struck Stan, the spirits vanished,
and felt humanity had him banished.
He seemed caught in the Americans' dreams,
as their consciousness gathered, patched in seams,
to guide and be guided through the battle,
with the awareness of bullied cattle.
He wished to explain to his audience
that war-craft is an art, not a science.
Human conduct goes beyond all theories,
what an opponent might do makes queries
into the whole history of the Earth,
from nativity to funeral berth.
Genghis Khan knew how to craft a war's plan,
yet he was a lone, exceptional man,
who formed an empire and fulfilled intent,

then rode off from it to his homeland's tent.
For all that could be gained then was intrigues
among his Gold Horde's conspiring leagues;
there was nothing left to do except lose,
or get drunk on fermented mare's milk booze.
So he rode his pony to the sunrise
as if the world was not enough a prize.
As Stan tried to shape his thoughts into words,
it seemed he could hear some bellowing herds,
like the bygone eras of that region
when soil was ripe for the farmers' legion.
He turned and saw three members of his squad
slinking across sand-dunes as though unshod.
"Christ, there you are. We have to get you back.
Now Sarajevo is under attack,
and we have orders to advise Muslims
on how to combat killer Christian whims."

18

Love and Weapons

Baal Clinton took a tremendous bribe
from a corporate monopoly tribe
that controlled the computer market's course,
so the government's lawsuit had no force.
The battles to end all competitions
was also a mandate among nations
that sought to incorporate in one soul
homogenous distractions for control
of their consumers' psyches through mandates
that globalized a trade center for states.
Corporations were granted the powers
of unlimited bribes from their towers,
destroying myths that nurtured the schism
of rugged individualism,
which Americans pride themselves upon,
as they are controlled like a chessboard pawn,
who is quickly sacrificed to distract
attention from the world-puppeteer's act.
When young, Bill Clinton had made it his chore
to protest his country's Vietnam War
while he studied at college in England
as a pacifist who had world peace planned.
While president, he enjoyed bombing sites
in Bosnia and Iraq, and their plights

were shown onscreen to a pleased audience,
glad for a distraction from Bill's dropped pants.
He would ensure peace among Bosnians
like a great deity who smote peons.
Russia was too deep in debt to respond,
as its new capitalist state had dawned,
and the Soviet empire was finished,
for satellite states found freedom as wished.
Yet in villages and among cities
people fought for their new identities,
and forced their images upon women,
which to Charles was an ironic omen
of rapine and murder that reflected
the moral core which Baal selected.
He was no fighter like Agamemnon,
though Baal demanded his seeds be sown,
and women were prizes who he would seize
like Agamemnon took from Achilles.
Charles had not replaced his old hate with love,
and the revenge-machine made him think of
Paris avenging brother Hector's death
by stealing away Achilles' last breath.
Clinton's supporters thought him civilized
for not marauding through the countryside
like the Bosnian and Serb Christian feasts
after years of being chained like wild beasts.
Charles predicted that as humans are caged,
like the global corporations have staged,
there will come a time of freedom's anger,
when tensions become an unleashed danger.
People would stay happy only so long
as they are given choices for a song,
but when a much-loved and favorite lay
is deemed subversive and taken away,
and replaced by weekly retarded tunes
mass-manufactured from parties of goons,

people will branch-out to invent their own,
and though they may have similar seeds sown,
vast original cultures will evolve
with new stars as the firmaments revolve.
As Mustafa decided on a plan,
judging his uncle's murder was by Stan
through oblique tracking of information
up for sale in the desperate nation,
Mustafa's excitement overcame fear
the wrong man might be slain; the case was clear.
Makya, the hotel clerk, could buy records
of the night Stan cut Al-Shaila's life cords.
Makya wanted hard justice to be done
to appease god for the lies Makya spun,
which had destroyed Shaklur through perjury,
and would bring down Allah's awesome fury.
Makya was approached by Shaklur's lawyer
and shown records of the hotel's foyer,
where Al-Shailah staggered in Stanley's grip
to keep from listing like a foundered ship.
Makya asked why videos were not shown
at trial, and the lawyer loosed a groan:
"It was obvious Shaklur was dead meat,
and I cannot do miracles of feat.
I work with those people for a living
and do not want them mad, but forgiving,
at least to me, if not my customers,
for the law is like a screen full of blurs.
What is popular one day changes soon,
like our calendar centered on the moon.
People now miss Shaklur and mourn his loss:
he is reformed by the media's gloss.
They would want blood for records you lied of,
wreck you for a false resurrection's love.
Why chance it when you can buy this vision
like a mullah on a sacred mission?

Now granted, it might not be from our god,
but it could be the destiny you trod.
So gather your wits and try to be nice.
I will return next week, please have my price."
In terror, Makya knew the lawyer's plot
would reduce Makya to a bloody clot,
nor would it end with just one extortion,
but steal his entire life saving's portion.
He accepted he deserved punishment
for lying to keep his life being rent,
yet it seemed it was out of symmetry
in a system run on false piety.
Truthfulness was demanded from the poor
and middle class, who were shown Heaven's door
by echelons who could not be trusted
to manage life on Earth, as they lusted
for possessions like jinn without justice.
So how could they know of Heavenly bliss,
except to base it on experience
of their large gardens, women, and mansions,
basing a Heaven on their crude passions?
Makya decided his back earned no rod,
taking his chance with leniency from god.
If Makya was to be punished for lies,
it would not be from jinn in lawyer's guise.
And to stoke Allah's wrath through the blackmail
would assure Makya's Last Judgment would fail
in keeping him from the grips of devils
like those at the hotel's highest levels.
As the clerk, he had witnessed many things
while the nations converged like drunken kings
celebrating a victory of loot.
Perhaps it was where their Heaven took root,
and it was Makya's job to bade welcome
with catamites, females, or opium.
He faced the truth and it was too gritty

to allow much space for integrity.
His fabrications were like a Black Hole
that threatened to destroy body and soul.
Each way Makya turned brought sorrow and grief,
so he went to Mustafa for relief,
whose heart's vigor leapt like a warrior.
A meeting was arranged with the lawyer.
Makya agreed on the price he was told,
and after the video had been sold
in a hotel room at Makya's work site,
the lawyer drank some gin, for he felt tight
and anxious that his scheme might go awry,
so cordially drank and loosened his tie.
Makya left the room with the door ajar,
and Mustafa entered, ready to spar.
There was an unwritten ethic for trade
that the hotel be safe from any raid,
as it was bad business to let murder
disrupt the strict, unnatural order
Saddam and Baal imposed on Iraq,
and both would levy a counterattack.
The lawyer believed this and let a yell
when he saw a foe would send him to Hell.
But Makya had chosen a soundproof room
that, like Hell, kept tight the fierce howls of doom.
Mustafa: "You studied the legal bar
where you learned to push Allah's law too far,
and even hotel clerks know right from wrong
better than you with your gibberish song.
If you want to live and continue deeds
of planting your destructive corrupt seeds,
hand over the rest of the videos
you plan to use in a blackmailer's pose
before you change again to a law sage
with a cultivated sneering image
before the cameras, as you defend

wealthy clients in a world of pretend,
full of disguises, like records you sold,
fleecing the flock in your pageantry fold."
The gin had effected the lawyer's head,
and his impulse of fear sank to mild dread:
"Our enemies use screens to mandate laws,
campaigning to rewrite their legal cause.
With a flick of a button each trial
can be watched to provoke tears or a smile.
It is bargained as an entertainment
and putrid versions of The Last Judgment.
Shakespeare wrote of a rebel named Jack Cade,
whose foremost law, until he was unmade:
'First thing, kill all the lawyers', but his purge
was drained of energy and lost its surge.
If an actor does not run out of lines,
and is just with foes, as the show entwines
various meetings with other players,
who may fancy themselves dragon-slayers;
as I say, when the situation comes,
one must change his tune to what the beat strums,
and be whatever justice passes for
as humans adapt to progressive lore.
And if that reasoning does not suffice,
I can howl some more, which is imprecise,
yet should be enough to rescue my life
from your active notions of bitter strife."
Mustafa disbelieved in this man's fame
and his conviction that truth was a game
to be bought as the only objective,
since justice and truth were both subjective.
Mustafa had his doubts of the *Koran*,
but that was just part of being human.
And he had done terrible things, which pride
may have been used to have it justified
by the faith that Allah was on his side

in the perpetual wars of Iraq,
where few were trusted from intrigue's attack.
It seemed each person in his loved nation
had suffered from a complete partition:
when the land is divided from the soul,
one goes insane or grabs another role.
Some clung to the *Koran* through fealty,
not knowing where else to place loyalty.
If personal relationships are wrecked,
it is natural for most to select
a greater form or divine entity
to bestow a stable identity.
And if that is hijacked by extremists
to guide the people from the darkened mists,
then radicals will also sow distrust,
and likewise be reaped into clouds of dust.
Mustafa wondered in vain at his role,
being used to behind-the-scenes control.
He would not return as a mere hired gun
when his revenge thirst was imbibed and done.
He did not think Allah a general
of wars or in fights that were personal,
because then Allah would have to switch sides
in human's fickle grope to where abides
any truth crafted in book metaphors
that promise journeys to Heavenly shores.
Honesty changed through various phases,
but Allah did not evolve by phrases
that were written to monopolize truth
in books, prayers, or the confession booth.
A wave of fatigue hit Mustafa's guts.
At one time he was like a bull that ruts,
and violence had come easy and quick,
guided by the state like carrot and stick.
The lawyer was still moving his vain lips,
revealing Allah's planned apocalypse,

and that Mustafa should not be a judge
or executioner who held a grudge.
For that was what Jews and Christians wanted
as they manipulated and haunted
Muslims into killing one another,
who should coexist as equal brother.
Mustafa said: "You think god caused the fight
among Ibrihim's kin to lead to light
whoever evolves to the newest faiths,
leaving the old behind, lost like jinn wraiths.
God does not abandon people or change
by breeding newer truths to rearrange
words and covenants like a packaged deal
that bribe with gifts to our senses' appeal.
You became so corrupt you are convinced
every one else also has the truth minced
into little pieces to use for gain,
and Allah also has that kind of stain.
I hope you better prepare your life's case
for your Last Judgment before truthful grace."
Mustafa did not stir up his kill urge,
though he wished to free the world in a purge
of people like the lawyer, lacking traits
of goodness, who hooked with lies of barbed baits
lost souls away from decent lawful states.
Yet if Mustafa did not kill the man,
it would harm the chance of murdering Stan.
For the lawyer would tell his legal friends
Mustafa was working to his own ends,
perhaps feral and going renegade
against systems that reflect what god made.
Mustafa had a vision of Helen's
vaunted beauty, her breasts like ripe melons,
a human portion of Aphrodite,
strong-willed but gregarious and flighty.
A god's love for its vain mirror image

shapes conflict even for the smallest midge
that thoughtlessly breeds the next lineage,
who is exterminated as it feeds
on the dreck of gnawed pomegranate seeds.
Who do I identify myself with,
Mustafa wondered: a fact or a myth?
Could he reinvent himself by an act
of revenge if he were careful in tact?
He shook his head to clear it and proceed
to cleanse his vengeance path of every seed,
so they could not grow like versions of him,
warped and monstrous in the past's light, so dim
in his conscious he forgets they mushroom
from rank manure, spreading forth to consume
all he holds dear through a vast explosion
when past cycles deny future vision.
Yet he was not a Hindu who believed
in cosmic karma, where it was perceived
that each thought and gesture caused contraries,
so meditate all day and eat berries.
He felt inactive enough, without force,
to fret about the universe's course,
and how his soul fit through for escape routes
into a Beingless Being that flouts
every human endeavor to wreckage,
just to prove it is beyond timeless age.
Those who tried to be free through positions
in various yoga meditations
had to listen to jargon and speeches
by acclaimed authority who teaches
that all is an illusion of some craft,
and bodies should be abandoned as daft.
Mustafa would rather receive hard hits
than contemplate a lecture while he sits.
He gazed at the lawyer, who babbled forth
Iraq had foes to the east, south, and north,

who must be confounded by any means
for Muslims to unite at Heaven's scenes.
Religious duty and family-ties
were appealed to Mustafa with crazed cries.
Mustafa decided not to explain
if Shaklur had been cleared of intrigue's stain
by the lawyer fulfilling his right task,
and Jacob was unveiled behind his mask,
there would be no need for further evil
and life could return to being civil,
or what passes for it in the nation
that reflects Allah's civilization:
evolved from nomad shepherds on the roam,
to lead Passover ghosts to people's home.
As it was, Mustafa's life had been leased,
and he had grown weary of being fleeced.
Too many blood-drops sprinkled too few doors,
and bombs fell as fighter-airplanes did tours.
Mustafa was his father's firstborn son,
and would get revenge on the right person.
The lawyer, through his guile, was in the way,
convinced by his own lies he deserved pay,
or at least be allowed to continue
his deceitful life in the court's venue.
But when he saw his words had no effect,
he pled as if to be humbly perfect,
admitting some flaws, but ignoring most,
in such a manner it seemed a great boast
that he would bring himself to low levels
of admitting he had dealt with devils,
yet could reform because he still felt pure
and in the hands of Allah, who can cure.
Mustafa no longer heard what was said,
and calmly shot the lawyer in his head.
When sure the body departed from soul,
Mustafa requested trash disposal,

and Makya sent up workers for the chore
of corpse removal and cleaning the gore.
It was part of the hotel's secret trade
to earn compensation and be well-paid
if the science of business turned to blood
and people were reduced to clay and mud,
and purify the rooms of evidence
to thwart all forensic mechanized sense.
The security videos were changed
so it would seem the lawyer rearranged
his day's schedule, in case someone was told
the lawyer had work, an hour to be sold
at the hotel, meeting a customer
who was happy to be a consumer.
All the proof of the lawyer's arrival,
and his failure to bid for survival,
was purged by the security sages
who erased his last living images.
Perhaps he was writ into the pages
of *The Book of the Dead*, and went to Hell,
where demons do not care what lawyer's sell,
but corruption can always recognize
itself in others, no matter the size.
Some react with hypocritical hate
when they see their own flaws in others' state.
A few thousand years of tilling the damned,
including celebrities full of hammed
self-importance for their posed swinish oinks,
would be as tiresome as self-induced poinks.
Mustafa's vocation entailed the art
of forcing victims and their wealth to part,
hunting them if they had fled from Iraq
because of the Coalition's attack.
While most surrendered their wealth at his threats,
others were tortured to their long regrets.
He tried to make it be impersonal,

detaching himself while staying stable,
watching as his victims faded then woke
to great pain their consciousness could not cloak.
When Mustafa saw how his uncle died
at someone's pleasure, without being tried,
Mustafa became aware his victims
had loving families that Hussein's whims
for comforts and a life of convenience
had split asunder with terrible rents.
Mustafa could no longer disengage
from his third-dimension's horrid image.
He saw who he was and bitterly wept
that his true ideals had somehow crept
away from him, leaving only the screen
which showed the hotel's security scene
of Stan guiding Al-Shailah from his room
and through the lobby to an oily doom.
Mustafa felt passion, deeming it strange
his life of violence could ever change
from cold calculation and detachment
to a loathing filled with self-resentment.
He watched the video play out fate's thread
in his patriarchs' library, and said:
"Just one more kill, god, then I will be through,
and shall adopt orphans to pay my due.
I worked and thought myself into madness,
living on other people's great duress,
as does this Stanley Jacob, who I blame
though I do not know who started this game,
where behind the scenes soldiers like me lurk,
also used as front-men for dirty work.
I tortured and killed more than one hostage
like Americans guard freedom's image."
Mustafa wiped his nose and crushed a tear,
then paused the screen at Stan in disguised leer.
Mustafa had contraband photographs

of Coalition leaders and their staffs.
He did not keep them on his computers
because of the professional looters
who would scan into Iraq's covert groups
to ferret information on the troops.
Mustafa had Stan as the prime suspect,
who traveled under a guise to inspect
sites for weapons being built or purchased,
like prior decades, at Hussein's behest.
Stan's true job was to sell information
to the high-bid from a corporation.
There were no weapons of mass destruction,
but global intrigue on oil production.
Mustafa felt he hung in the balance
as he matched Stan's pictures of resemblance.
He said softly: "Your armor is gone now,
and Allah will help me fulfill my vow."
Mustafa sat calmly to clear his head,
then contacted his informant who said
the inspectors and troops were leaving soon,
but Stan was found drunk upon a sand-dune,
and though his comrades tried to get him straight,
insane echoes resounded a bad state,
so they took him to a woman he had,
to bring him back from the worlds of the mad.
Stan's squad did not report to high command
his condition because he might be banned
from duties, and his rank could be broken,
losing his title and medal's token.
Mustafa asked for and got the address
of the woman with healing strength to dress
Stan's mental terrors, which were self-induced
in seeking a great spiritual boost.
The informant took what Mustafa paid,
and calmly commented, stoic and staid:
"If you and this fellow mix up a storm,

and I feel any heat, or even warm
from the blast of an investigation,
and you are caught in an inquisition
to be tortured to tell all your contacts,
like you use to collect wealth from bad wracks,
I will have you killed by inside sources
who work both sides of the engaged forces.
They will gladly take such a bounty fee,
so your best bet is to leave that house free
if you gamble on a conflict's campaign,
as you seem intent on inflicting pain."
Mustafa gazed at the man who sold death,
and felt passions stir, but with a calm breath
said: "We are like a parasite and host
feeding on each other until a ghost
is all that is left of our relation,
which is certain to find no elation
when Allah decrees a final judgment,
for both of us are filled with bad intent."
The informant laughed: "You sound like you mull
as sinner become evangelical.
You must be getting too old for the job,
or have heard too many penitents sob
when you take their wealth like an angry bawd
for our cheated whore country, which you laude.
We drink the foam down to the bitter dregs
like a fallen drunkard ascetic begs
for fuel to go onward in actions,
as resources are stolen by factions
who play us off against one another,
though you call us all a Muslim brother.
If they desire to make us fight ourselves,
I say we take a playbook from their shelves
and use espionage against the foes,
making them choke, like Shiva, on our woes."
Mustafa: "I do not deny the hue

of the gorged necks should turn a mottled blue.
It happens now as they gag on the fumes
of the genies' gas that also consumes
the world's atmosphere to a rolling boil,
as life's deathly ocean drowns the tilled soil.
Yet I search for a greater loyalty
than a promised Heaven bought for a fee.
I have spent my life doing such labor,
being the edge our nation's saber,
so I no longer differentiate
myself from those who I am paid to hate."
The other: "The common American
believes in the ancient Rome god, Vulcan,
who forges great weapons for special folks,
and wed to laughter's darling, whose sex jokes
with the war-god caught them in a net's snare
of machinery hid in Vulcan's lair.
And though he and Venus were god and wife,
they worked against each other at Troy's strife.
The point of my tale is we all get caught
in intrigue for death's tools or sex we bought.
Choose what you want to invest and how much,
but thick armor cannot prevent love's touch.
Achilles was destined to lose trophies
like Briseis in the *Iliad* strophes,
and yet Achilles was granted a boon
for revenge at Patroclus' ruin:
Vulcan's armor that Achilles received
as his fate's course, for which he was conceived.
Here is a pistol, American-made,
for you to turn a body into shade."
Mustafa took the gun and walked away:
stones to throw at a kingdom's feet of clay.
When he was home, he made sure it fired right,
and settled accounts the rest of the night.
He arranged the finances in order,

having cash sent within the Swiss border,
knowing the irony of what he did,
as it was his job to retrieve wealth hid
in other nations by a countryman
who rigged accounts at the isles of Cayman.
He completed paperwork for a tithe,
a large sum that would make Ashia writhe.
He laid next to Sofia for an hour,
perhaps for the last time in their bower.
She awoke and he kissed her on the cheek,
then asked her to dance before she could speak.
She became excited and spun and whirled
as she forgot the dream that had unfurled
while she slept, seeking to make an escape
from a single eye that took fiery shape,
which gazed at her with unrelenting glare,
laying all of her hopes and desires bare.
When she finished dancing she stretched her limbs
while Mustafa talked as if on crazed whims,
saying their family must leave that morn,
and if he was killed soon, she was to mourn
properly, and then open the letter
he sent to an Egyptian investor.
They would be safe in Cairo at his home,
and travel to Mecca to see the dome,
making the pilgrimage each Muslim ought,
after touring pyramids gone to rot.
He did not want them to have enemies
who would grab all their cash and quickly seize
the family's assets and their estates,
driven by greed that gobbling never sates.
Then call it justice to pay a blood-price,
as Americans loot, not thinking twice
of the debt they incur against god's laws,
believing they channel the Causeless Cause.
He did not go with her to the airport,

but sat alone in the house garden's court,
smelling her sleepy scent on his fingers
like a lilac smell a soft breeze lingers
on a spring evening, when new life awakes
and is enjoyed, for 'tis known summer takes
it to a dormant state, and only thought
can resurrect the odor the wind brought.
He licked his lips, reveling the savor
of when she brushed her teeth with mint flavor,
and how she quietly urged the children
to hug him then sit in the cab's sedan.
There had been no luggage, except the veils,
which she adorned with Arabian tales
in stitching that glowed with many details.
She only wore them at open functions
where the married women shared conjunctions,
and colorful apparel could be worn
to display fruits an active brain had borne.
Mustafa watched the sun rise through the trees,
his mind stirred by conflicting reveries.
The dead were gone and he owed them no debt,
but to his land's poor, whom he sometimes met,
he owed payments he did not want to make,
and core systems had a blood-price at stake.
He must settle the past to continue,
and death would open another venue.
He had watched the wealth of Iraq's nation
passed along to the next generation
with little or no fealty to god's
commandment the poor not be struck with rods,
rather, lifted and embraced as Muslims,
all voices together in *Koran* hymns.
Instead, the wealthy gave counsel to foes,
as well as the resources god bestows,
while reliant on global charities,
and even those goods, the wealthy would seize.

He did his duty by Saddam Hussein,
taking a solemn oath that turned profane.
Mustafa was done with the baroque masque,
he would no longer hide behind wealth's mask.
He checked his weapons and cleaned the pistol,
then inhaled a garden flower's pistil.

19

The Birthplace of Countless Lies

Stan met Marge at his troops' Catholic Mass,
and her neighborhood was once middle-class
that had slowly eroded to a slum,
with outlaw murmurs like a bee-hive's hum.
She wanted a better neighborhood's house
instead of stockings, a negligee blouse,
and other cheap gifts he brought in visits,
buying her food requests on ration-chits.
He sent most of his paycheck to his wife,
telling Margaret he was bound for life.
She often mentioned the chance of divorce;
though he did not want to mislead their course,
he sometimes played along with her vain hope
so she would be vivacious and not mope.
Hostilities occurred when they last met,
for she felt his promises owed a debt.
Stanley was leaving her and the nation's
war-torn and strung-out wicked sensations.
She followed him around her living-room
as he packed, noticing she lost her bloom.
Margaret spoke English and native tongue,
with military lingo as she sung
hymns of her dreams turning into nightmares,
and her lusterless fields were thick with tares

that he had planted among her rich grain,
plowing her to seed an unholy stain.
She said: "I told them not to leave you here,
babbling insanely of your darkest fear,
and now that I helped you, you leave again,
keeping me trapped in this spidery den."
Stan: "You do not understand my nation's
enthrallment by image reputations.
I wish not to be of the hypocrites
who rave of family values, then splits
from a tiresome wife and children to chase
the first skirt to come along, like a race
competition to spread a gene-tag's trace.
Too, we would be excommunicated
if we were to be legally mated,
and that would make my father disown me.
I do not want a banishment decree."
She replied: "You could get an annulment
from your wife and achieve our fulfillment.
You said they are granted in your region
to keep churches stocked with a faith's legion.
I am sure the upper-hierarchies
prefer their own order than anarchies,
so make a deal with them for us to wed.
You are not Henry the Eighth with a bed
of revolving wives, trying to maintain
a lineage of a Papal blessed reign."
Stan: "My intentions were not to deceive,
it was your ill-fated star to receive
what I had to offer in love's disguise,
which seemed to fit us in a real size.
You are too good for me in some matters,
but trust too much in a tongue that flatters.
Consider this a learning exercise,
and when I am gone you can exorcise
the demons I planted so deep it hurt,

hoeing the weeds I sowed in fertile dirt."
Margaret crumpled in a heap and wept,
but Stan had no time to think how adept
he had become at watching lives destroyed,
for his own balance teetered on a void.
His strength returned and his hands did not shake,
yet he felt an interior earthquake.
He functioned on intelligent instinct,
though felt desert wraiths still had him chain-linked.
Near his hometown he camped in the Badlands,
where strata of rocks revealed fossil strands,
and the various evolving ages
seemed an open volume of Earth's pages.
Maddox and he admired what glaciers made,
which no human could compete with in trade.
He handed to Margaret Charles' gold ring
for respite from the barbed, unpleasant sting.
She could give it to someone with no vow
of raging hate and vengeance to endow.
She threw the ring into a far corner
and hung her head like an angry mourner.
She could not bring herself to chant verses
in a litany of dreaded curses
in hopes of destroying Stan with god's help.
As if Jesus Christ answered every yelp,
and a god of love could be used for hate,
which Margaret thought of as Satan's bait,
winning her over to the demons' side,
where vengeance is gained but no lights abide.
Margaret: "You will get what you deserve,
Stan, though I shall not be the one to serve
your banquet of misfortune and despair.
I will laugh in Heaven while demons tear
you into little pieces to be sold
like you use global markets to unfold
the plans and schemes for your greedy nation

in their efforts to buy domination.
My countrymen are split by your plunder,
but you also will be torn asunder,
because it is not just you and your peers,
your nation consists of war-profiteers
as Clinton sold you cheap oil for eight years.
Despite the claims you build peaceful world tribes,
you are like a Communist who takes bribes.
Everything in your country is packaged
and sold as if it is what god imaged
for your ambition of a perfect soul,
and there is no script for me in a role."
Stan: "Our tales guide us to something better,
adapting to spirits' law of letter,
not sticking to one book's order of rule,
which is warped to the whims of a cruel
tyrant whose land reflects his sordid grace,
with no hope to escape his glaring face.
You would not be happy in my nation,
my region scowls at miscegenation.
I would have to move from Rapid City,
to them, our love is an audacity.
I only give you their own opinion,
which pervades my family's dominion,
and I would resent you for their hatred
that marriage to you will have spun and bred.
My brother got involved with an Asian,
and he was disowned for the occasion.
Now he works on a corporate farm-land,
losing the dairy business he had planned
on inheriting, working for long years,
making profits for my dad and his peers
who had invested in our dairy trade.
That was Reuben's reward for being staid."
Margaret: "You create vast excuses
like poets invent beautiful Muses,

all the while hiding behind crafted light
to justify hateful things poets write.
You blame destiny or even a god,
while you covertly venerate and laude
your self-image for keeping clear and free
as you evade responsibility.
Go somewhere else to find a new life's lease.
Get out now before I call the police."
Mustafa parked his car three blocks away
from Margaret's house, and he heard the fray
of hysteria, though Stan's voice was clear.
Mustafa strolled languidly, drawing near.
A member of Stan's squad sat in a jeep
outside the house, and it was time to reap
his aspiring military life
with the cut-throat blade of Mustafa's knife,
who deliberately wore tattered clothes
to suit the neighborhood and fulfill oaths.
He was barely glanced at by Stan's squad-ride,
who saw Mustafa in a beggar's hide.
The driver dead, Mustafa breathed relief,
his revenge compulsion was a belief.
He stood outside the wall, near the front door,
and raised his pistol, hearing the old floor
of the house creak as Stan made his way out,
his subconscious thought prepared for a bout
as Stan left, putting on his steel helmet,
the bullet careening as forces met.
Stan fell in a deaf faint from the missile,
but Mustafa did not linger or mill.
He saw Stan down and the helmet dented,
knowing revenge and death were prevented.
Mustafa aimed again at Stanley's chest,
but Margaret leaped forth, trying to wrest
the weapon with a frantic move, though bold,
and the two stumbled over the threshold.

She bit at his face and grappled to scratch,
but for his skilled talent she was no match.
She fell to the ground and grabbed at his legs,
like sick pariahs at the bottom dregs
cling to passersby for relief or cure,
'til driven away to keep the land pure.
So Mustafa kicked at her hands and head,
blurring her vision from gashes that bled.
Stan faded in and out of a stupor,
dreaming he was amidst a thick vapor,
with dim lights above that glittered as guides,
promising 'twas where love's knowledge abides.
Warning voices steered him away from it,
saying the light tempted him to a pit,
so Stan awoke from the waning deep dream.
His commander had sent men of the team
to the neighborhood to investigate
the cause for delaying flight from the state,
convinced that Stan wanted one last embrace
with a familiar lover in smooth lace
before going to Bosnia's ripped land,
where finding a new lover could be banned.
The women there suffered rapine traumas,
and might avoid any love-play dramas.
Troops' good luck might hold if hurt women think,
offered food, comfort, and something to drink,
carnal love is the reward men desire,
thus be sacrifices on a sex-pyre.
Some people's work is to make others fit,
destroying self-esteem or bloating it.
Thus the squad traveled to Stanley's safe-home,
hoping Stan had been allowed no beer foam,
for his boozing had increased as months passed,
and he had been warned so he felt harassed.
Mustafa broke free of Margaret's grip,
as Stan leveled the pistol from his hip.

He fired, barely conscious, and saw the fall
of his wounded foe, who let out no call.
Mustafa was hit on his left torso,
and the bullet went through from the fierce blow.
Margaret crawled away from the combat,
and neighbors stayed clear, used to the format
of violent rituals, like herd beasts
Americans prepared for ghastly feasts.
Stan tried to adjust his vision for death
to descend on his foe, drawing last breath.
Mustafa gasped, laying flat on his back,
and his fingers probed the wound for the flak,
unaware that it had passed through his shape.
He plotted murder and how to escape,
while Stan staggered at him to end the fight,
though Stan could not focus hearing or sight.
He fired blindly, the missile struck the floor,
as Mustafa quickly sat up and tore
at Stan's legs, hoping to reach a weapon,
for the pistols were dropped as the foes spun.
Stan fell atop Mustafa and they rolled
like a heap of flesh, bound into one mold,
being reduced to beasts' survival states,
each releasing his fierce animal traits.
Stan's fingers drilled one of Mustafa's eyes,
so they fought blindly, intent on demise.
Mustafa grabbed Stan's hair and yanked his head,
while their fluids mingled from wounds that bled,
which weakened them to bitter exhaustion,
draining energy's life-giving potion.
Stan gripped Mustafa's ears, trying to pound
and fracture his skull against the tiled ground.
Mustafa grabbed a knife from Jacob's sheath,
wanting to stab the liver from underneath
Stan's bulk, but there was no space between them,
as if sewn together by fated hem.

Stan's squad arrived and saw the driver dead,
so set up a perimeter instead
of invading where Margaret cried out,
as she gave Mustafa a brutal clout.
He lost awareness for a dire moment,
watching past scenes whirl as if Heaven-sent.
Stan staggered to his feet and almost fell,
not hearing the command his squad let yell
for all persons in the house to lay flat,
with hands on their heads or be a death stat.
Margaret dropped down and grabbed Jacob's knees,
but he did not comprehend her wild pleas.
She pointed outside but he could not look,
while Mustafa saw angels he forsook.
He stirred awake and his hand found a gun,
firing blind at Stan, who thought the fight done.
The shot broke a mirror, which was a gift
Stan bought to heal her vain emotions' rift.
He spun back to Mustafa's broken form
as the squad's leader ordered a fire-storm
in response to the shot inside the house,
and the fusillade was a heavy douse.
The missiles tore through Stan and he collapsed,
moments later his time on Earth elapsed.
The squad was unaware Stan was murdered,
and after a cease-fire had been ordered,
they went through the house by front and back-doors,
finding mayhem that shook them to their cores.
A medic was demanded with a cry,
but an Iraq hospital was nearby,
and the Coalition's medical groups
were airlifted before inspector troops.
Stan's shattered body revealed no life-signs,
bullets cratered him like Earth by strip-mines.
A pulse was found in Mustafa, though faint,
and death gave the close air a wicked taint.

Margaret told them of how the foes strived,
and in brief time the ambulance arrived.
The leader ordered three men to travel
to the clinic and try to unravel
the mystery of the chaotic fight
by questioning Mustafa at first sight
of him regaining any conscious states,
as Margaret denied she knew his traits.
At the hospital Doctor Ib Karzan
recognized Mustafa, and formed a plan.
The doctor knew a battle had occurred,
and wasting time on Stan would be absurd.
Mustafa went often to the clinics
to amuse the children with his antics,
and joke or tell ancient Iraq fables,
working at puzzles on the ward tables.
Doctor Karzan checked Mustafa's bashed head,
then to the American soldiers said:
"I doubt there is much hope in saving him,
he lost much blood and his pupil is dim.
Wheel him into the operating room,
where it is certain he will meet his doom."
Once there, Ib Karzan said to his nurses
they could have his love or angry curses,
depending on if Mustafa survived,
free of enemies, as Karzan contrived.
The nurses knew Mustafa and agreed
they would aid Karzan with what he might need.
Karzan: "Take him to the morgue and give word
to Doctor Fasil, and make him assured
that I take responsibility for
what happens, but because his surgeon's lore
is better than mine, we need his skilled poise.
Do not let our patient move or make noise.
A sedative now might kill our fellow,
so we must risk he stays in his dream-flow

as you wheel him, well-covered, past the guards.
I will scatter their wits like broken shards."
It was accomplished while Karzan argued
with soldiers whose wrath was also imbued
by knowing they had killed Stan, and vengeance
was required, but Karzan kept a firm stance:
"The Iraqi is dead. We will perform
the proper rituals for his mauled form.
It is against our religion to slice
a dead body, no matter how precise.
He is Muslim, I gather from your hate,
let him go to Heaven in a full state.
You have your own man to prepare for rites,
and this is my clinic and we have rights,
just as you defend the democracies
for micro-managed world oligarchies.
You must obey rules or show cause why not,
as we civilians are tired of your rot.
I answer to the Chief Staff Director,
and my wife who sits as queen of my core.
You are neither of them, so take your leave
and go where 'tis most fitting to bereave."
The troops lacked orders from chain-of-command,
thus Mustafa escaped as it was planned,
for the squad was not accustomed to strong
Iraqi resistance, despite the wrong
suffered by the legal occupation
mandated through the world's Coalition.
At another hospital surgery
was done on Mustafa, and he went free.
Stanley's squad did not know the protocol
of Islamic burial and death-shawl.
Karzan said the corpse was mutilated
by the battle, so it was cremated,
which relieved the squad with revenge sated.
Stan's body was processed and then returned

home for burial, where the Black Hills burned,
scorching trees and underbrush, with smoking
swirls as if shades summoned by an invoking.
Reuben did not attend the funeral,
his father's harsh words sank in Reuben's skull.
He was weary of his kin's racism,
thus detached in a family schism.
He managed a corporate farm with Ahn,
who compared the fields to Eden's green lawn.
He smiled and kissed her fascinating head,
but his reasoning demurred, so he said:
"Though we evolve and hybrids are mated,
still god cannot be domesticated.
We fool ourselves as a loving nation
who can purchase the world's evolution."
Friends and relatives went to the Church Mass,
where psalms were sung by the Sunday school class
to help Stan achieve a higher Heaven,
guiding him toward the fate he was driven.
Saints were called forth to steer Stan on the road,
as was Christ the Shepherd and his sheepfold.
Forgiveness of Stan's sins were also pled,
stains washed clean by what the lamb of god bled.
The votive change of wafer bread and wine
to Christ's flesh and blood by a priest's design
were partaken as a deity's fare
teaching to carry the crosses they bear.
The military's investigation
cleared Stan's questionable reputation
by changing Margaret's testimony,
thus honored him in full ceremony
at the burial lot of the Jacobs',
after dining on Christ with plates and cups.
It was hard to accept their men were not
superheroes who ever faced death's rot.
Instead, bequeathed their citizens with gifts,

which raised the nation through trophies' war-rifts
garnered by conquering other countries
in global corporate murdering sprees.
As the funeral procession drove past
burned pine trees falling like a wrecked ship's mast,
Charles observed, gazing at the line of cars,
chariots of Christ and the war-god Mars.
The acrid smoke hovered in a thick haze
like the land was cremated by a blaze.
Charles thought: So Stan's family raises Hell
to greet him for his overdue death-knell,
and ends a resentment I can release,
which adds to the joy of my new life's lease.
Yet what will I be without my old hate
that led me near a self-destructive fate?
I try not to make many enemies
I want assassinated with decrees
to spoiler spirits I think I command
with nod of my head or gesture by hand.
I lost the battle for complete control,
not even the five senses or my soul
are truly part of my shell's possessions
as they are addicted to obsessions
when I am left to my own devices
in a vacuum of vanity vices.
I sold three paintings today, and my tale
insists I operate behind a veil,
away from society to fulfill
the visions I change to products and shill.
Media forums breed and multiply,
and artists get lost in cults as they ply
their craftwork to a global audience,
with faith in the praises for great genius.
'Tis easy to be snared in such acclaim,
feeding on the energy of bright fame.
People work for satellite and screen lives

like drones collecting honey to queen hives,
which plot a network with their buzzing tunes,
abandoning history as ruins.
And when 'tis their turn for power to rule
they send messages like a mundane fool
using media forums to complain
they have no private lives to hide a stain
which threatens Heavenly satellite's reign.
I do not know what occurred in Iraq
when Stanley met his death by an attack.
The official story fits well his myth,
harvested by an abusive man's scythe,
who turned on Stan when he tried to protect
the man's wife from an extreme Muslim sect,
which wanted to clip her orgasm part,
or bargain her off at an open-mart
if she did not comply with their edict
and allow her pudendum to be nicked.
A great American was there to save
her from misery as a crushed sex-slave,
but her husband was a cowardly man,
who feared the loss of esteem by his clan.
He waited until Jacob turned his back,
ending his patriot tour of Iraq.
Stan was hailed as a hero and emblem
of truth in the American system.
Wrecking whore Babylon's lies deserved thanks,
thus buried with medals and higher ranks.
Anti-heroes and figures without flaws
are mass-produced for a self-righteous cause,
and they represent both sides of the laws.
Redemption is offered at retail cost,
buying new roles to avoid being lost.
Charles was reformed from a wandering shade,
and felt freedom through art that was well-paid.
He took a college business class and learned

the checks-and-balances he had once spurned.
In *Ethics* Charles heard Aristotle sing
money is the measure of everything,
which was meant as a caution against greed,
but was adapted by those who would lead
to teach money as signs of pure success,
which can hide one's flaws with make-up and dress,
spawning imitations around the sphere,
polluting the airwaves and atmosphere.
A good society's best fulfillment
is philosophy, not entertainment.
Charles had no pride in his moderation,
accepting his part in god's planned ration.
Charles considered his sordid history
as lessons taught by the Great Mystery,
who allowed Charles to blunder on his own,
without scapegoats as a redemptive loan.
He tried not to humble any human,
though had secret glee at the death of Stan.
Charles was still learning from an oppressive
culture of when to take and how to give.
At times he went directly opposite
when he reasoned that love and hate would split.
He did some good unto the strong but meek,
avoiding the enemy-of-the-week,
disengaged from media rhetoric
inventing foes from a dangerous clique.
He would not watch consumers' enmities
be directed to hang scapegoats from trees.
If the audience should ever return
to the third-dimension their heads would churn
at their psychic energy gone to waste
for crafted resentments in public taste.
'Tis not so much choosing one's own battle,
as investing to be herded cattle.
Charles surrendered as lord of self-control

and bull of Heaven to have a man's role.
Only then did he find a real freedom
against the dramatic whirling maelstrom.
His higher power had a tradition
that was immutable unambition.
Karen Buffalo Who Mourns did not tame
his occasional beast-like urge for fame,
and be the greatest at his endeavors,
displaying his wit in artistic wars.
He knew his Alpha-male role was conceit,
so he would not bully or have deceit,
but used competition to self-improve,
not fitting people in a niche or groove.
He painted Classical Lakota scenes
connected to Mother Earth as she weans
people to be independent and free,
'til they return on a burial tree.
The natural resources of feathers,
beads, pelts, hides, and buckskin creates tethers
to the spiritual realms of the past
when great hunters and warriors would fast
and pray for visions that spanned each era
to modern consumption of the terra.
The gear-grinding noise seemed incessant rot,
so Charles also painted cogs' drunk gavotte
from when he wanted to dance to each tune,
and when that failed, conduct his fate's ruin.
Much time was spent being proud of his pride,
with Soma cultivated myths that lied
of fertile breeding-grounds for fantasies,
which indiscriminately killed to seize
new worlds wherein he could craft his legends,
not caring about the means or the ends.
As communication became abstract
through devices that were meant to distract,
Charles grew aware that it was not his path

to understand metaphysical math.
The language seemed like his drunk monologues
when he had been sinking deep into bogs.
He had tried that trail's void, nor did he seek
to invest vigor in computer-speak.
Revolutions whirled onwards and each flung
promised enlightenment from Mother Tongue.
Groups and cliques formed, seeming only to live
for bantering words that were exclusive.
Competition may elevate the soul,
yet leaves behind people without a role.
The Word may indeed have been One with god,
and as satellites soar the terra's sod
'tis easy to want to look at futures,
or peer into the past with time's sutures
when the present offers only a numb
vacation into a senses' kingdom.
He went to Karen's house and watched them sort
art in a collaborative effort.
Betsy mixed computer-designed planets
with Karen's painting of what Earth begets.
They made plans that night for a chili-fest
at a program dance with a speaker-guest.

20

City of Humans

Life is not just purchases to sample,
nor a morality tale example.
When eternity is canonical,
entropy feeds on the Host, never full.
If religions fail through lack of sages,
nations form in corporate images.
For fees, modern consumers have access
to chosen scribes as faithful audience.
Myths and histories by men like Plutarch
changed to inventions for Augustine's arc,
which soared through several hundred years in shows
gleaned from fables of their earlier foes.
The base of power creates images
that rise to the top with privileges.
Persia, now known as Iran, freed the Jews
from Babylon, though it was called a ruse
by god, which changed to Egypt's inglory
because it made for a better story.
The pyramids were awesome to behold,
more than the ziggurats where Jews were sold
in ancient Iraq, then called Babylon,
where Baal was used to fertilize lawn.
The Jews absorbed much of that religion,
so when they left and reached Canaan's region,

priests tempted Jews to redefine their past
with laws, rites, and tales written down to last.
The Jews' tribute to the Persian god-king
was retold to be votives they would bring
as part of the land-deal with Adoni,
god of ideal fictions one must buy
in hopes to make truth seem less horrible
by justifying it in the *Bible*.
Oral stories and screen-worlds quickly change;
written words adopt and engrave the strange.
Individual consciousness conforms
to scripture that supplies role-playing forms,
'til immigrants appear like thunderstorms
with new words and variations of tales
on covenants for god's Heavenly sales.
The Lakota had no written language,
and I do not cast myself as their sage.
There is a widespread foolish mania
that when all else fails, blame the media.
People pray for or demand pageantry
to escape their characters and feel free.
A church procession or native dances
grant people a change of appearances,
though some go too far and begin to fade,
casting out their souls and turning to shade.
Others try to dominate every sense,
tossing their demons in the audience.
Muse, let me not perform that foul mistake
in a sincerity which becomes fake.
What my dark side reveals has me tempted
to claim rewards for what I attempted
in this verse I seek to share with readers,
whom I try to impress with rhyme meters.
I admire processions of great writers,
though some don themselves with gowns and miters,
dubbed as script-formers for the universe,

yet now ignored with their forgotten verse.
Charles no longer believed life was futile.
His mind, though set free of wrath's harsh stifle,
had to be trained to explore new frontiers
without hate for himself or pioneers
in their modern garb and technology,
whose mixture in him began to agree
that void's madness can be a contagion
which people try to fill with a legion
until they lose their own identity.
So he moved away from Rapid City,
where tourist trade bought cowboys yearly roles,
and the Lakota washed up on the shoals.
After two years, Karen and Charles were wed,
and moved to a house she inherited,
which underwent a large renovation
at the Natives' Pine Ridge Reservation.
Charles earned degrees in business math and art,
teaching students to paint and draw with heart
and reasoning skills of the intellect,
as well as lessons in how to protect
money from others who would try to rob
the pupils if they ever got a job.
Education is a business work-loom,
training Capitalists how to consume.
Charles stumbled through his youth, seeking knowledge
that changed to entropy, then broke his pledge
of fidelity to what tempted him
into pursuit until empty and dim.
He tried to stay out of the wars between
gangs of light and dark because both could wean,
in safe pockets, a weary traveler
to tell the tale's past and what might occur.
Identities get shuffled in the mix,
and each side vows it can cure with a fix.
Perhaps that is why covert agencies

run the wars for world conglomerate fees,
for when no one knows who is in command,
scapegoats are not crushed by the public's hand,
except the chosen who go opposite
to business as usual as 'tis writ.
Choosing ignorance is still culpable
in creating a religious fable.
Intelligence is sold, with none to blame
but selected people to take the shame
and feel the weight of society's sin,
then karma balances for them to win
by similar fashions as oppressors,
ambition for glory eats at their cores.
If eternal Heaven does not exist
for those who suffer the world's iron fist,
then why not be enthroned expediters
selling decrees through commercial writers?
One can have intrigues properly unfurled,
with promised rewards for wrecking the world
from a god who plots a great destruction,
with a new Eden under construction.
When a cycle seemed ready to condemn,
Charles sought another enlightened system.
Relations are what make the world distinct,
senses on the prowl with innate instinct
to consume familiar gods or new tales
churned from Samsara by subconscious whales.
So Charles hunted for great visions to paint:
in the belly of the beast is a saint
who welcomes the sinners to communion
from every known and unknown religion.
Energy consumed, Charles and Karen made
a child during a conscious-sharing raid
into the Bardos, and the fetus grew
so thick and heavy Karen called it stew,
which seemed to mix all of her components,

needing tusk calcium like elephants.
Charles did not place honor and dignity
in temporal things like an art-trophy.
It became less difficult to define
and express his concord with the divine.
Yet sometimes he did not use astute stealth
in arguments with Karen about wealth.
Money made it easier to control
those he loved, fitting them to the right role.
The fetus' head was out of proportion,
draining her calcium with absorption.
Charles said the capsules were too expensive
to replace elements she had to give
their unborn child, who demanded great growth,
consuming the resources of them both.
Karen: "I do not care if insurance
will not cover what I need in defense
of my body against this sponge-creature.
I want to keep an attractive feature.
Or do you want me as a toothless hag,
who you divorce because you cannot brag
of my good looks and smile, as calcium
loss makes my hair and teeth go to the drum
kicking in my womb with an appetite,
which I shall not hit with a famine blight?
You still enjoy it when I preen and pose,
despite weight-gain and slightly damaged nose."
Betsy observed them in amused wonder,
then went to her room to read and ponder.
Charles felt he would lose his territory
if he surrendered to his wife's story.
Yet she made him seem like an idiot
for raising his voice in a wrathful fit,
and knowing that, he felt only more rage
in not being his ideal image.
He suddenly burst into laughing tones

as he thought of her losing parts of bones.
Karen suffered a greater debt than he,
yet Charles had issued a stupid decree.
He said: "I will go to the pharmacy,
as our child could absorb Samsara's sea.
Perhaps it can be employed in the fights
over the Lakota mineral rights,
because it takes them all into its form,
and could well be an elemental storm."
Karen: "He will be worth his weight in gold,
if we can ever get him from my mold.
His name will be Julius as a star,
and for my Caesarean section scar."
Charles: "That would be an interesting name,
though bad portents were part of his great fame.
If we have a son, let us not foster
ambition for a lineage monster,
like was spawned with the Antichrist, Nero,
Caligula dressed as a war-hero,
or the other scoundrels of that heir-line
who wrecked their nation's Republic design.
Plutonium, a fashioned element
made to unveil the god of Hell's intent,
is artificial, much like the cultures
of composite identity sutures.
We can all burn in Hell, one fiery stew
Pluto reigns over with a demon crew.
Not that votes matter much here in our lands,
as leaders heed world corporate commands
that turn people on each other, then bet
in global stocks on the weapons' market.
We wash ourselves from the whole bloody mess
like Pilate did Christ for Tiberius.
Betsy has a basketball game tonight,
we can pretend 'tis a stadium fight.
Urged to battle our fellows by white crowds

as the audience, like Passover clouds,
which swoop in to establish their order
after we are wrecked by rape and murder.
If we swear at Heaven with a vile cuss,
maybe there shall arise a Spartacus
to lead us gladiators in revolt
against the standard television jolt
of vacuous sporting entertainments,
while we pay for high-priced advertisements."
Karen: "We already had a debate
on the television networks you hate.
They seem to possess you like greedy ghosts,
with Christian channels as the lord of hosts.
You keep quoting that goofy Augustine
from his book on Roman gods as unclean,
especially in their theater rites.
Then you compare it to pageantry sites
of modern Christians, who love a big show
with glittering stars in a spotlight's glow,
but they are not all like that, as you know.
You still have resentments for religions
that tried to wreck the faith of our regions.
As you might quote Saint Thomas Aquinas,
good potency is real among us.
You use your knowledge as a hatred tool,
but things changed at the Christian boarding-school.
Your mom was abused there, like bloody chum
turned into Communion for Christ's kingdom,
but she let go of her anger and found
it almost consumed her like Heaven's hound."
Charles: "I still have an urge to find a cause,
even one without reason or just laws.
And when I focus my mind on money,
I can buy a future bright and sunny,
where family and friends are protected
from those who form gods to be reflected."

Charles had considered the use others made
of past dirty-tricks taught by a foe's shade,
who was held in esteem and was well-paid.
Covert agencies are hired to protect
celebrities of the Israelite sect,
who get their comrades to invest in shows
of covert intrigues fighting Jewish foes.
So the agencies enjoy their repute,
and get advice fees for ignorant fruit.
They learned propaganda from the Nazis,
now American brains are programmed keys
turned and locked to aim at the latest threat
to stupid bliss with no blood-stain regret.
Fictional shows with fake blood splattering
the camera avoids a shattering.
So 'tis easy to go to Last Judgment
and testify against the violent,
dead or found guilty. Then seize the rewards,
having gamed them off each other, like lords,
and blood-minerals they shed doom their state,
while the meek innocent inherit Fate.
Karen: "You need to get your noggin clear
and out of the manure in your rear.
You study so many theologies
you do not know where lies your loyalties,
except with the almighty dollar bill,
which leaves a vacuum you can never fill."
Charles: "I certainly am not reticent
on views critiquing each dollar and cent.
I spend so much time teaching the topic
that it seems immersed in my life's epic,
like a dragon hoarding gold I must slay,
before I am corrupted by its sway.
Coyote is more friendly than Fenris
when Ragnorok brings a new garden's bliss.
Culling the herds on a global level

becomes the work of the machine's devil,
programmed from the instincts of predators,
as if still animals from ancient lores.
We must put a lock on the computer,
so Betsy is not prey to a looter."
Karen: "Now you are thinking like a man
ready to guide the courses of our clan,
knowing that some trails demand craft and stealth,
which cannot be purchased by any wealth."
Charles: "High-finances are based on poaching,
and they do not want others encroaching
on subsidized estate territories,
and their plans to steal Lakota stories,
replacing them with world conglomerates'
tales of salvation from greedy pirates
by ripping the elements from our land,
and bombing enemies into glass-sand.
Global corporations promise safe homes,
if we heed screen-madness of rabid foams.
We learn dirty-tricks from our role-models.
Should we turn and punish them with throttles?"
Karen: "This week I watched a bunch of hams,
police and covert agency programs,
who saved the world many times from the plots
of Muslim terrorists turned to blood clots
in bad fictions that tried to be gritty
with gore and our heroes' integrity."
Charles: "Since most Muslims do not eat ham-pork,
what do they think of television's work?
Are the only jobs for our great nation's
Muslims is to act on the screen-stations
as crazed jihadists who want to destroy
decadence with a nefarious ploy?"
Karen: "That is not a good role-model
for our children to learn while they toddle.
It used to be cowboys and Indians,

now some one else has to pay for fake sins.
The media sponsors want us to hate
those they wish to plunder with hook and bait."
Charles laughed: "Resentments can become abstract,
which devolve to a truth not based on fact.
I used to form them and watch them possess
all beauty 'til there was no safe egress.
Trapped in committees of my spirit's mind,
the third-dimension was deeply entwined
with cave shadows like Plato invented,
and a paranoid rage was fomented,
which was not commanded by satellites
that direct ongoing staged global fights.
I wanted total freedom and received
jail-time with police orders, where I grieved.
Folks are partitioned by corporate strife,
yet the sweetest revenge is a good life."
Karen: "I, too, was caught in that system,
and was quick to blame others and condemn
those who made money from my legal woes,
not wanting to face my own inner-foes.
Contraries worked in the institutions
to pay for freedom or prosecutions.
Both gave orders in and out of my head,
like my Higher Power's terms could be read.
Bad craft imitating even worse art
is like you trying to run the Earth's mart.
I chose a god not made in my image,
one writing me on *The Book of Life's* page."
Charles: "Life demands independent sentries,
as we return to the landed gentries.
Like freedom founded by George Washington,
with slaves on his tobacco plantation.
Perhaps he tried some miscegenation,
then sold his own children with the year's crop,
a true Capitalist who loved to shop.

Reuben telephoned last week from the farm,
he and Ahn are now blessed with a son's charm.
Reuben has been disowned by his parents,
and cut-off from his land inheritance,
though he does not say he is in bondage
as we begin a new pharaonic age."
Karen: "That reminds me we have to sit
and discuss how my mom wants to visit.
She believes she can dry-out in our home,
as she grows too old to wander and roam.
I know you do not like to take in strays,
but she will only be here a few days.
She gave us this house instead of my kin,
which my siblings complain was a gross sin.
If she drinks here, we can make her depart,
though she vows she is taking a new start."
Charles: "We both know a wet-drunk will promise
anything to escape their awful bliss.
It is a rapture hard to understand
by so-called normal people who command
and control any alcohol habits,
not riding stallions without reins or bits.
Convinced we can break it, we quickly mount,
scoring an apocalypse body-count:
a bleak vision after terrible storms,
with the landscape littered by broken forms.
It is foolish to think we can control
the Soma people believe guides their soul.
And alcoholics are quite resourceful,
until their brain gets too damp in the skull."
Karen: "I do not want my mom to think
she has bred her own foes to make her sink.
Sometimes it seems we have children for wars
in America or on other shores.
One child-rearing message that we are taught,
love for them is proved by how much is bought.

They learn that people can be purchased for use
in work, wars, or to consume a false truce.
We will fail to pass traditions along
if the world is extinct of human song.
Status symbols become superstitious
machinery tokens guiding the conscious.
The competition to reach satori
is a language chant computer story.
Freedom exchanged for new status symbols
evolves to possessions by unclean souls.
I feel caught between the satellite world,
where roles change fast to not be pigeon-holed,
and the third-dimension's shifting orders
of destroying all natural borders.
I hate being both parents to my mom,
the roles are like an abnormal maelstrom.
The four seasons also alter so quick
that weather gods must be mentally sick
from all the pollution that they digest
as our sacrifice to see who is best."
Charles: "'Tis hard to separate the dramas
of comic laughs and disaster traumas.
It spins around like a crazy machine
leased from the Mafia as a debt lien
to draw suckers into our casinos,
attracting third-rate celebrity shows.
Even a presidential candidate
will not campaign in South Dakota's state.
The loan sharks have legalized usury
through government lobbyists to curry
favor, which includes the tourism trade
of keeping Natives locked up and unmade.
White casinos want no competition
from the Lakota's sovereign nation.
We hurt money-changing chips when we booze,
so the police are busy with their crews.

There are three choices for a way of life:
prison, school, or the military's strife,
all of which involve global corporate
churning of Samsara with their trap's net:
each way of life has its own languages
that form people into mold images.
When Adam began to call things by name,
he did not say Eve was a whore of shame."
Karen: "I have a superstitious state
of you saying such things while I gestate,
as it absorbs my intake and senses,
building its walls and immune defenses
through cell-layers, which I hope do not lead
to jail-cells for a criminal's misdeed
by habits that lead to a life of dread,
which cannot be rehabilitated.
Some choose a lifestyle at an early age,
though all want a share of the spotlight's stage.
Shortly after the sun dance ritual,
with a part played by a buffalo skull,
we mated and I conceived in my dark
some of the Great Mystery's glowing spark."
Charles: "It was a sacred and fun mission,
not love-play in front of television.
We wean our children like computer cubs,
even serial-killers have fan clubs.
One thing about America's drama,
we have various choices of Soma
manufactured to heighten distractions
or escape into our oblivions,
and are extinct through trivialities,
then reformed to start new cosmic stories,
where life and death do not hang on a strand
of fate invented by a broadcast band.
The current pantheon of deities
shall be washed away as will their cities.

The speed and efficiency of machines
has those who rule try to hold on to scenes,
but the tides of Samsara revolve fast,
not even the moon helps steer a ship's mast.
The world's greatest energy goes to waste
to satisfy an artificial taste."
Karen: "When South and North America
ores were drained like blood from a body's ka,
it left a corpse to fertilize new tales,
creating beliefs in Somatic grails.
A cast was bred of staggering zombies,
who still consume, though but rotten mummies.
So the fight is rewritten to dramas
watched onscreen of the battle for Somas."
Charles: "Some black-outs are best left forgotten,
evolving to gin mills to pick cotton,
and on the other side of a black-out
we hope there is no anger, fear, or doubt.
Then, returning to the third-dimension,
we find we have sold our comprehension.
So 'tis with our Information Ages,
history replaced by myth images,
who teach Earth's resources last forever,
so get lost in screens that will not sever
deserving folks from the highest powers,
built on those at the base of the towers.
Nor should one fear their primitive weapons,
but turn them against each other like pawns.
After reaping where elements reside,
sell mineral munitions to each side,
and use the funds for crafting a safe place,
while trying to create a new role's face."
Karen: "I will go put on my war-paint,
known as lip-gloss a celebrity saint
sells onscreen to snare a sexy suitor,
while you put a lock on our computer

so Betsy does not find a predator
who lurks in the airwaves like a germ spore.
I will tell her of our decided deed,
that we shall select her screen-modem's seed.
She knows how to get around your advice,
and will not quickly give up her device.
She is mad her friends call her a phony
because you promised to buy a pony,
and have not fulfilled her endless wish-list
that leads through the stardust of ether's mist.
Like a swarm of locusts or grasshoppers,
Betsy can make us eternal shoppers
ranging round the world on computer sites
as a compelled mind for consumptive blights."
Charles: "It is easier to make her spoil,
for disciplining can be too much toil.
My mom did the same when I was a child,
then drunk, she would turn on me and be wild.
I try to be more consistent than that,
and not have whims like a savage tomcat.
I want people to expect the good in me,
not a vicious clown whose jests are crazy.
It is hard to learn how to sacrifice
the proper amount with what will suffice."
Karen: "All of your studies in those books
and still you want to evade their god-hooks
as if they hide some sort of self-treason,
but their rites are passed on for a reason.
So try to focus on the good of them
instead of vainly building a system
where you have all superiority
to guide others through your eternity."
Charles: "Those are humbling words to take to heart;
my self-induced angst can drive me apart
from all that I love and want to cherish,
hoping in my art they will not perish.

Yet when I return from crafting visions,
I still feel alone with sacred missions
that are hard to explain, and not be daft
or angry no one understands my craft.
As if I can explain the world away,
or my version of it, which should hold sway.
I cannot carry the globe on my back,
a horse sacrifice to guide our dreams' track.
Another era in our lives begins
with twined superstitious virtues and sins."
My muse ends the song of Charles Standing Horse,
a young man who wandered a sundry course,
looking for freedom outside each system
to be at the roots where new growth would stem
beyond promising words of salvation,
or the foul curses of condemnation.
Perhaps 'tis a gift of free will god sent
to choose between passion and detachment,
and be a partaker or audience
to the stimuli that evolves each sense.
And children carry on our consciousness,
exploring individuality
of the world's contrary duality.
Caught in systems of prefabrication,
being taught 'tis free will's destination,
then use any means for a vacation
from the invented tales and oracles
that promise a good end with miracles,
but instead snare with deities' shackles.
One has to have money to buy a berth
in the screen-stories of magnetic worth,
drawing one on to abandon the globe
for subliminal messages that probe
the minds of the audience to create
ignorant love and intelligent hate.
Stupid consumers of blissful Eden,

or disobey and not weed the garden
when lords try to organize clean-up crews
after they lay waste to bodies in pews.
It is how they form a resurrection,
while investing in means of pollution.

Epilogue

Iraq's gang-rape helped build a relation
in the fraternal thieves' Coalition.
The countries fight among themselves again,
so they need a whore to corral and pen
to victimize as incarnate evil
who goes against their laws that are civil,
and spread profits among the pimping clan
united to plunder. I bet Iran
will be our slut, like Lilith of Iraq,
Babylon's succubus with an oiled crack.
A Bush would contrive a vicious gang-rape,
so vote one in to burn and not lose shape.
Get the propaganda-machine cranking:
deus ex machina prepares a spanking
which results in a peace of luxuries:
rewards of cheap gas from refineries.
Perhaps Russia can be appeased to join
a nations' league with Iran to purloin.
If Iranians starve, then oil for food
will keep their rich conniving with our brood.

Printed in the United States
by Baker & Taylor Publisher Services